Handbook of Multibiometrics

International Series on Biometrics

Consulting Editors

Professor David D. Zhang

Department of Computer Science
Hong Kong Polytechnic University
Hung Hom, Kowloon, Hong Kong

email: csdzhang@comp.polyu.edu.hk

Professor Anil K. Jain

Dept. of Computer Science& Eng.
Michigan State University
3115 Engineering Bldg.
East Lansing, MI 48824-1226, U.S.A.
Email: jain@cse.msu.edu

In our international and interconnected information society, there is an ever-growing need to authenticate and identify individuals. Biometrics-based authentication is emerging as the most reliable solution. Currently, there have been various biometric technologies and systems for authentication, which are either widely used or under development. The International Book Series on Biometrics will systematically introduce these relative technologies and systems, presented by biometric experts to summarize their successful experience, and explore how to design the corresponding systems with in-depth discussion.

In addition, this series aims to provide an international exchange for researchers, professionals, and industrial practitioners to share their knowledge of how to surf this tidal wave of information. The International Book Series on Biometrics will contain new material that describes, in a unified way, the basic concepts, theories and characteristic features of integrating and formulating the different facets of biometrics, together with its recent developments and significant applications. Different biometric experts, from the global community, are invited to write these books. Each volume will provide exhaustive information on the development in that respective area. The International Book Series on Biometrics will provide a balanced mixture of technology, systems and applications. A comprehensive bibliography on the related subjects will also be appended for the convenience of our readers.

Additional titles in the series:

UNCONSTRAINED FACE RECOGNITION *by Shaohua Kevin Zhou, Rama Chellappa, Wenyi Zhao;* ISBN: 0-387-26407-8

HUMAN IDENTIFICATION BASED ON GAIT *by Mark S. Nixon, Tieniu Tan and Rama Chellappa;* ISBN: 0-387-24424-7

PALMPRINT AUTHENTICATION *by David D. Zhang;* ISBN: 1-4020-8096-4

HUMAN-COMPUTER INTERFACE *by Antonio J. Colmenarez, Ziyou Xiong and Thomas S. Huang;* ISBN: 1-4020-7802-1

FACIAL ANALYSIS FROM CONTINUOUS VIDEO WITH APPLICATIONS TO COMPUTATIONAL ALGORITHMS FOR FINGERPRINT RECOGNITION *by Bir Bhanu and Xuejun Tan;* ISBN: 1-4020-7651-7

Additional information about this series can be obtained from our website:
springer.com

Handbook of Multibiometrics

by

Arun A. Ross
Lane Department of Computer Science and Electrical Engineering
West Virginia University, USA

Karthik Nandakumar
Department of Computer Science and Engineering
Michigan State University, USA

Anil K. Jain
Department of Computer Science and Engineering
Michigan State University, USA

 Springer

Arun A. Ross
West Virginia University
Dept. of Computer Science & Electrical Eng.
751 ESB
Morgantown WV 26506-6109
ross@csee.wwu.edu

Karthik Nandakumar
Michigan State Univ.
Dept. of Computer Science & Eng.
PRIP Lab
3208 Engineering Bldg.
East Lansing MI 48824
nandakum@cse.msu.edu

Anil K. Jain
Michigan State University
Dept. of Computer Science & Eng.
3115 Engineering Building
East Lansing MI 48824
jain@cse.msu.edu

Library of Congress Control Number: 2006923240

Handbook of Multibiometrics
by Arun A. Ross, Karthik Nandakumar and Anil K. Jain

ISBN-13: 978-0-387-22296-7
ISBN-10: 0-387-22296-0
e-ISBN-13: 978-0-387-33123-2
e-ISBN-10: 0-387-33123-9

Printed on acid-free paper.

Printed in the United States of America.

9 8 7 6 5 4 3 2 1

springer.com

Contents

List of Figures

List of Tables

Preface

The pronounced need for reliably determining or verifying the identity of a person has spurred active research in the field of biometric authentication. Biometric authentication, or simply biometrics, is the science of establishing an identity based on the physical or behavioral attributes of an individual, including fingerprint, face, voice, gait, iris, signature, hand geometry and ear. It is becoming increasingly apparent that a single biometric trait (used in a unibiometric system) is not sufficient to meet a number of system requirements - including matching performance - imposed by several large-scale authentication applications. Multibiometric systems seek to alleviate some of the drawbacks encountered by unibiometric systems by consolidating the evidence presented by multiple biometric sources. These systems can significantly improve the recognition performance of a biometric system besides improving population coverage, deterring spoof attacks, and reducing the failure-to-enroll rate. Although the storage requirements, processing time and the computational demands of a multibiometric system can be significantly higher (than a unibiometric system), the above mentioned advantages present a compelling case for deploying multibiometric systems in large-scale authentication systems (e.g., border crossing) and systems requiring very high accuracies (e.g., access to a secure military base).

The field of multibiometrics has made rapid advances over the past few years. These developments have been fueled in part by recent government mandates stipulating the use of biometrics for delivering crucial societal functions. The US-VISIT program (United States Visitor and Immigration Status Indicator Technology) is a border security system that validates the travel documents of foreign visitors to the United States. Currently, fingerprint images of left- and right-index fingers of a person are being used to associate a visa with an individual entering the United States; in the future, all ten fingers may be used thereby necessitating the development of efficient data capture as well as fusion algorithms. The International Civil Aviation Organization (ICAO) has unanimously recommended that its member States use Machine Readable Travel Documents (MRTDs) that incorporate at least the face biometric (some combination of face, fingerprint and iris can also be used) for purposes of establishing the identity of a passport holder. Thus, research in multibiometrics has the potential to impact several large-scale civilian and commercial applications.

From an academic perspective, research in multibiometrics has several different facets: identifying the sources of multiple biometric information; determining the type of information to be fused; designing optimal fusion methodologies; evaluating and comparing different fusion methodologies; and building robust multimodal interfaces that facilitate the efficient acquisition of multibiometric data. One of the goals of this book is to lend structure to the amorphous body of research work that has been conducted in the field of multibiometrics. To this end, we have attempted to assemble a framework that can be effectively used to understand the issues and progress being made in multibiometrics while identifying the challenges and potential research directions in this field.

The book is organized as follows. Chapter 2 introduces the notion of information fusion in the context of biometrics and enumerates the advantages imparted by multibiometric systems. The various sources of biometric information that can be integrated in a multibiometric framework, such as multiple sensors, multiple algorithms and multiple samples, are then discussed with examples from the literature. This chapter also examines different types of acquisition and processing schemes that are relevant to multibiometric systems. Finally, the types of information (also known as the levels of fusion) that can be accommodated in a fusion architecture are briefly visited. In Chapter 3, the sensor-level, feature-level, rank-level and decision-level fusion schemes are explored in detail along with examples highlighting the pros and cons of each fusion level. Integration strategies for each of these fusion levels are presented, both from the multibiometric as well as the multiple classifier system literature. The chapter concludes by categorizing some of the representative publications in multibiometrics on the basis of the sources of biometric information used and the level of fusion adopted. Chapter 4 is entirely dedicated to score-level fusion, since fusion at this level has been elaborately studied in the literature. The integration strategies pertinent to this level are presented under three distinct categories: (i) density-based score fusion, (ii) transformation-based score fusion, and (iii) classifier-based score fusion. This chapter discusses examples embodying each of these categories; a mathematical framework is adopted in order to assist the reader in understanding the differences between the three categories. The chapter concludes by indicating how the performance of a score fusion system can be further enhanced by utilizing user-specific parameters. In Chapter 5, the possibility of incorporating ancillary information, such as the quality of the biometric data and the soft biometrics of individuals, in a biometric fusion framework is discussed. Soft biometric traits include characteristics such as gender, height, weight, eye color, etc. that provide added information about an individual, but lack the distinctiveness and permanence to sufficiently differentiate between multiple individuals. The chapter presents an information fusion framework to include soft biometric traits in the authentication process. The final contribution of this book is an Appendix that lists some of the databases that have been used for evaluating the performance of various multibiometric algorithms.

We are grateful to a number of individuals who lent their generous support to this project. Julian Fierrez-Aguilar, Universidad Autonoma de Madrid, Patrick Flynn, University of Notre Dame, Lawrence Hornak, West Virginia University, Richard Lazarick, Computer Sciences Corporation, Norman Poh, IDIAP, Salil Prabhakar, Digital Persona, Inc., Choonwoo Ryu, INHA University, Marios Savvides, Carnegie Mellon University, Yunhong Wang, Beihang University and James Wayman, San Jose State University reviewed and provided valuable comments on preliminary drafts of this book. We had a number of useful discussions with Josef Bigun, Halmstad University, Sarat Dass, Michigan State University, Josef Kittler, University of Surrey, Sharath Pankanti, IBM T. J. Watson Research Center and David Zhang, Hong Kong Polytechnic University. Arun George, West Virginia University and Yi Chen, Michigan State University designed several of the illustrations in this book. Thanks to Samir Shah and Rohan Nadgir, West Virginia University and Umut Uludag, Michigan State University for proofreading the manuscript. We would also like to thank the Center for Identification Technology Research (CITeR), West Virginia University, the National Science Foundation (NSF) and the Department of Homeland Security (DHS) for supporting our research in multibiometrics.

This book has been written for researchers, engineers, students and biometric system integrators who are keen on exploring the fundamentals of multibiometrics. It can be used as a reference guide for a graduate course in biometrics. Some of the concepts presented in this book are applicable to the general domain of information fusion and, hence, students of this field will also benefit from the book. We hope that the concepts and ideas presented in the following pages will stimulate the reader's curiosity and help develop an appreciation for this rapidly evolving field, called Multibiometrics.

ARUN ROSS, MORGANTOWN, WV
KARTHIK NANDAKUMAR, EAST LANSING, MI
ANIL K. JAIN, EAST LANSING, MI

Chapter 1

BIOMETRICS: WHEN IDENTITY MATTERS

1.1   Introduction

A reliable identity management system is a critical component in several applications that render services to only legitimately enrolled users. Examples of such applications include sharing networked computer resources, granting access to nuclear facilities, performing remote financial transactions or boarding a commercial flight. The proliferation of web-based services (e.g., online banking) and the deployment of decentralized customer service centers (e.g., credit cards) have further enhanced the need for reliable identity management systems.

The overarching task in an identity management system is the determination (or verification) of an individual's identity (or claimed identity).[1] Such an action may be necessary for a variety of reasons but the primary intention, in most applications, is to prevent impostors from accessing protected resources. Traditional methods of establishing a person's identity include knowledge-based (e.g., passwords) and token-based (e.g., ID cards) mechanisms, but these surrogate representations of the identity can easily be lost, shared, manipulated or stolen thereby undermining the intended security. Biometrics[2] offers a natural and reliable solution to certain aspects of identity management by utilizing fully automated or semi-automated schemes to recognize individuals based on their inherent physical and/or behavioral characteristics (Jain et al., 2004c). By using biometrics it is possible to establish an identity based on *who you are*, rather than by *what you possess*, such as an ID card, or *what you remember*, such as a password (Figure 1.1). In some applications, biometrics may be used to supplement ID cards and passwords thereby imparting an additional level of security. Such an arrangement is often called a dual-factor authentication scheme. Thus, biometrics does not have to replace tokens and passwords in all applications.

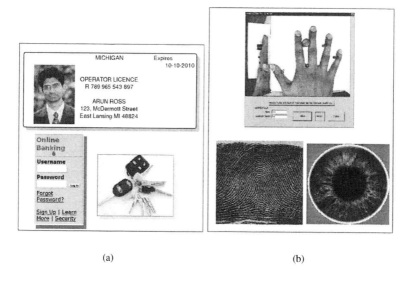

(a)   (b)

Figure 1.1. Authentication schemes. (a) Traditional schemes use ID cards, passwords and keys to validate individuals and ensure that system resources are accessed by a legitimately enrolled individual. (b) With the advent of biometrics, it is now possible to establish an identity based on "who you are" rather than by "what you possess" or "what you remember".

The effectiveness of an authenticator (biometric or non-biometric) is based on its robustness to various types of malicious attacks as well as its relevance to a particular application. O'Gorman, 2003 lists a number of attacks that can be launched against authentication systems based on passwords and tokens: (a) client attack (e.g., guessing passwords, stealing tokens); (b) host attack (e.g., accessing plain text file containing passwords); (c) eavesdropping (e.g., "shoulder surfing" for passwords); (d) repudiation (e.g., claiming that token was misplaced); (e) trojan horse attack (e.g., installation of bogus log-in screen to steal passwords); and (f) denial of service (e.g., disabling the system by deliberately supplying an incorrect password several times). While some of these attacks can be deflected by designing appropriate defense mechanisms, it is not possible to handle all the problems associated with the use of passwords and tokens.

Biometrics offers certain advantages such as negative recognition and non-repudiation that cannot be provided by tokens and passwords (Prabhakar et al., 2003). Negative recognition is the process by which a system determines that a certain individual is indeed enrolled in the system although the individual might deny it. This is especially critical in applications such as welfare disbursement where an impostor may attempt to claim multiple benefits (i.e., double dipping) under different names. Non-repudiation is a way to guarantee that an individual who accesses a certain facility cannot later deny using it (e.g., a person accesses a certain computer resource and later claims that an impostor must have used it under falsified credentials).

Biometric systems use a variety of physical or behavioral characteristics (Figure 1.2), including fingerprint, face, hand/finger geometry, iris, retina, signature, gait, palmprint, voice pattern, ear, hand vein, odor or the DNA information of an individual to establish identity (Jain et al., 1999a; Wayman et al., 2005). In the biometric literature, these characteristics are referred to as *traits*, *indicators*, *identifiers* or *modalities*. While biometric systems have their own limitations (O'Gorman, 2002) they have an edge over traditional security methods in that they cannot be easily stolen or shared. Besides bolstering security, biometric systems also enhance user convenience by alleviating the need to design and remember passwords.

The use of biological traits to confirm the identity of an individual is certainly not a new concept. In the late 19th century, Alphonse Bertillon, a French law enforcement officer, advocated a personal identification system that associated a set of anthropometric measurements with an individual (Moenssens, 1971). The Bertillonage system entailed the precise measurement of certain bony parts of the body (including the ear); a morphological description of the appearance and shape of the body; and a listing of peculiar marks such as moles, scars and tattoos on the surface of the body. These measurements were then recorded on a card and filed in a central repository that was partitioned into several categories based on the acquired measurements. This indexing ability permitted the quick retrieval of an individual's card when a repeat offender was booked by the police. But the system was cumbersome to administer uniformly (making it prone to error) and did not guarantee uniqueness across individuals (Figure 1.3). It was, therefore, abandoned in the wake of rapid developments in forensic fingerprint examination thanks to the pioneering works of Henry Faulds, William Herschel and Sir Francis Galton (Faulds, 1880; Herschel, 1880; Galton, 1888). Although the Bertillonage system cannot be considered as a biometric system because of its lack of automation, it has nevertheless laid the foundation for modern day biometrics.

The advent of digital signal processing saw the design of automated systems in the 1960s and 1970s that were capable of processing fingerprint (Trauring, 1963; Grasselli, 1969; Shelman, 1967), voice (Kersta, 1962; Pruzansky, 1963; Luck, 1969), hand (Ernst, 1971; Miller, 1971; Jacoby et al., 1972) and face (Kanade, 1973) data. The availability of faster computers and improved sensing technology (Figure 1.4) coupled with significant advances in statistical pattern recognition and computer vision has resulted in the development

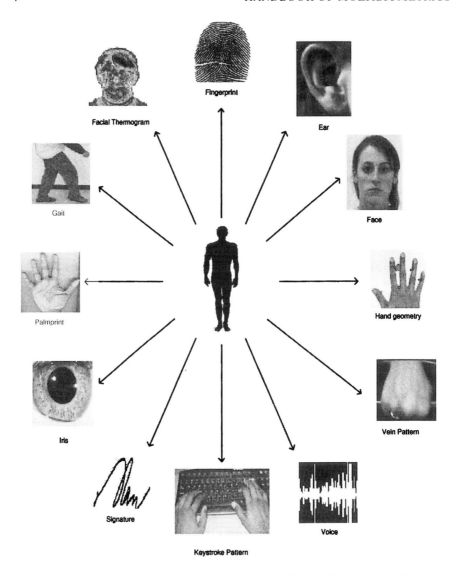

Figure 1.2. Examples of biometric traits that can be used for authenticating an individual. Physical traits include fingerprint, iris, face and hand geometry while behavioral traits include signature, keystroke dynamics and gait.

of sophisticated schemes to process and match the biometric data of several modalities including iris, retina, gait and signature. Furthermore, advances in 3D modeling and graphics in recent years have paved the way for processing 3D biometric data such as range images of the hand, face and ear.

Figure 1.3. The Bertillonage system, so named after its inventor Alphonse Bertillon, relied on the precise measurement of various attributes of the body for identifying recidivists. These measurements included the height of the individual, the length of the arm, geometry of the head and the length of the foot. The process was tedious to administer and did not guarantee uniqueness across individuals.

1.2 Operation of a biometric system

How does a biometric system operate? A biometric system is essentially a pattern recognition system that acquires biometric data from an individual, extracts a salient feature set from the data, compares this feature set against the feature set(s) stored in the database, and executes an action based on the result of the comparison. Therefore, a generic biometric system can be viewed as having four main modules: a sensor module; a quality assessment and feature extraction module; a matching module; and a database module. Each of these modules is described below.

1 **Sensor module**: A suitable biometric reader or scanner is required to acquire the raw biometric data of an individual. To obtain fingerprint images, for example, an optical fingerprint sensor may be used to image the friction ridge structure of the fingertip. The sensor module defines the human machine interface and is, therefore, pivotal to the performance of the biometric system. A poorly designed interface can result in a high failure-to-acquire rate (see Section 1.4) and, consequently, low user acceptability. Since most biometric modalities are acquired as images (exceptions include voice which is audio-based and odor which is chemical-based), the quality of the raw

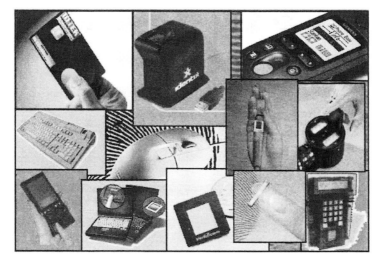

Figure 1.4. A variety of fingerprint sensors with different specifications (e.g., sensing technology, image size, image resolution, image quality, etc.) are now available. These rather compact sensors may be embedded in computer peripherals and other devices to facilitate user authentication.

data is also impacted by the characteristics of the camera technology that is used.

2 **Quality assessment and feature extraction module**: The quality of the biometric data acquired by the sensor is first assessed in order to determine its suitability for further processing. Typically, the acquired data is subjected to a signal enhancement algorithm in order to improve its quality.

However, in some cases, the quality of the data may be so poor that the user is asked to present the biometric data again. The biometric data is then processed and a set of salient discriminatory features extracted to represent the underlying trait. For example, the position and orientation of minutia points (local ridge and valley anomalies) in a fingerprint image are extracted by the feature extraction module in a fingerprint-based biometric system. During enrollment, this feature set is stored in the database and is commonly referred to as a *template*.

3 **Matching and decision-making module**: The extracted features are compared against the stored templates to generate match scores. In a fingerprint-based biometric system, the number of matching minutiae between the input and the template feature sets is determined and a match score reported. The match score may be moderated by the quality of the presented biometric data. The matcher module also encapsulates a decision making module, in which the match scores are used to either validate a claimed identity or provide a ranking of the enrolled identities in order to identify an individual.

4 **System database module**: The database acts as the repository of biometric information. During the enrollment process, the feature set extracted from the raw biometric sample (i.e., the template) is stored in the database (possibly) along with some biographic information (such as name, Personal Identification Number (PIN), address, etc.) characterizing the user. The data capture during the enrollment process may or may not be supervised by a human depending on the application. For example, a user attempting to create a new computer account in her biometric-enabled workstation may proceed to enroll her biometrics without any supervision; a person desiring to use a biometric-enabled ATM, on the other hand, will have to enroll her biometrics in the presence of a bank officer after presenting her non-biometric credentials.

The template of a user can be extracted from a single biometric sample, or generated by processing multiple samples. Thus, the minutiae template of a finger may be extracted after mosaicing multiple samples of the same finger. Some systems store multiple templates in order to account for the intra-class variations associated with a user. Face recognition systems, for instance, may store multiple templates of an individual, with each template corresponding to a different facial pose with respect to the camera. Depending on the application, the template can be stored in the central database of the biometric system or be recorded on a token (e.g., smart card) issued to the individual.

In the face recognition literature, the raw biometric images stored in the database are often referred to as *gallery images* while those acquired during authentication are known as *probe images*. These are synonymous with the terms *stored images* and *query* or *input images*, respectively.

1.3   Verification versus identification

Depending on the application context, a biometric system may operate either in the verification or identification mode (see Figure 1.5). In the verification mode, the system validates a person's identity by comparing the captured biometric data with her own biometric template(s) stored in the system database. In such a system, an individual who desires to be recognized claims an identity, usually via a PIN, a user name or a smart card, and the system conducts a one-to-one comparison to determine whether the claim is true or not (e.g., "Does this biometric data belong to Bob?"). Verification is typically used for positive recognition, where the aim is to prevent multiple people from using the same identity.

In the identification mode, the system recognizes an individual by searching the templates of all the users in the database for a match. Therefore, the system conducts a one-to-many comparison to establish an individual's identity (or fails if the subject is not enrolled in the system database) without the subject having to claim an identity (e.g., "Whose biometric data is this?"). Identification is a critical component in negative recognition applications where the system establishes whether the person is who she (implicitly or explicitly) denies to be. The purpose of negative recognition is to prevent a single person from using multiple identities. Identification may also be used in positive recognition for convenience (the user is not required to claim an identity). While traditional methods of personal recognition such as passwords, PINs, keys, and tokens may work for positive recognition, negative recognition can only be established through biometrics.

Throughout this book, we will use the generic terms recognition or authentication where we do not wish to make a distinction between the verification and identification modes.

The verification problem may be formally posed as a two-category classification problem as follows: given an input (query) feature set X_Q and a claimed identity I, determine if (I, X_Q) belongs to ω_1 or ω_2, where ω_1 indicates that the claim is true (a "genuine" user) and ω_2 indicates that the claim is false (an "impostor"). Typically, X_Q is matched against X_I, the stored biometric template corresponding to user I, to determine its category. The resulting decision rule is,

$$(I, X_Q) \in \begin{cases} \omega_1 & \text{if } \mathcal{S}(X_Q, X_I) \geq \eta, \\ \omega_2 & \text{otherwise,} \end{cases} \quad (1.1)$$

where $\mathcal{S}$ is the function that measures the similarity between X_Q and X_I, and η is a predefined threshold. The value $\mathcal{S}(X_Q, X_I)$ is termed as a similarity score or match score between the feature vectors of the query and the stored template corresponding to identity I. Every claimed identity in a verification scenario is

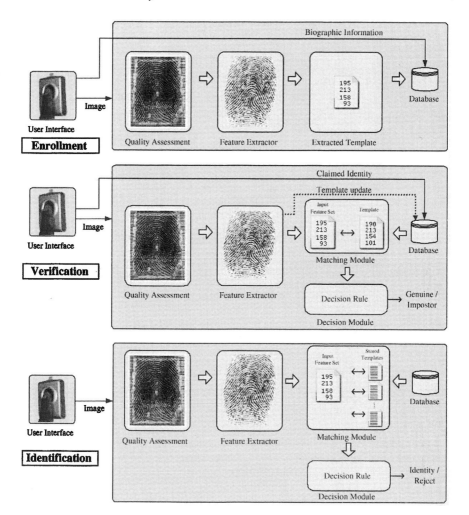

Figure 1.5. Enrollment and recognition (verification and identification) stages of a biometric system. The quality assessment module determines if the sensed data can be effectively used by the feature extractor. Note that the process of quality assessment in itself may entail the extraction of some features from the sensed data.

classified as ω_1 or ω_2 based on the variables X_Q, I, X_I and η, and the function $\mathcal{S}$.

The identification problem, on the other hand, may be stated as follows: given an input feature set X_Q, determine the identity I_k, $k \in \{1, 2, \ldots M, M+1\}$, where $I_1, I_2, \ldots I_M$ are the M identities enrolled in the system, and I_{M+1} indicates the reject case where no suitable identity can be determined for the input. Hence,

$$X_Q \in \begin{cases} I_K & \text{if } K = \arg \max_k \{\mathcal{S}(X_Q, X_{I_k})\} \text{ and } \mathcal{S}(X_Q, X_{I_K}) > \eta, \\ I_{M+1} & \text{otherwise}, \end{cases}$$

$$(1.2)$$

where X_{I_k} is the biometric template corresponding to identity I_k, and η is a predefined threshold on the match score.

In the above formulation, we assume that the match score, $\mathcal{S}(X_Q, X_I)$, indicates how *similar* X_Q and X_I are. It is also possible to view the match score as a *dissimilarity* measure or a *distance* score. A large distance score would imply a poor match between X_Q and X_I, while a large similarity score would imply a good match.

1.4   Performance of a biometric system

Unlike password-based systems, where a *perfect* match between two alphanumeric strings is necessary in order to validate a user's identity, a biometric system seldom encounters two samples of a user's biometric trait that result in exactly the same feature set. This is due to imperfect sensing conditions (e.g., noisy fingerprint due to sensor malfunction), alterations in the user's biometric characteristic (e.g., respiratory ailments impacting speaker recognition), changes in ambient conditions (e.g., inconsistent illumination levels in face recognition) and variations in the user's interaction with the sensor (e.g., occluded iris or partial fingerprints). Thus, the distance between two feature sets originating from the same biometric trait of a user is typically non-zero (a distance score of zero would indicate that the feature sets are identical). Figure 1.6 shows the minutia features extracted from three different impressions of the same finger. It is quite apparent that the features extracted from these fingerprint samples differ significantly from each other, and it is factitious to expect a perfect match between any two pairs. In fact, a perfect match might indicate the possibility that a replay attack (see Section 1.7) is being launched against the system.

The variability observed in the biometric feature set of an individual is referred to as *intra*-class variation, and the variability between feature sets originating from two different individuals is known as *inter*-class variation. A useful feature set exhibits small intra-class variation and large inter-class variation.

A similarity match score is known as a *genuine* or *authentic* score if it is a result of matching two samples of the same biometric trait of a user. It is known as an *impostor* score if it involves comparing two biometric samples originating from different users. An impostor score that exceeds the threshold η results in a false accept (or, a false match), while a genuine score that falls below the threshold η results in a false reject (or, a false non-match). The *False Accept Rate (FAR)* (or, the False Match Rate (FMR)) of a biometric system can

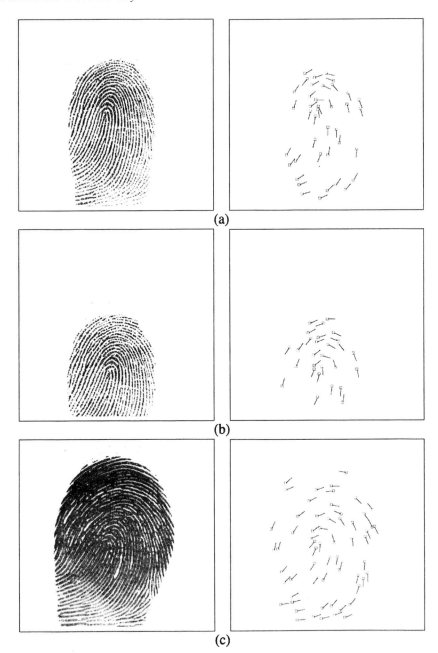

Figure 1.6. Multiple feature sets of the same biometric trait seldom result in an exact match. Here, three fingerprint impressions of a person's finger (left) and the corresponding minutia points (right) are shown. Due to variations in finger placement, elasticity of the skin and finger pressure, the minutiae distributions of the three impressions are observed to be quite different. A perfect match between two samples of the same finger is almost impossible to achieve.

therefore be defined as the fraction of impostor scores exceeding the threshold η. Similarly, the *False Reject Rate (FRR)* (or, the False Non-match Rate (FNMR))[3] of a system may be defined as the fraction of genuine scores falling below the threshold η. The *Genuine Accept Rate (GAR)* is the fraction of genuine scores exceeding the threshold η. Therefore,

$$GAR = 1 - FRR. \qquad (1.3)$$

Regulating the value of η changes the FRR and the FAR values, but for a given biometric system, it is not possible to decrease both these errors simultaneously. When a large number of genuine and impostor scores is available, one could *estimate* the probability density functions of the two sets of scores in order to analytically derive the FAR and FRR. Let $p(s|genuine)$ and $p(s|impostor)$ represent the probability density functions (or, probability distributions) of the score s under the genuine and impostor conditions, respectively. Then for a particular threshold, η,

$$FAR(\eta) = \int_{\eta}^{\infty} p(s|impostor)ds, \qquad (1.4)$$

$$FRR(\eta) = \int_{-\infty}^{\eta} p(s|genuine)ds. \qquad (1.5)$$

If the match score represents a distance or dissimilarity value, then $FAR(\eta)$ and $FRR(\eta)$ may be expressed as follows:

$$FAR(\eta) = \int_{-\infty}^{\eta} p(s|impostor)ds, \qquad (1.6)$$

$$FRR(\eta) = \int_{\eta}^{\infty} p(s|genuine)ds. \qquad (1.7)$$

Figure 1.7 illustrates the genuine and impostor distributions corresponding to a face biometric system. The similarity scores, in this case, are taken from the NIST BSSR1 database (see Appendix) and originate from a matcher identified as Face-G.

The FAR and FRR at various values of η can be summarized using a Detection Error Tradeoff (DET) curve (Martin et al., 1997) that plots the FRR against the FAR at various thresholds on a *normal deviate* scale and interpolates between these points (Figure 1.8(a)). When a linear, logarithmic or semi-logarithmic scale is used to plot these error rates, then the resulting graph is known as a Receiver Operating Characteristic (ROC) curve (Egan, 1975). In many instances, the ROC curve plots the GAR (rather than the FRR) against the FAR (see Figure

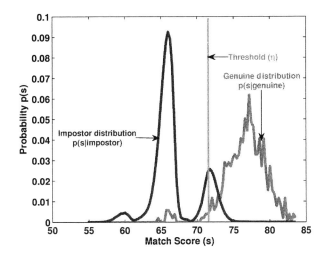

Figure 1.7. The genuine and impostor distributions corresponding to the Face-G matcher in the NIST BSSR1 database. The threshold, η, determines the FAR and FRR of the system. Note that given these two distributions, the FAR and the FRR cannot be reduced *simultaneously* by adjusting the threshold.

1.8(b) and (c)). The primary difference between the DET and ROC curves is the use of the normal deviate scale in the former.

It is important to note that the occurrence of false accepts and false rejects is not evenly distributed across the users of a biometric system. There are inherent differences in the "recognizability" of different users. Doddington et al., 1998 identify four categories of biometric users based on these inherent differences. Although this categorization (more popularly known as Doddington's zoo) was originally made in the context of speaker recognition, it is applicable to other biometric modalities as well.

1 Sheep represent users whose biometric feature sets are very distinctive and exhibit low intra-class variations. Therefore, these users are expected to have low false accept and false reject errors.

2 Goats refer to users who are prone to false rejects. The biometric feature sets of such users typically exhibit large intra-class variations.

3 Lambs are users whose biometric feature set overlaps extensively with those of other individuals. The biometric feature sets of these users have low inter-class variations. Thus, a randomly chosen user (from the target population) has a high probability of being accepted as a lamb than as a sheep. The false accept rate associated with these users is typically high.

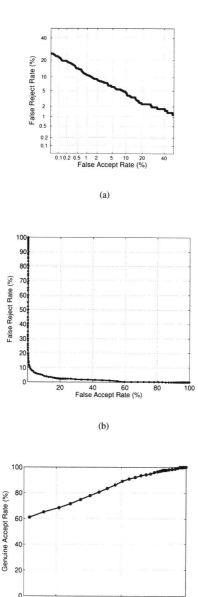

Figure 1.8. The performance of a biometric system can be summarized using DET and ROC curves. In this example, the performance curves are computed using the match scores of the Face-G matcher from the NIST BSSR1 database. The graph in (a) shows a DET curve that plots FRR against FAR in the normal deviate scale. In (b) a ROC curve plots FRR against FAR in the linear scale, while in (c) a ROC curve plots GAR against FAR in a semi-logarithmic scale.

4 Wolves indicate individuals who are successful in manipulating their biometric trait (especially behavioral traits) in order to impersonate legitimately enrolled users of a system. Therefore, these users can increase the false accept rate of the system.

Doddington et al., 1998 discuss the use of statistical testing procedures to detect the presence of goats, lambs and wolves in a voice biometric system. A combination of the F-test, Kruskal Wallis test and Durbin test is used to establish the occurrence of these categories of users in the 1998 NIST database of speech segments that was used in the evaluation of speaker recognition algorithms (http://www.nist.gov/speech/tests/spk/1998/current_plan.htm).

Besides the two types of errors (viz., false accept and false reject) indicated above, a biometric system can encounter other types of failures as well. The *Failure to Acquire (FTA)* (also known as Failure to Capture (FTC)) rate denotes the proportion of times the biometric device fails to capture a sample when the biometric characteristic is presented to it. This type of error typically occurs when the device is not able to locate a biometric signal of sufficiently good quality (e.g., an extremely faint fingerprint or an occluded face image). The FTA rate is also impacted by sensor wear and tear. Thus, periodic sensor maintenance is instrumental for the efficient functioning of a biometric system. The *Failure to Enroll (FTE)* rate denotes the proportion of users that cannot be successfully enrolled in a biometric system. User training may be necessary to ensure that an individual interacts with a biometric system appropriately in order to facilitate the acquisition of good quality biometric data. This necessitates the design of robust and efficient user interfaces that can assist an individual both during enrollment and recognition.

There is a tradeoff between the FTE rate and the perceived system accuracy as measured by FAR/FRR. FTE errors typically occur when the system rejects poor quality inputs during enrollment; consequently, if the threshold on quality is high, the system database contains only good quality templates and the perceived system accuracy improves. Because of the interdependence among the failure rates and error rates, all these rates (i.e., FTE, FTC, FAR, FRR) constitute important performance specifications of a biometric system, and should be reported during system evaluation along with the target population using the system.

The performance of a biometric system may also be summarized using other single-valued measures such as the Equal Error Rate (EER) and the d-prime value. The EER refers to that point in a DET curve where the FAR equals the FRR; a lower EER value, therefore, indicates better performance. The d-prime value (d') measures the separation between the means of the genuine and impostor probability distributions in standard deviation units and is defined as,

$$d' = \frac{\sqrt{2} \mid \mu_{genuine} - \mu_{impostor} \mid}{\sqrt{\sigma_{genuine}^2 + \sigma_{impostor}^2}},$$

where the μ's and σ's are the means and standard deviations, respectively, of the genuine and impostor distributions. A higher d-prime value indicates better performance. If the genuine and impostor distributions indeed follow a normal (Gaussian) distribution with equal variance (a very unlikely situation in the practical biometric domain), then d' reduces to the normal deviate value (Swets et al., 1961). Poh and Bengio, 2005b introduce another single-valued measure known as F-Ratio which is defined as,

$$\text{F-ratio} = \frac{\mu_{genuine} - \mu_{impostor}}{\sigma_{genuine} + \sigma_{impostor}}.$$

If the genuine and impostor distributions are Gaussian, then the EER and F-ratio are related according to the following expression:

$$\text{EER} = \frac{1}{2} - \frac{1}{2}\text{erf}\left(\frac{\text{F-ratio}}{\sqrt{2}}\right),$$

where

$$\text{erf}(x) = \frac{2}{\sqrt{\pi}} \int_0^x e^{-t^2} dt.$$

In the case of identification, the input feature set is compared against all templates residing in the database in order to determine the top match (i.e, the best match). The top match can be determined by examining the match scores pertaining to all the comparisons and reporting the identity of the template corresponding to the largest similarity score. The *identification rate* indicates the proportion of times a previously enrolled individual is successfully mapped to the correct identity in the system. Here, we assume that the question being asked is, "Does the top match correspond to the correct identity?" An alternate question could be, "Does any one of the top k matches correspond to the correct identity?" (see Moon and Phillips, 2001). The rank-k identification rate, R_k, indicates the proportion of times the correct identity occurs in the top k matches as determined by the match score. Rank-k performance can be summarized using the Cumulative Match Characteristic (CMC) curve (Moon and Phillips, 2001) that plots R_k against k, for $k = 1, 2, \ldots M$ with M being the number of enrolled users. The relationship between CMC and DET/ROC curves has been discussed by Grother and Phillips, 2004 and Bolle et al., 2005.

The biometric of choice for a particular application is primarily dictated by the error rates and failure rates discussed above. Other factors such as the cost of the system, throughput rate, user acceptance, ease of use, robustness

Table 1.1. Authentication solutions employing biometrics can be used in a variety of applications which depend on reliable user authentication mechanisms.

FORENSICS	GOVERNMENT	COMMERCIAL
Corpse identification	National ID card	ATM
Criminal investigation	Driver's license; voter registration	Access control; computer login
Parenthood determination	Welfare disbursement	Mobile phone
Missing children	Border crossing	E-commerce; Internet; banking; smart card

of the sensor, etc. also determine the suitability of a biometric system for an application.

1.5   Applications of biometrics

Establishing the identity of a person with high confidence is becoming critical in a number of applications in our vastly interconnected society. Questions like "Is she really who she claims to be?", "Is this person authorized to use this facility?" or "Is he in the watchlist posted by the government?" are routinely being posed in a variety of scenarios ranging from issuing a driver's licence to gaining entry into a country. The need for reliable user authentication techniques has increased in the wake of heightened concerns about security, and rapid advancements in networking, communication and mobility. Thus, biometrics is being increasingly incorporated in several different applications. These applications can be categorized into three main groups (see Table 1.1):

1 Commercial applications such as computer network login, electronic data security, e-commerce, Internet access, ATM or credit card use, physical access control, mobile phone, PDA, medical records management, distance learning, etc.

2 Government applications such as national ID card, managing inmates in a correctional facility, driver's license, social security, welfare-disbursement, border control, passport control, etc.

3 Forensic applications such as corpse identification, criminal investigation, parenthood determination, etc.

Examples of a few applications where biometrics is being used for authenticating individuals are presented below (also see Figure 1.9).

1 The *Schiphol Privium* scheme at Amsterdam's Schipol airport employs iris scan smart cards to speed up the immigration procedure. Passengers who are voluntarily enrolled in this scheme insert their smart card at the gate and peek into a camera; the camera acquires the eye image of the traveler and processes it to locate the iris, and computes the Iriscode (Daugman, 1999); the computed Iriscode is compared with the data residing in the smart card to complete user verification. A similar scheme is also being used to verify the identity of Schiphol airport employees working in high-security areas. This is a good example of a biometric system that is being used to enhance user convenience while improving security.

2 The Ben Gurion International Airport at Tel Aviv employs automated hand geometry-based identification kiosks to enable Israeli citizens and frequent international travelers to rapidly go through the passport inspection process. Currently more than 160,000 Israeli citizens are enrolled in this program. The kiosk-based system uses the credit card of the traveler to begin the verification process. The hand geometry information is then used for validating the traveler's identity and ensuring that the individual is not a security hazard. The automated inspection process takes less than 20 seconds and has considerably reduced the waiting time for passengers.

3 Some financial institutions in Japan have installed palm-vein authentication systems in their ATMs to help validate the identity of a customer intending to conduct a transaction. A contactless sensor is used to image the vein pattern pertaining to the customer's palm using a near infrared lighting source. Thus, a person does not have to directly place the palm on the device.

4 Kroger, a US supermarket chain, has deployed fingerprint scanners in some of its stores in order to help customers cash payroll checks or render payment after a purchase. Interested customers can enroll their index finger along with details of their credit/debit card (or electronic check); the customer's driver's licence is used to validate the identity during the time of enrollment.

5 Season pass holders accessing theme park facilities at Disney World, Orlando, have their finger geometry information stored in a central repository. When a visitor presents her pass to access a facility in the theme park, the biometric information presented at the entrance is compared with the data in the repository. This ensures that multiple individuals do not use the same season pass fraudulently. The personal details of the visitor are not associated with the finger geometry data in the repository thereby imparting security without compromising privacy.

6 The United States Visitor and Immigration Status Indicator Technology (US-VISIT) is a border security system that has been deployed at 115 airports,

15 seaports and in the secondary inspection areas of the 50 busiest land ports of entry. Foreign visitors entering the United States have their left and right index fingers scanned by a fingerprint sensor. The biometric data acquired is used to validate an individual's travel documents at the port of entry. A biometric exit procedure has also been adopted in some airports and seaports to facilitate a visitor's future trips to the country. Although two-print information is currently being used, the system might employ all ten fingers of a person in the future; this would ensure that the US-VISIT fingerprint database is compatible with the ten-print database maintained by the FBI in its Integrated Automated Fingerprint Identification System (IAFIS - see `http://www.fbi.gov/hq/cjisd/iafis.htm`).

1.6   Biometric characteristics

A number of biometric characteristics are being used in various applications. Each biometric has its pros and cons and, therefore, the choice of a biometric trait for a particular application depends on a variety of issues besides its matching performance. Jain et al., 1999a have identified seven factors that determine the suitability of a physical or a behavioral trait to be used in a biometric application.

1 **Universality**: Every individual accessing the application should possess the trait.

2 **Uniqueness**: The given trait should be sufficiently different across individuals comprising the population.

3 **Permanence**: The biometric trait of an individual should be sufficiently invariant over a period of time with respect to the matching algorithm. A trait that changes significantly over time is not a useful biometric.

4 **Measurability**: It should be possible to acquire and digitize the biometric trait using suitable devices that do not cause undue inconvenience to the individual. Furthermore, the acquired raw data should be amenable to processing in order to extract representative feature sets.

5 **Performance**: The recognition accuracy and the resources required to achieve that accuracy should meet the constraints imposed by the application.

6 **Acceptability**: Individuals in the target population that will utilize the application should be willing to present their biometric trait to the system.

7 **Circumvention**: This refers to the ease with which the trait of an individual can be imitated using artifacts (e.g., fake fingers), in the case of physical traits, and mimicry, in the case of behavioral traits.

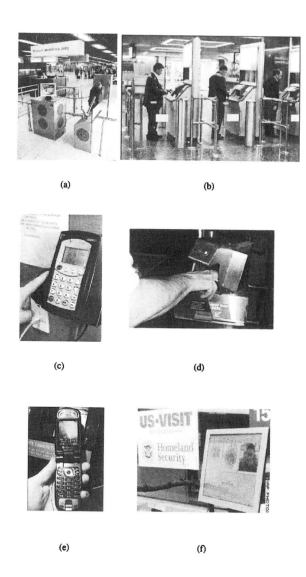

Figure 1.9. Biometric systems are being deployed in various applications. (a) The Schiphol Privium program at the Amsterdam airport uses iris scans to validate the identity of a traveler (www.airport-technology.com). (b) The Ben Gurion airport in Tel Aviv uses Express Card entry kiosks fitted with hand geometry systems for security and immigration (www.airportnet. org). (c) A few Kroger stores in Texas use fingerprint verification systems that enable customers to render payment at the check-out counter. The fingerprint information of a customer is linked with her credit or debit card (www.detnews.com). (d) Finger geometry information is used in Disney World, Orlando to ensure that a single season pass is not fraudulently used by multiple visitors. (e) A cell-phone that validates authorized users using fingerprints and allows them access to the phone's special functionalities such as mobile-banking (www.mobileburn.com). (f) The US-VISIT program currently employs two-print information to validate the travel documents of visitors to the United States (www.dhs.gov).

No single biometric is expected to effectively meet all the requirements (e.g., accuracy, practicality, cost) imposed by all applications (e.g., Digital Rights Management (DRM), access control, welfare distribution). In other words, no biometric is *ideal* but a number of them are *admissible*. The relevance of a specific biometric to an application is established depending upon the nature and requirements of the application, and the properties of the biometric characteristic. A brief introduction to some of the commonly used biometric characteristics is given below:

1 **Face**: Face recognition is a non-intrusive method, and facial attributes are probably the most common biometric features used by humans to recognize one another. The applications of facial recognition range from a static, controlled "mug-shot" authentication to a dynamic, uncontrolled face identification in a cluttered background. The most popular approaches to face recognition (Li and Jain, 2005) are based on either (i) the location and shape of facial attributes, such as the eyes, eyebrows, nose, lips, and chin and their spatial relationships, or (ii) the overall (global) analysis of the face image that represents a face as a weighted combination of a number of canonical faces. While the authentication performance of the face recognition systems that are commercially available is reasonable (Phillips et al., 2003), they impose a number of restrictions on how the facial images are obtained, often requiring a fixed and simple background with controlled illumination. These systems also have difficulty in matching face images captured from two different views, under different illumination conditions, and at different times. It is questionable whether the face itself, without any contextual information, is a sufficient basis for recognizing a person from a large number of identities with an extremely high level of confidence. In order that a facial recognition system works well in practice, it should automatically (i) detect whether a face is present in the acquired image; (ii) locate the face if there is one; and (iii) recognize the face from a general viewpoint (i.e., from any pose).

2 **Fingerprint**: Humans have used fingerprints for personal identification for many decades. The matching (i.e., identification) accuracy using fingerprints has been shown to be very high (Wilson et al., 2004; Maio et al., 2004). A fingerprint is the pattern of ridges and valleys on the surface of a fingertip whose formation is determined during the first seven months of fetal development. It has been empirically determined that the fingerprints of identical twins are different and so are the prints on each finger of the same person (Maltoni et al., 2003). Today, most fingerprint scanners cost less than US $50 when ordered in large quantities and the marginal cost of embedding a fingerprint-based biometric in a system (e.g., laptop computer) has become affordable in a large number of applications. The accuracy of

the currently available fingerprint recognition systems is adequate for authentication systems in several applications, particularly forensics. Multiple fingerprints of a person (e.g., ten-prints used in IAFIS) provide additional information to allow for large-scale identification involving millions of identities. One problem with large-scale fingerprint recognition systems is that they require a huge amount of computational resources, especially when operating in the identification mode. Finally, fingerprints of a small fraction of the population may be unsuitable for automatic identification because of genetic factors, aging, environmental or occupational reasons (e.g., manual workers may have a large number of cuts and bruises on their fingerprints that keep changing).

3 **Hand geometry**: Hand geometry recognition systems are based on a number of measurements taken from the human hand, including its shape, size of palm, and the lengths and widths of the fingers (Zunkel, 1999). Commercial hand geometry-based authentication systems have been installed in hundreds of locations around the world. The technique is very simple, relatively easy to use, and inexpensive. Environmental factors such as dry weather or individual anomalies such as dry skin do not appear to adversely affect the authentication accuracy of hand geometry-based systems. However, the geometry of the hand is not known to be very distinctive and hand geometry-based recognition systems cannot be scaled up for systems requiring identification of an individual from a large population. Furthermore, hand geometry information may not be invariant during the growth period of children. In addition, an individual's jewelry (e.g., rings) or limitations in dexterity (e.g., from arthritis), may pose challenges in extracting the correct hand geometry information. The physical size of a hand geometry-based system is large, and it cannot be embedded in certain devices like laptops. There are authentication systems available that are based on measurements of only a few fingers (typically, index and middle) instead of the entire hand. These devices are smaller than those used for hand geometry, but still much larger than those used for procuring certain other traits (e.g., fingerprint, face, voice).

4 **Palmprint**: The palms of the human hands contain pattern of ridges and valleys much like the fingerprints. The area of the palm is much larger than the area of a finger and, as a result, palmprints are expected to be even more distinctive than the fingerprints (Zhang et al., 2003; Kumar et al., 2003). Since palmprint scanners need to capture a large area, they are bulkier and more expensive than the fingerprint sensors. Human palms also contain additional distinctive features such as principal lines and wrinkles that can be captured even with a lower resolution scanner, which would be cheaper (Duta et al., 2002). Finally, when using a high-resolution palmprint scanner,

all the features of the hand such as geometry, ridge and valley features (e.g., minutiae and singular points such as deltas), principal lines, and wrinkles may be combined to build a highly accurate biometric system.

5 **Iris**: The iris is the annular region of the eye bounded by the pupil and the sclera (white of the eye) on either side. The visual texture of the iris is formed during fetal development and stabilizes during the first two years of life (the pigmentation, however, continues changing over an extended period of time Wasserman, 1974). The complex iris texture carries very distinctive information useful for personal recognition (Daugman, 2004). The accuracy and speed of currently deployed iris-based recognition systems is promising and support the feasibility of large-scale identification systems based on iris information. Each iris is distinctive and even the irises of identical twins are different. It is possible to detect contact lenses printed with a fake iris (see Daugman, 1999). The hippus movement of the eye may also be used as a measure of liveness for this biometric. Although early iris-based recognition systems required considerable user participation and were expensive, the newer systems have become more user-friendly and cost-effective (Negin et al., 2000; Fancourt et al., 2005). While iris systems have a very low False Accept Rate (FAR) compared to other biometric traits, the False Reject Rate (FRR) of these systems can be rather high (International Biometric Group, 2005).

6 **Keystroke**: It is hypothesized that each person types on a keyboard in a characteristic way. This biometric is not expected to be unique to each individual but it may be expected to offer sufficient discriminatory information to permit identity verification (Monrose and Rubin, 1997). Keystroke dynamics is a behavioral biometric; one may expect to observe large intra-class variations in a person's typing patterns due to changes in emotional state, position of the user with respect to the keyboard, type of keyboard used, etc. The keystrokes of a person could be monitored unobtrusively as that person is keying in information. This biometric permits "continuous verification" of an individual's identity over a session after the person logs in using a stronger biometric such as fingerprint or iris.

7 **Signature**: The way a person signs her name is known to be a characteristic of that individual (Nalwa, 1997; Lee et al., 1996). Although signatures require contact with the writing instrument and an effort on the part of the user, they have been accepted in government, legal, and commercial transactions as a method of authentication. With the proliferation of PDAs and Tablet PCs, on-line signature may emerge as the biometric of choice in these devices. Signature is a behavioral biometric that changes over a period of time and is influenced by the physical and emotional conditions of the signatories. Signatures of some people vary substantially: even successive

impressions of their signature are significantly different. Further, professional forgers may be able to reproduce signatures that fool the signature verification system (Harrison, 1981).

8 **Voice**: Voice is a combination of physical and behavioral biometric characteristics (Campbell, 1997). The physical features of an individual's voice are based on the shape and size of the appendages (e.g., vocal tracts, mouth, nasal cavities, and lips) that are used in the synthesis of the sound. These physical characteristics of human speech are invariant for an individual, but the behavioral aspect of the speech changes over time due to age, medical conditions (such as common cold), emotional state, etc. Voice is also not very distinctive and may not be appropriate for large-scale identification. A text-dependent voice recognition system is based on the utterance of a fixed predetermined phrase. A text-independent voice recognition system recognizes the speaker independent of what she speaks. A text-independent system is more difficult to design than a text-dependent system but offers more protection against fraud. A disadvantage of voice-based recognition is that speech features are sensitive to a number of factors such as background noise. Speaker recognition is most appropriate in telephone-based applications but the voice signal is typically degraded in quality by the communication channel.

9 **Gait**: Gait refers to the manner in which a person walks, and is one of the few biometric traits that can be used to recognize people at a distance. Therefore, this trait is very appropriate in surveillance scenarios where the identity of an individual can be surreptitiously established. Most gait recognition algorithms attempt to extract the human silhouette in order to derive the spatio-temporal attributes of a moving individual. Hence, the selection of a good model to represent the human body is pivotal to the efficient functioning of a gait recognition system. Some algorithms use the optic flow associated with a set of dynamically extracted moving points on the human body to describe the gait of an individual (Nixon et al., 1999). Gait-based systems also offer the possibility of tracking an individual over an extended period of time. However, the gait of an individual is affected by several factors including the choice of footwear, nature of clothing, affliction of the legs, walking surface, etc.

1.7   Limitations of biometric systems

While biometric systems impart several advantages to both civilian and government authentication applications over password- and token-based approaches, it is imperative that the vulnerabilities and limitations of these systems are considered when deploying them in real-world applications involving a large number of users (viz., in the order of millions). Some of the challenges commonly encountered by biometric systems are listed below.

1 **Noise in sensed data**: A fingerprint image with a scar, or a voice sample altered by cold are examples of noisy data. Noisy data may also result from defective or improperly maintained sensors (e.g., accumulation of dirt on a fingerprint sensor) or unfavorable ambient conditions (e.g., poor illumination of a user's face in a face recognition system). Noisy biometric data may not be successfully matched with corresponding templates in the database, resulting in a genuine user being incorrectly rejected.

2 **Intra-class variations**: Intra-class variations in biometric systems are typically caused by an individual who is incorrectly interacting with the sensor (e.g., incorrect facial pose - see Figure 1.10), or due to changes in the biometric characteristics of a person over a period of time (e.g., change in hand geometry). These variations can be handled by storing multiple templates for every user and updating these templates over time (Uludag et al., 2004). Template update is an essential ingredient of any biometric system since it accounts for changes in a person's biometric with the passage of time. The face, hand and voice modalities, in particular, can benefit from suitably implemented template update mechanisms.

Intra-class variations are more prominent in behavioral traits since the varying psychological makeup of an individual might result in vastly different behavioral characteristics at different time instances. For example, depending on the stress level of an individual, the voice sample presented by the person at the time of authentication may be significantly different from the enrolled template. Similarly, an inebriated person's gait and signature may be substantially altered resulting in false rejects.

3 **Inter-class similarities**: Inter-class similarity refers to the overlap of feature spaces corresponding to multiple classes or individuals. In an identification system comprising of a large number of enrolled individuals, the inter-class similarity between individuals will increase the false match rate of the system. Therefore, there is an upper bound on the number of individuals that can be effectively discriminated by the biometric system. Golfarelli et al., 1997 state that the number of distinguishable patterns in two of the most commonly used representations of hand geometry and face are only of the order of 10^5 and 10^3, respectively (also see Table 1.2). This implicit (upper) bound on the number of distinguishable patterns indicates that the capacity of an identification system (i.e., the number of enrolled users) cannot be arbitrarily increased for a fixed feature set and matching algorithm.

4 **Non-universality**: The biometric system may not be able to acquire meaningful biometric data from a subset of users. A fingerprint biometric sys-

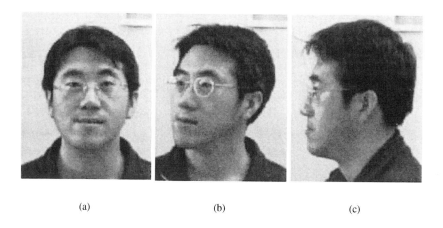

(a)   (b)   (c)

Figure 1.10. Intra-class variation associated with an individual's face image. Due to change in pose, an appearance-based face recognition system is unlikely to match these three images successfully, although they belong to the same individual (Hsu, 2002).

tem, for example, may extract incorrect minutia features from the finger-prints of certain individuals, due to the poor quality of the ridges (Figure 1.11). Thus, there is a failure to enroll (FTE) rate associated with using a single biometric trait. The International Biometric Group (IBG) recently evaluated the performance of a specific iris recognition software (Iridian KnoWho OEM SDK) on iris images obtained using three different iris cameras (LG IrisAccess 3000, OKI Electronics IRISPASS-WG and Panasonic BM-ET300) from 1,224 subjects. It was reported that between 1.6% and 7% of the participants could not be successfully enrolled based on the camera that was used (International Biometric Group, 2005).

5 **Interoperability issues**: Most biometric systems operate under the assumption that the biometric data to be compared are obtained using the same sensor and, hence, are restricted in their ability to match or compare biometric data originating from different sensors. For example, a speaker recognition system may find it challenging to compare voice prints originating from two different handset technologies such as electret and carbon-button (Martin et al., 2000). Phillips et al., 2000a state that the performance of face recognition algorithms is severely affected when the images used for comparison are captured using different camera types. Similarly, fingerprints obtained using multiple sensor technologies cannot be reliably compared (Ross and Jain, 2004) due to variations in sensor technology, image resolution, sensing area, distortion effects, etc. Although progress has been made in the development of common data exchange formats to facilitate the exchange

Table 1.2. The false accept and false reject error rates associated with the fingerprint, face, voice and iris modalities. The accuracy estimates of biometric systems depend on a number of test conditions including the sensor employed, acquisition protocol used, subject disposition, number of subjects, number of biometric samples per subject, demographic profile of test subjects, subject habituation, time lapse between data acquisition, etc.

Biometric Trait	Test	Test Conditions	False Reject Rate	False Accept Rate
Fingerprint	FVC 2004 (Maio et al., 2004)	Exaggerated skin distortion, rotation	2%	2%
Fingerprint	FpVTE 2003 (Wilson et al., 2004)	US Government operational data	0.1%	1%
Face	FRVT 2002 (Phillips et al., 2003)	Varied lighting, outdoor/indoor, time	10%	1%
Voice	NIST 2004 (Przybocki and Martin, 2004)	Text independent, multi-lingual	5-10%	2-5%
Iris	ITIRT 2005 (International Biometric Group, 2005)	Indoor environment, multiple visits	0.99%	0.94%

of feature sets between vendors (Podio et al., 2001), very little effort has been invested in the actual development of algorithms and techniques to match these feature sets. The US-VISIT program for example, obtains fingerprint (and face) information of millions of travelers arriving at U.S. airports and seaports. An optical fingerprint sensor is currently being used during the enrollment phase to procure fingerprint images. However, it is not guaranteed that a similar type of sensor will be used at a later time when verifying the same individual. It is possible that due to advancements in sensor technology, it will be more desirable and cost effective to use newer types of sensors. The cost and time involved in re-enrolling individuals every time the sensor is changed will be tremendous, and could potentially lead to huge bottlenecks in the system resulting in user inconvenience. In cases such as these, the need for feature extraction and matching algorithms that oper-

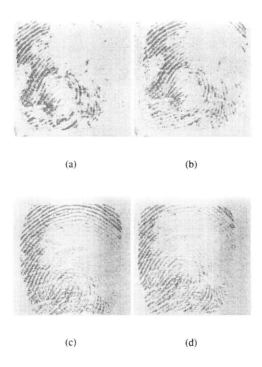

(a)   (b)

(c)   (d)

Figure 1.11. Non-universality of fingerprints. The four impressions of a user's fingerprint shown here cannot be enrolled by most fingerprint systems due to the poor image quality of the ridges. Consequently, alternate methods must be adopted in order to include this user in the biometric authentication system.

ate seamlessly across different sensors is paramount and will significantly impact the usability of the system over a period of time.

6 **Spoof attacks**: Spoofing involves the deliberate manipulation of one's biometric traits in order to avoid recognition, or the creation of physical biometric artifacts in order to take on the identity of another person. This type of attack is especially relevant when behavioral traits such as signature (Harrison, 1981) and voice (Eriksson and Wretling, 1997) are used. However, physical traits such as fingerprints and iris are also susceptible to spoof attacks (Matsumoto et al., 2002; Matsumoto et al., 2004). The possibility of generating digital artifacts of biometric characteristics in order to circumvent a biometric system has also been demonstrated (see Hill, 2001; Adler, 2003; Uludag and Jain, 2004; Ross et al., 2005). Spoof attacks, when successful, can severely undermine the security afforded by a biometric system. There are several ways to address issues related to spoofing. In the case of physical traits, such as fingerprint and iris, a liveness detection

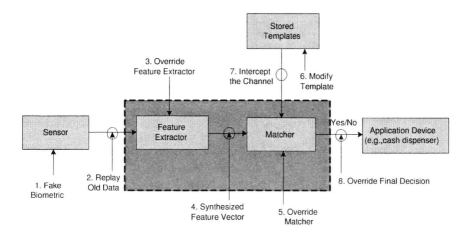

Figure 1.12. A biometric system is vulnerable to a variety of attacks (adapted from Ratha et al., 2001). For functional integrity, there should be protocols in place that deflect, detect and rectify the consequences of these attacks.

scheme may be used to detect artifacts; in the case of behavioral traits, a challenge-response mechanism may be employed to detect spoofing (United Kingdom Biometric Working Group, 2003).

7 **Other vulnerabilities**: A biometric system, like any other security application, is vulnerable to a broad range of attacks. Ratha et al., 2001 identify several levels of attacks that can be launched against a biometric system (Figure 1.12): (i) a fake biometric trait such as an artificial finger may be presented at the sensor, (ii) illegally intercepted biometric data may be re-submitted to the system, (iii) the feature extractor may be replaced by a Trojan horse program that produces pre-determined feature sets, (iv) legitimate feature sets may be replaced with synthetic feature sets, (v) the matcher may be replaced by a Trojan horse program that always outputs high scores thereby defying system security, (vi) the templates stored in the database may be modified or removed, or new templates may be introduced in the database, (vii) the data in the communication channel between two modules of the system may be altered, and (viii) the final decision output by the biometric system may be overridden. This demands the design of effective countermeasures that can be used to prevent or detect these attacks.

1.8 Biometric standards

With the increased deployment of biometric-based authentication solutions in several civilian and government applications, there is a definite need for standardization of biometric systems in order (a) to facilitate interoperability between vendors, and (b) to ensure that biometric sub-systems can be easily integrated into a variety of applications. To this end, there have been concerted efforts to draft biometric standards, a few of which are listed below.

1 **INCITS M1**: The International Committee for Information Technology Standards (INCITS) in the United States is involved in the standardization of Information and Communication Technology (ICT). It is accredited by the American National Standards Institute (ANSI) and operates under the rules instituted by ANSI. In November 2001, INCITS established a Technical Committee for Biometrics called M1 (http://www.ncits.org/tc_ home/m1.htm) in order to develop biometric standards for application program interfaces, security mechanisms, data interchange formats, common file formats, data quality, performance testing, etc. M1 consists of several task groups: (i) M1.2 deals with the interfaces between biometric components and sub-systems; (ii) M1.3 handles data interchange formats for fingerprint, face, iris, signature and hand geometry; (iii) M1.4 focuses on biometric application profiles pertaining to transportation workers, border management and point-of-sale transactions; (iv) M1.5 develops metrics for measuring and reporting biometric performance; and (v) M1.6 investigates the use of technical solutions, such as privacy enhancing measures, to address cross jurisdictional and societal issues related to the implementation of biometrics. Apart from these task groups, M1 also supports ad-hoc groups working on multibiometric systems (M1 ad-hoc group), biometric data quality (M1.3 ad-hoc group) and e-authentication (M1.4 ad-hoc group).

2 **ISO/IEC JTC1 SC37**: The International Standards Organization (ISO) and the International Electrotechnical Commission (IEC) established the Joint Technical Committee 1 (JTC1) to help in the standardization of Information Technology. In June 2002, JTC1 initiated a new sub-committee, SC37, on biometrics (see http://isotc.iso.org). This sub-committee has six Working Groups (WGs) dealing with biometric vocabulary and definitions (WG01), biometric technical interfaces (WG02), biometric data interchange formats (WG03), application profiles for biometric applications (WG04), biometric testing and reporting (WG05) and the societal aspects of biometric implementation (WG06). The M1 Technical Committee on biometrics, in fact, serves as the United States Technical Advisory Group (US-TAG) for ISO/IEC JTC1 SC37.

3 **CBEFF**: The Common Biometric Exchange File Format (CBEFF) is intended to facilitate exchange of biometric data between vendors or even between different components of a biometric system (Podio et al., 2001). The information to be exchanged may be raw data (e.g., a fingerprint image), processed data (e.g., an enhanced fingerprint image), or a feature set representing the raw data (e.g., minutiae points in a fingerprint image). CBEFF

defines a set of data elements that are common across multiple biometric technologies. These data elements are placed under three major sections: (i) the Standard Biometric Header (SBH), (ii) the Biometric Specific Memory Block (BSMB), and (iii) the Signature Block (SB). By adopting such a storage format, CBEFF facilitates the co-existence of multiple biometric technologies in a single system.

4 **BioAPI**: The BioAPI standard embraces specifications for a standardized Application Programming Interface (API) that would accommodate a wide range of biometric modalities, devices and applications (`http://www.bioapi.org/`). This API is intended for biometric integrators and application programmers to develop device independent biometric solutions. Currently, there are two different versions of the API. The BioAPI 1.1 standard is an American National Standard (ANSI/INCITS 358:2002) developed by the BioAPI Consortium comprising of over 120 companies and organizations; the BioAPI 2.0 standard, on the other hand, is an international standard (ISO/IEC 19794-1:2005) that was developed by the standards committee for biometrics within ISO (i.e., ISO/IEC JTC1 SC37). These standards define an interface for executing tasks related to enrollment, verification and identification of users. The Biometric Identification Record (BIR) of the BioAPI standard conforms to CBEFF requirements.

5 **ANSI X9.84**: The X9.84 standard by the American National Standards Institute (ANSI) deals with the secure collection, storage, management and transmission of biometric data. X9.84 supports different types of key-management methods (e.g., *constructive key management*) and digital certificates (e.g., *domain certificate*). Thus, this protocol extends confidentiality, integrity and non-repudiation to the biometric data pertaining to various modalities (American National Standards Institute, 2003). The biometric object specified by ANSI X9.84 conforms to CBEFF requirements and can, in principle, operate with the Biometric Identification Record (BIR) of BioAPI.

1.9 Multibiometric systems

As discussed in Section 1.2, the biometric trait of an individual is characterized by a set of discriminatory features or attributes. In many instances, this feature set can be represented by a fixed d-dimensional feature vector, with d denoting the number of feature values used (exceptions include (i) fingerprint minutiae, where the number of features can vary across images, and (ii) Hidden Markov Model (HMM) for speech recognition, where the number of state transitions may vary across utterances). The d-dimensional feature set of an arbitrary individual often resides in a subspace manifold that overlaps with those of other individuals enrolled in the system. Thus, for a fixed identification error rate, the number of unique users that can be accommodated in the biometric system is naturally restricted due to this inherent constraint. Population characteristics such as non-universality and operational factors such as noisy input data further restrict this number. Hence, fine tuning the system parameters (of the feature extractor and matcher) cannot be expected to provide continuous performance improvement. Consider a scenario that necessitates every living individual in the planet ($\sim$ 6 billion) to be enrolled in a single biometric system operating in the identification mode. If the face modality is used, then an upper bound on the performance of the system will be based on the number of identical twins. Similarly, if the voice biometric is used, the performance will be limited by the number of people who are unable to speak coherently. Therefore, the performance of a biometric system employing a single trait is constrained by these intrinsic factors.

This inherent limitation can be alleviated by fusing the information presented by multiple sources. For example, the face and gait traits, or multiple images of the face, or the fingerprints of the right and left index fingers of an individual may be used together to resolve the identity of an individual. Fusion in biometrics helps "expand" the feature space used to represent individuals. This increases the number of people that can be effectively enrolled in a certain personal identification system. A system that consolidates the evidence presented by multiple biometric sources (i.e., cues) is known as a *multibiometric* system. These systems are also expected to be more reliable due to the availability of multiple pieces of evidence (Hong et al., 1999).

The use of multiple biometric sources for authentication was originally referred to as *layered* biometrics (Atick, 2002; Most, 2003). The term was used to indicate the integration of decisions (i.e., "match" or "no-match") rendered by multiple biometric systems. However, it is possible to integrate other types of information also, such as match scores, feature sets, raw data, etc. (besides the individual decisions) originating from multiple biometric sources. The term multibiometrics denotes the fusion of different types of information and is, therefore, much broader in scope than layered biometrics. The problem of consolidating the information or evidence presented by multiple biometric sources is known as *information fusion*, which is the main focus of this book. One of the goals of this book is to lend structure to the amorphous body of research that has been conducted in the field of multibiometrics. To this end, we have attempted to outline a framework that can be effectively used to understand the issues and progress being made in multibiometrics while identifying the challenges and potential research directions in this field.

1.10   Summary

Rapid advancements in the field of communications, computer networking and transportation, coupled with heightened concerns about identity fraud and national security, has resulted in a pronounced need for reliable and efficient identity management schemes in a myriad of applications. The process of identity management in the context of a specific application involves the creation, maintenance and obliteration of identities while ensuring that an impostor does not fraudulently gain privileges associated with a legitimately enrolled individual. Traditional authentication techniques based on passwords and tokens are limited in their ability to address issues such as negative recognition and non-repudiation. The advent of biometrics has served to address some of the shortcomings of traditional authentication methods. Biometric systems use the physical and behavioral characteristics of an individual such as fingerprint, face, hand geometry, iris, gait and voice to establish identity. A broad spectrum of establishments can engage the services of a biometric system including travel and transportation, financial institutions, health care, law enforcement agencies and various government sectors.

The deployment of biometrics in civilian and government applications has raised questions related to the privacy accorded to an enrolled individual (Davies, 1994). Specifically, questions such as (i) "Will biometric data be used to track people covertly thereby violating their right to privacy?", (ii) "Can the medical condition of a person be surreptitiously elicited from the raw biometric data?", (iii) "Will the acquired biometric data be used only for the intended purpose, or will it be used for previously unexpressed functions, hence resulting in *functionality creep*?", (iv) "Will various biometric databases be linked in order to deduce an individual's social and financial profile?", and (v) "What are the consequences of compromising a user's biometric data?", have advocated societal concerns about the use of biometric solutions in large-scale applications. The promotion of Privacy-Enhancing Technologies (PETs) can assuage some of the legitimate concerns associated with biometric-enabled technology (Rejman-Greene, 2005; Kenny and Borking, 2002). For example, the use of personal smart cards to store and process the biometric template of an individual can mitigate public concerns related to placing biometric information in a centralized database. Apart from technological solutions to address privacy concerns, government regulations are also required in order to prevent the inappropriate transmission, exchange and processing of biometric data.

The matching performance of a biometric system is affected by several factors including noisy data, large intra-class variations, and improper user interaction (Bolle et al., 2003). There is an implicit upper bound on the matching accuracy of any biometric system. Jain et al., 2004b suggest three primary reasons for this inherent constraint:

1 **Information limitation**: The magnitude of discriminatory information available in a biometric trait is naturally restricted. For example, hand geometry measurements can distinguish fewer identities than, say, fingerprints (Pankanti et al., 2002).

2 **Representation limitation**: The ideal representation scheme for a particular biometric trait should be designed to retain all invariant and discriminatory information in the sensed measurements. Practical feature extraction systems, typically based on simplistic models of biometric data, fail to capture the richness of information in a realistic biometric input resulting in the inclusion of redundant or spurious features, and the exclusion of salient features. Consequently, a significant fraction of legitimate feature space cannot be handled by the biometric system resulting in authentication errors (FAR and FRR).

3 **Matcher limitation**: Given a particular representation scheme, the design of an ideal matcher should perfectly model the invariant relationship between different patterns (i.e, biometric samples) originating from the same class (i.e, identity). In practice, however, a matcher may not correctly model the invariance (e.g., due to non-availability of sufficient number of training samples) resulting in poor matcher accuracy.

Multibiometrics is expected to alleviate some of the limitations of unibiometric systems by consolidating the evidence presented by multiple biometric sources. This integration of evidence is known as information fusion and, if appropriately done, can enhance the matching accuracy of a recognition system. Thus, a properly designed multibiometric system can improve matching accuracy, increase population coverage and deter spoofing activities. With biometrics already being chosen to deliver crucial societal functions, it is only a matter of time before multibiometric systems begin to impact the way we perform identity management in the 21st century.

Notes

1 The *identity* of an individual may be viewed as the information associated with that person in a particular identity management system. For example, a bank issuing credit cards typically associates a customer with her name, password, social security number, address and date of birth. Thus, the identity of the customer in this application will be defined by these personal attributes (i.e., name, address, etc.). The interested reader is referred to Kent and Millett, 2003 for a discussion on this terminology.

2 The term *biometric authentication* is perhaps more appropriate than *biometrics* since the latter has been historically used in the field of statistics to refer to the analysis of biological (particularly medical) data (Wayman et al., 2005). For brevity sake, we adopt the term *biometrics* in this book.

3 It behooves us to point out that, strictly speaking, FMR and FNMR are not always synonymous with FAR and FRR, respectively (see Mansfield and Wayman, 2002 and Maltoni et al., 2003). However, in this book we treat them as being equivalent.

Chapter 2

INFORMATION FUSION IN BIOMETRICS

2.1 Introduction

Information fusion has a long history and the theory of multiple classifier systems (MCS) has been rigorously studied over the past several years (Ghosh, 2002). In fact information fusion is an integral part of various application domains ranging from automatic target recognition (ATR) and remote sensing to weather forecasting, object tracking and robotics. The concept of fusion has been studied under several different terminologies (Ho, 2002; Kuncheva et al., 2001), including

- stacked generalizations (Wolpert, 1990)

- classifier ensembles (Drucker et al., 1994)

- hybrid methods (Bunke and Kandel, 2002)

- cooperative agents (Tan, 1997)

- dynamic classifier selection (Woods et al., 1997)

- opinion pool (Benediktisson and Swain, 1992)

- sensor fusion (Iyengar et al., 1995)

- mixture of experts (Jacobs et al., 1991)

- consensus aggregation (Benediktisson and Swain, 1992)

- divide-and-conquer classifiers (Chiang and Fu, 1994)

- social choice functions (Arrow, 1963).

Ho, 2002 states that there has been a paradigm shift in the approach to solving pattern recognition problems:

> Instead of looking for the best set of features and the best classifier, now we look for the best set of classifiers and then the best combination method.

The goal of information fusion, therefore, is to determine the best set of experts in a given problem domain and devise an appropriate function that can optimally combine the decisions rendered by the individual experts (Figure 2.1). A similar philosophy has been advocated by several researchers, including Minsky (Minsky, 1991) who states

> To solve really hard problems, we'll have to use several different representations ....

and,

> It is time to stop arguing over which type of pattern classification technique is best because that depends on our context and goal. Instead we should work at a higher level of organization and discover how to build managerial systems to exploit the different virtues and evade the different limitations of each of these ways of comparing things.

We briefly examine the role of data fusion in different applications. The purpose is to indicate to the reader the diversity of scientific fields that rely on information fusion schemes.

1. **Weather forecasting**: An elaborate weather forecasting system relies on the evidence provided by diverse sources of information such as geostationary meteorological satellites, weather balloons/planes, ground stations, radars, automated buoys, etc. in order to compute geophysical parameters of interest. These geophysical parameters are then collectively interpreted by an automated system to facilitate weather forecasting. The system also relies on previous results of weather prediction (temporal information) to continually refine its outputs (Palmer, 2000).

2. **UAV swarms**: A group of unmanned aerial vehicles (UAVs), searching for a mobile evasive target in a potentially hazardous environment, has to determine a flight arrangement that optimizes the integrated sensing capability of component UAVs (Vachtsevanos et al., 2004). In this type of scenario, an optimal flight configuration has to be derived based on the nature of the data acquired by the individual UAVs, constraints on the amount of information that can be transmitted between UAVs and the possibility of losing a UAV (e.g., UAV missing in action). An appropriate fusion architecture is necessary to accommodate the dynamics of the topology as well as the reliability of the sensor data obtained in order to generate efficient actions.

3. **Object detection**: Many applications attempt to detect and establish the trajectories of objects based on the evidence supplied by multiple image modalities. The fusion of visible and non-visible information pertaining to

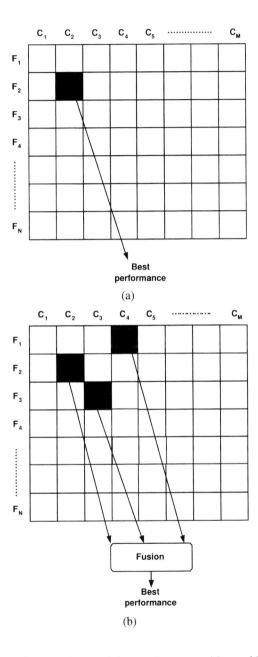

Figure 2.1. Two general approaches to solving a pattern recognition problem. Each cell in this diagram indicates the application of a particular classifier, C_i, to a specific pattern representation (i.e., feature set), F_j. The approach in (a) is to determine the best set of features and the best classifier, while in (b) the goal is to determine the best set of classifiers and an optimal fusion algorithm to integrate these classifiers. The feature sets $F_1, F_2, \ldots, F_N$ do not have to be mutually exclusive.

different wavelengths in the electromagnetic spectrum (e.g., radar and infrared images, or thermal and visible spectrum images) can assist in estimating the location and kinematic features of objects such as T-72 tanks or a squad of soldiers in a night-time battlefield. These applications rely on image fusion methodologies to combine multiple modalities (Blum and Liu, 2006).

4 **Robot navigation**: A robot is typically fitted with a variety of sound, light, image, range, proximity and force sensors that permit it to record its environment. In order to determine a suitable action (e.g., move right or tilt camera at a certain angle), the data acquired using these multiple sensors are processed simultaneously (Abidi and Gonzalez, 1992). Sensor integration in a modular framework is a challenging task since it entails the reconciliation of non-commensurate data.

5 **Land mine detection**: Several types of sensor technologies are being used to detect buried land mines. These include electromagnetic induction (EMI), ground penetrating radar (GPR), infra-red imaging (IR), quadrupole resonance (QR), chemical detectors and sensors of acoustically induced surface vibrations (Gunatilaka and Baertlein, 2001). In many cases, the data presented by these multiple sensors are concurrently used to improve the accuracy of land mine detection algorithms.

2.2   Fusion in biometrics

Humans recognize one another based on the evidence presented by multiple biometric characteristics (behavioral or physical) in addition to several contextual details associated with the environment. The recognition process itself may be viewed as the reconciliation of evidence pertaining to these multiple modalities. Each modality on its own cannot always be reliably used to perform recognition. However, the consolidation of information presented by these multiple experts can result in the accurate determination or verification of identity.

Biometric systems can also be designed to recognize a person based on information acquired from multiple biometric sources. Such systems, known as *multibiometric* systems, can be expected to be more accurate due to the presence of multiple pieces of evidence (Hong et al., 1999). Multibiometric systems offer several advantages over traditional (uni)biometric systems. Some of these advantages are listed below.

1 Multibiometric systems can offer substantial improvement in the matching accuracy of a biometric system depending upon the information being combined and the fusion methodology adopted. Thus, the FAR and the FRR of the verification system can be reduced simultaneously. Furthermore, the availability of multiple sources of information increases the feature space

available to individuals and, hence, the capacity of an identification system may be increased in order to accommodate more individuals.

2 Multibiometrics addresses the issue of non-universality or insufficient population coverage. If a person's dry fingers prevent him from successfully enrolling into a fingerprint system, then the availability of another biometric trait, say iris, can aid in the inclusion of this individual in the identity management system. A certain degree of flexibility is achieved when a user enrolls into the system using several different traits (e.g., face, voice, fingerprint, iris, hand) while only a subset of these traits (e.g., face and voice) is requested during authentication based on the nature of the application under consideration and the convenience of the user.

3 It becomes increasingly difficult (if not impossible) for an impostor to spoof multiple biometric traits of a legitimately enrolled individual. If each subsystem indicates the probability that a particular trait is a 'spoof', then appropriate fusion schemes can be employed to determine if the user, in fact, is an impostor. Furthermore, by asking the user to present a random subset of traits at the point of acquisition, a multibiometric system facilitates a challenge-response type of mechanism, thereby ensuring that the system is interacting with a *live* user. Note that a challenge-response mechanism can be initiated in unibiometric systems also (e.g., system prompts "Please say 1-2-5-7", "Blink twice and move your eyes to the right", "Change your facial expression by smiling", etc.).

4 Multibiometric systems also effectively address the problem of noisy data. When the biometric signal acquired from a single trait is corrupted with noise, the availability of other (less noisy) traits may aid in the reliable determination of identity. Some systems take into account the *quality* of the individual biometric signals during the fusion process. This is especially important when recognition has to take place in adverse conditions where certain biometric traits cannot be reliably extracted. For example, in the presence of ambient noise, when an individual's voice characteristics cannot be accurately measured, the facial characteristics may be used by the multibiometric system to perform authentication. Estimating the quality of the acquired data is in itself a challenging problem but, when appropriately done, can reap significant benefits in a multibiometric system.

5 These systems also help in the *continuous* monitoring or tracking of an individual in situations when a single trait is not sufficient. For example, a person walking down a crowded aisle can be recognized using his face and gait cues. However, depending upon the distance and pose of the subject with respect to the camera, both these characteristics may not be simultaneously

available. Therefore, either (or both) of these traits can be used depending upon the situation.

6 A multibiometric system may also be viewed as a fault tolerant system which continues to operate even when certain biometric sources become unreliable due to sensor or software malfunction, or deliberate user manipulation. The notion of fault tolerance is especially useful in large-scale authentication systems handling a large number of users (e.g., a border control system).

2.3   Issues in designing a multibiometric system

Multibiometric systems rely on the evidence presented by multiple sources of biometric information. An information fusion scheme in the context of biometrics raises several design questions as we will see shortly. Primary among these is the design of a suitable human computer interface (HCI) that would permit the efficient acquisition of an individual's biometric information. An appropriately designed interface can ensure that multiple pieces of evidence pertaining to an individual's identity are reliably acquired whilst causing minimum inconvenience to the user (Oviatt, 2003). Consider the user interface shown in Figure 2.2 which acquires the face, fingerprint and hand geometry information of an individual. This particular arrangement of the scanners might make it tedious for the person to interact with the system since the hand geometry and fingerprint sensors are spatially separated requiring the individual to explicitly interact with these two sensors. A better arrangement would be to integrate these two sensors into a single device thereby capturing the hand and fingerprint modalities simultaneously with minimum user inconvenience. As one moves from unimodal to multimodal systems, it is imperative that HCIs be carefully designed.

Some of the other factors that impact the design and structure of a multibiometric system are described below.

1 **Cost benefits**: What is the tradeoff between the added cost and the improvement in matching performance? The cost is a function of the number of sensors deployed, the time taken to acquire the biometric data, the storage requirements, the processing time of the algorithm and the perceived (in)convenience experienced by the user.

2 **Determining sources of biometric information**: What are the various sources of biometric information that can be used in a multibiometric system? Which of these sources are relevant to the application at hand?

3 **Acquisition and processing sequence**: Should the data corresponding to multiple information sources (e.g., modalities) be acquired simultaneously or at different time instances, as the need arises, in a serial fashion? Simi-

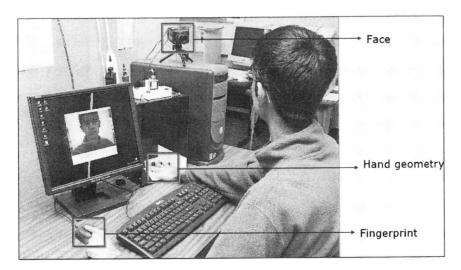

Figure 2.2. A multimodal interface to acquire face, fingerprint and hand geometry images of a person. A well designed interface can enhance user convenience and ensure that multiple sources of evidence are reliably acquired. In this example, integrating the hand and fingerprint input devices into a single unit may be beneficial as it would reduce the burden on the individual to explicitly interact with two spatially separated devices.

larly, should the information acquired be processed sequentially or simultaneously?

4 **Type of information**: What type of information or attributes (i.e., features, match scores, decisions, etc.) is to be fused? What is the impact of correlation among the sources of information on the performance of the fusion system?

5 **Fusion methodology**: What fusion scheme should be employed to combine the information presented by multiple biometric sources? Is it possible to predict the performance gain obtained using different fusion methodologies in order to determine the optimal one?

To make a business case for multibiometric systems, it is necessary to measure the performance gain as a function of the cost incurred in deploying such a system. The addition of multiple sensors, for example, would increase the cost of the system significantly especially if the user interface has to be altered in order to accommodate new devices. Furthermore, the throughput of the system can potentially decrease if the time taken to acquire the biometric data corresponding to multiple traits is high. While it is possible to quantify the additional cost of sensors and the increased authentication time, it is substantially difficult to quantify the system's ability to deter potential impostors from launching a spoof attack (if multiple traits are used). Similarly, it may not be possible to quantify the time needed (number of authentication attempts) for user habituation and the potential inconvenience as perceived by the user. In light of this, the benefit of a multibiometric system is often evaluated based on its matching accuracy, the number of users that can be accommodated in the system, the cost of adding new sensors and the additional time required for acquiring and processing multiple traits both during enrollment and authentication.

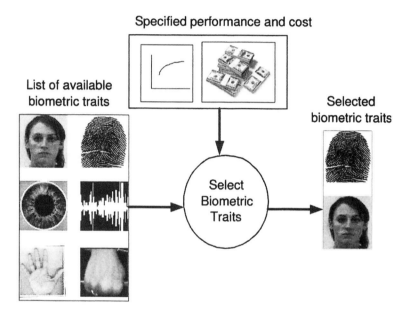

Figure 2.3. Multimodal biometric systems utilize different body traits to establish identity. In principle, a large number of traits can be used to improve the identification accuracy. In practice, factors such as cost of deployment, finite training sample size, throughput time and user training will limit the number of traits used in a particular application.

2.4   Sources of multiple evidence

What are the *sources* of information that can be considered in a multibiometric system? We address this question by introducing some terminology to describe the various scenarios that are possible to obtain multiple sources of evidence (see Figure 2.4). In the first four scenarios described below, information fusion is accomplished using a single trait, while in the fifth scenario multiple traits are used.

1 **Multi-sensor systems**: In these systems, a single biometric trait is imaged using multiple sensors in order to extract diverse information from

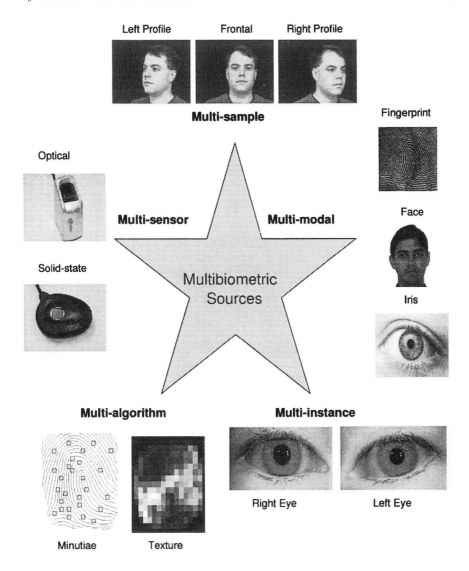

Figure 2.4. The various sources of information in a multibiometric system: multi-sensor, multi-algorithm, multi-instance, multi-sample and multimodal. In the first four scenarios, a single biometric trait provides multiple sources of evidence. In the fifth scenario, different biometric traits are used to obtain evidence.

(spatially) registered images. For example, a system may record the two-dimensional texture content of a person's face using a CCD camera and the three-dimensional surface shape of the face using a range sensor in order to perform authentication. The introduction of a new sensor (in this case, the range sensor) to measure the facial surface variation increases the cost of the multibiometric system. However, the availability of multi-sensor data pertaining to a single trait can assist the *segmentation* and *registration* procedures also (Bendjebbour et al., 2001) besides improving matching accuracy.

Marcialis and Roli, 2004a discuss a scheme to fuse the fingerprint information of a user obtained using an optical and a capacitive fingerprint sensor (spatial registration between the two sensors is not necessary in this case). The authors, in their work, indicate that the two sensors provide complementary information thereby resulting in better matching accuracy. They also suggest the possibility of employing a dynamic sensor selection scheme (Woods et al., 1997; Giacinto and Roli, 2001) wherein, based on the nature of the input data obtained from the two sensors, the information from only one of the sensors may be used to perform recognition. Chen et al., 2005a examine the face images of an individual obtained using a thermal infrared camera and a visible light camera. They demonstrate that integrating the evidence supplied by these two images (both at the score-level and rank-level) improves matching performance. Socolinsky and Selinger, 2004 and Heo et al., 2004 also demonstrate the benefits of using thermal infrared and visible light imagery for face recognition.

2 **Multi-algorithm systems**: In these systems, the same biometric data is processed using multiple algorithms. For example, a texture-based algorithm and a minutiae-based algorithm can operate on the same fingerprint image in order to extract diverse feature sets that can improve the performance of the system (Ross et al., 2003). This does not require the use of new sensors and, hence, is cost-effective. Furthermore, the user is not required to interact with multiple sensors thereby enhancing user convenience. However, it does require the introduction of new feature extractor and/or matcher modules which may increase the computational requirements of the system (Figure 2.5).

A multi-algorithm system can use multiple feature sets (i.e., multiple representations) extracted from the same biometric data or multiple matching schemes operating on a single feature set. Lu et al., 2003 discuss a face recognition system that employs three different feature extraction schemes (Principal Component Analysis (PCA), Independent Component Analysis (ICA) and Linear Discriminant Analysis (LDA)) to encode (i.e., represent) a single face image. The authors postulate that the use of different feature sets makes the system robust to a variety of intra-class variations normally associated with the face biometric. Experimental results indicate that combining multiple face classifiers can enhance the identification rate of the biometric system. Han and Bhanu, 2005 present a context-based gait recognition system which invokes and combines two gait recognition classifiers based on the walking surface. A probabilistic approach is used to combine the participating classifiers. The authors demonstrate that using context information in a fusion framework has the potential to improve the identification rate of the system. Jain et al., 1999c fuse the evidence of three different fingerprint matchers to determine the similarity between two minutiae sets. The three minutiae matchers considered in their system are based on the Hough transform, one-dimensional string matching and two-dimensional dynamic programming. They observe that the matching performance obtained by combining two of the three matchers is comparable to combining all the three matchers. Factors such as the correlation between component algorithms, the disparity in their matching accuracies, and the fusion methodology adopted significantly impact the performance obtained after fusion.

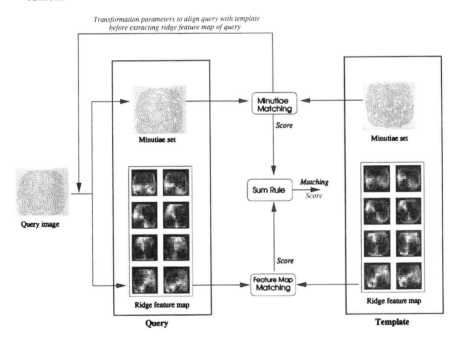

Figure 2.5. The multi-algorithm fingerprint matcher designed by Ross et al., 2003. The system utilizes both minutiae and texture information to represent and match two fingerprint images (query and template). The minutiae matching module provides the transformation parameters necessary to align the query image with the template before extracting the texture information from the former. The texture information is represented using ridge feature maps.

3 **Multi-instance systems**: These systems use multiple instances of the same body trait and are also referred to as multi-unit systems in the literature. For example, the left and right index fingers, or the left and right irises of

an individual may be used to verify an individual's identity. These systems generally do not necessitate the introduction of new sensors nor do they entail the development of new feature extraction and matching algorithms and are, therefore, cost efficient. However, in some cases, a new sensor arrangement might be necessary in order to facilitate the simultaneous capture of the various units/instances. Automated Fingerprint Identification Systems (AFIS), that obtain ten-print information from a subject, can benefit from sensors that are able to rapidly acquire impressions of all ten fingers. Multi-instance systems are especially beneficial for users whose biometric traits cannot be reliably captured due to inherent problems. For example, a single finger may not be a sufficient discriminator for a person having dry skin. However, the integration of evidence across multiple fingers may serve as a good discriminator in this case. Similarly, an iris system may not be able to image significant portions of a person's iris due to drooping eyelids. The consideration of both the irides will result in the availability of more texture information that can be used to establish the individual's identity in a more reliable manner. Multi-instance systems are often necessary in applications where the size of the system database (i.e., the number of enrolled individuals) is very large (FBI's database currently has $\sim$ 50 million ten-print images and multiple fingers provide additional discriminatory information).

4 **Multi-sample systems**: A single sensor may be used to acquire multiple samples of the same biometric trait in order to account for the variations that can occur in the trait, or to obtain a more complete representation of the underlying trait. A face system, for example, may capture (and store) the frontal profile of a person's face along with the left and right profiles in order to account for variations in the facial pose. Similarly, a fingerprint system equipped with a small size sensor may acquire multiple dab prints of an individual's finger in order to obtain images of various regions of the fingerprint. A mosaicing scheme may then be used to stitch the multiple impressions and create a composite image. One of the key issues in a multi-sample system is determining the *number* of samples that have to be acquired from an individual. It is important that the procured samples represent the *variability* as well as the *typicality* of the individual's biometric data. To this end, the desired relationship between the samples has to be established before-hand in order to optimize the benefits of the integration strategy. For example, a face recognition system utilizing both the frontal- and side-profile images of an individual may stipulate that the side-profile image should be a three-quarter view of the face (Hill et al., 1997; O'Toole et al., 1995). Alternately, given a set of biometric samples, the system should be able to automatically select the "optimal" subset that would best represent

the individual's variability. Uludag et al., 2004 discuss two such schemes in the context of fingerprint recognition.

5 **Multimodal systems**: These systems combine the evidence presented by different body traits for establishing identity. For example, some of the earliest multimodal biometric systems utilized face and voice features to establish the identity of an individual (Brunelli and Falavigna, 1995). Physically uncorrelated traits (e.g., fingerprint and iris) are expected to result in better *improvement* in performance than correlated traits (e.g., voice and lip movement). The cost of deploying these systems is substantially more due to the requirement of new sensors and, consequently, the development of appropriate user interfaces. The identification accuracy can be significantly improved by utilizing an increasing number of traits although the *curse-of-dimensionality* phenomenon would impose a bound on this number. The curse-of-dimensionality limits the number of attributes (or features) used in a pattern classification system when only a small number of training samples is available (Jain and Chandrasekaran, 1982). The number of traits used in a specific application will also be restricted by practical considerations such as the cost of deployment, enrollment time, throughput time, expected error rate, user habituation issues, etc.

6 **Hybrid systems**: Chang et al., 2005 use the term *hybrid* to refer to systems that integrate a subset of the five scenarios discussed above. For example, Brunelli and Falavigna, 1995 describe an arrangement in which two speaker recognition algorithms are combined with three face recognition algorithms at the match score and rank levels via a HyperBF network. Thus, the system is multi-algorithmic as well as multimodal in its design. Similarly, the NIST BSSR1 dataset (National Institute of Standards and Technology, 2004) has match scores pertaining to two different face matchers operating on the frontal face image of an individual (multi-algorithm), and a fingerprint matcher operating on the left- and right-index fingers of the same individual (multi-instance). Hybrid systems attempt to extract as much information as possible from the various biometric modalities.

Besides the above scenarios, it is also possible to use biometric traits in conjunction with non-biometric identity tokens in order to enhance the authentication performance. For example, Jin et al., 2004 discuss a dual factor authenticator that combines a pseudo random number (present in a token) with a facial feature set in order to produce a set of user-specific compact codes known as BioCode. The pseudo random number and the facial feature sets are fixed in length and an iterated inner product is used to generate the BioCode. When an individual's biometric information is suspected to be compromised, then the token containing the random data is replaced, thereby revoking the previous authenticator. The use of biometric and non-biometric authenticators in tandem is a powerful way of enhancing security. However, some of the inconveniences associated with traditional authenticators remain (such as "Where did I leave my token?").

Beattie et al., 2005 discuss a scenario in which biometric sensors are placed at various locations in a building in order to impart security to individual facilities/rooms (Figure 2.6). The building is partitioned into various zones based on access privileges assigned to different users of the building. The authentication decision rendered at a particular zone (for a specific user) may depend on the decisions made previously in other zones (for the same user). Furthermore, in very sensitive zones, a combination of biometric evidences may be used to validate an individual's identity, while in less sensitive zones, a single biometric evidence may be sufficient to establish identity. The fusion scheme used to combine the decisions of multiple sensors can also vary depending upon the zone that a user intends to enter. For example, the AND decision rule may be used in high security areas - a user can enter such a zone only when *all* the sensors successfully confirm the individual's identity (see Varshney et al., 2002). Therefore, the scenario described by Beattie et al., 2005 permits the inclusion of multiple fusion rules involving multiple sensors in a dynamic architecture. The presence of biometric sensors in various zones can also aid in determining an individual's location within the building.

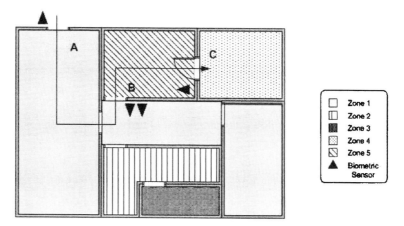

Figure 2.6. The scenario envisioned by Beattie et al., 2005 in which biometric sensors are installed at various locations within a building that is partitioned into various zones. The authentication decision rendered at a particular location for a specific user, is a function of the decisions generated at other locations previously visited by the same user. Thus, there is an integration of evidence across space and time. Moreover, the fusion rule employed at a particular site can vary depending upon the security level of the associated zone. For example, in the above illustration, a user entering site **B** has to be verified using two biometric sensors whose decisions may be combined using the AND decision rule.

2.5 Acquisition and processing architecture

As indicated earlier, the nature of the human computer interface adopted by a multibiometric system impacts its usability. Specifically, the order or sequence of biometric data acquisition has a bearing on the convenience imparted to the user. The enrollment time and the failure to enroll (FTE) rate can be substantially reduced by designing an acquisition protocol that enhances user convenience while ensuring that good quality biometric data is obtained from the user. Also, the sequence in which the procured biometric data is processed can significantly impact the throughput time in large-scale identification systems (involving millions of enrolled users) since it may be possible to arrive at an identification decision rapidly. The various types of acquisition and processing architectures are discussed below.

2.5.1 Acquisition sequence

The acquisition sequence in a multibiometric system refers to the order in which the various sources of evidence are acquired from an individual (in the case of multi-algorithm systems, only a single biometric sample is required and, therefore, the acquisition methodology is not an issue). Typically, the evidence is gathered sequentially, i.e., each source is independently obtained with a short time interval between successive acquisitions. In some cases, the evidence may be acquired simultaneously. For example, the face and iris information of a user may be obtained nearly simultaneously by utilizing two cameras housed in the same unit. Similarly, the face, voice and lip movements of a user may be acquired simultaneously by using a video camera (Frischholz and Dieckmann, 2000). Simultaneous procurement of information presents the possibility of (spatially) registering the information gleaned from multiple sources. In a multimodal face and iris system, the face image may be used to estimate the gaze direction which can then assist in localizing the iris image (in several instances, eye localization precedes face detection; therefore, the system might first detect the eyes of the subject before attempting to locate the face). Socolinsky et al., 2003 discuss a face acquisition setup that is capable of obtaining face images pertaining to the visible as well as the longwave infrared (LWIR) spectrum. The sensor captures video sequences of an individual's face by employing a CCD array and a LWIR microbolometer. The procured image pair (each of size 240x320) is co-registered to sub-pixel accuracy. This makes it possible to have a one-to-one correspondence between salient facial features present in both the images. Kumar et al., 2003 present a setup that acquires the palmprint and hand geometry details of an individual using a single camera. Simultaneously procuring multiple modalities can decrease enrollment time in multibiometric systems.

2.5.2   Processing sequence

The processing sequence adopted by a multibiometric system refers to the order in which the acquired information is used in order to render a decision. Here, the focus is not on the order of acquisition, but on the order in which information is processed. Thus, information may be *acquired sequentially* but *processed simultaneously*.

In the serial or cascade mode, the processing of information takes place sequentially. In Figure 2.7, the fingerprint information of the user is first processed; if the fingerprint sub-system is unable to determine the identity, then the data corresponding to the face biometric is processed. In such an arrangement, the processing time can be effectively reduced if a decision is made before going through all the biometric subsystems. In the parallel mode, on the other hand, each sub-system processes its information independently at the same time and the processed information is combined using an appropriate fusion scheme (see Figure 2.8).

The cascading scheme can improve user convenience as well as allow fast and efficient searches in large scale identification tasks. For example, when a cascaded biometric system has sufficient confidence on the identity of the user after processing the first modality, the user may not be required to provide the other traits. The system can also allow the user to decide which modality he/she would present first. Finally, if the system is faced with the task of identifying the user from a large database, it can utilize the outcome of each modality to successively prune the database, thereby making the search faster and more efficient. Thus, a cascaded system may be more convenient to the user and it generally requires a shorter recognition time compared to its parallel counterpart. However, robust algorithms are essential to efficiently handle the various sequence of events that are possible. Hong and Jain, 1998 propose a cascaded system in which face recognition is used to retrieve the top n matching identities while fingerprint recognition is used to determine the final identity based on the retrieved identities only. This is significant because (i) face matching using fixed length feature vectors is generally faster than fingerprint matching; (ii) fingerprint identification is more accurate than face identification. Thus, the advantages of both modalities are exploited in this scheme (Figure 2.9).

A multibiometric system designed to operate in the parallel mode generally has a higher accuracy because it utilizes more evidence about the user for recognition. Of course, in the cascade mode, as information from multiple sources is progressively accumulated, the system is also expected to have a higher accuracy. Most multibiometric systems proposed in the literature have a parallel architecture because the primary goal of system designers has been to reduce the error rates of biometric systems (see Ross and Jain, 2003, Snelick et al., 2005 and the references therein) and not necessarily the throughput and/or processing time.

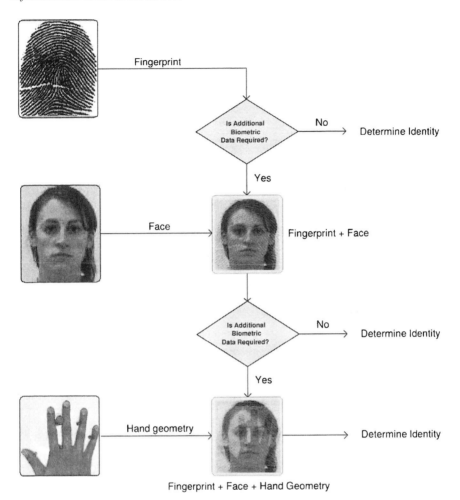

Figure 2.7. In the cascade (or serial) mode of operation, evidence is incrementally processed in order to establish identity. This scheme is also known as sequential pattern recognition. It enhances user convenience while reducing the average processing time since a decision can be made without having to acquire all the biometric traits.

Besides the two modes of operation discussed above, it is also possible to have a hierarchical (tree-like) architecture to combine the advantages of both cascade and parallel architectures (Maltoni et al., 2003). In such a scheme, a subset of the acquired modalities may be combined in parallel, while the remaining modalities may be combined in a serial fashion. Such an architecture can be dynamically determined based on the quality of the individual biometric samples as well as the possibility of encountering missing biometric data.

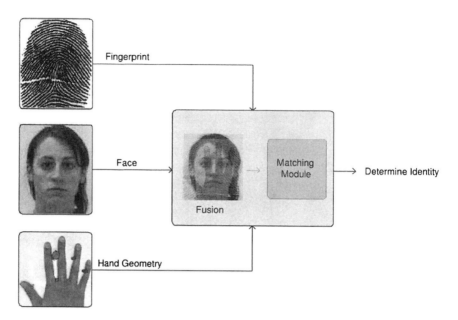

Figure 2.8. In the parallel mode of operation, the evidence acquired from multiple sources is simultaneously processed in order to establish identity. Note that the evidence pertaining to the multiple sources may be acquired in a sequential fashion.

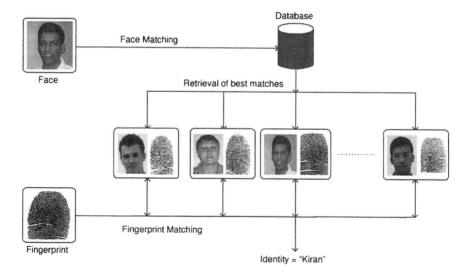

Figure 2.9. The cascade mode of processing permits database indexing where one modality can be used to retrieve a subset of identities while the second modality determines the best match. In this example, the face system is employed to recover the top n matches while the fingerprint system decides the identity of the user based on the n retrieved matches.

However, the design of a hierarchical multibiometric system has not received much attention from researchers.

2.6 Levels of fusion

In a typical pattern recognition system, the amount of information available to the system gets compressed as one proceeds from the sensor module to the decision module (see Figure 3.1). In a multibiometric system, fusion can be accomplished by utilizing the information available in any of these modules. Figure 2.10 indicates the various levels of fusion that are possible in the context of a biometric system. These levels can be broadly classified as (i) fusion prior to matching, and (ii) fusion after matching (Sanderson and Paliwal, 2002). This distinction is made because once the matcher (of a biometric system) is invoked, the amount of information available to the system drastically decreases. In this section we briefly introduce the various levels of fusion. In the next chapter, a more detailed description is provided.

2.6.1 Fusion prior to matching

Prior to matching, integration of information from multiple biometric sources can take place either at the sensor level or at the feature level. The raw data from the sensor(s) are combined in *sensor level fusion* (Iyengar et al., 1995). Sensor level fusion is applicable only if the multiple sources represent samples of the same biometric trait obtained either using a single sensor or different compatible sensors. For example, 2D face images of an individual obtained from several cameras can be combined to form a 3D model of the face. Another example of sensor level fusion is the mosaicing of multiple fingerprint impressions of a subject in order to construct a more elaborate fingerprint image (Jain and Ross, 2002a; Moon et al., 2004). In sensor level fusion, the multiple cues must be compatible and the correspondences between points in the raw data must be either known in advance or reliably estimated.

Feature level fusion refers to combining different feature sets extracted from multiple biometric sources. When the feature sets are homogeneous (e.g., multiple measurements of a person's hand geometry), a single resultant feature vector can be calculated as a weighted average of the individual feature vectors. When the feature sets are non-homogeneous (e.g., features of different biometric modalities like face and hand geometry), we can concatenate them to form a single feature vector. Feature selection schemes are employed to reduce the dimensionality of the ensuing feature vector (Ross and Govindarajan, 2005). Concatenation is not possible when the feature sets are incompatible (e.g., fingerprint minutiae and eigen-face coefficients).

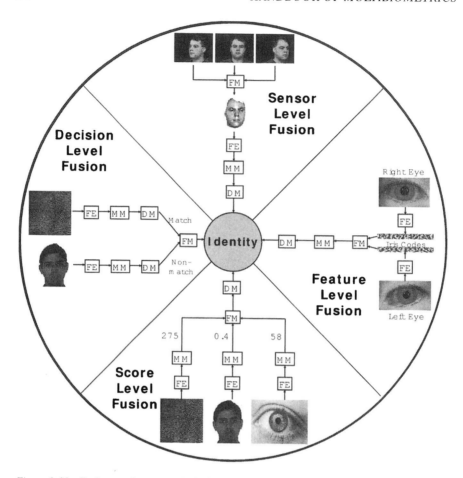

Figure 2.10. Fusion can be accomplished at various levels in a biometric system. Most multi-biometric systems fuse information at the match score level or the decision level. More recently researchers have begun to fuse information at the sensor and feature levels. In biometric systems operating in the identification mode, fusion can be done at the rank level (not shown here). FE: feature extraction module; MM: matching module; DM: decision-making module; FM: fusion module.

2.6.2   Fusion after matching

Schemes for integration of information after the classification/matcher stage can be divided into four categories: dynamic classifier selection, fusion at the decision level, fusion at the rank level and fusion at the match score level. A *dynamic classifier selection* scheme chooses the results of that biometric source which is most likely to give the correct decision for the specific input pattern (Woods et al., 1997). This is also known as the winner-take-all approach and the module that performs this selection is known as an associative switch (Chen et al., 1997).

When each biometric system outputs a match score indicating the proximity of the input data to a template, integration can be done at the *match score level*. This is also known as fusion at the *measurement level* or *confidence level*. Next to the feature vectors, the match scores output by biometric matchers contain the richest information about the input pattern. Also, it is relatively easy to access and combine the scores generated by the different matchers. Consequently, integration of information at the match score level is the most common approach in multibiometric systems.

Integration of information at the *abstract* or *decision level* can take place when each biometric system independently makes a decision about the identity of the user (in an identification system) or determines if the claimed identity is true or not (in a verification system). Methods like majority voting (Lam and Suen, 1997), behavior knowledge space (Lam and Suen, 1995), weighted voting based on the Dempster-Shafer theory of evidence (Xu et al., 1992), AND/OR rules (Daugman, 2000), etc. can be used to consolidate the decisions rendered by individual systems. Since most commercial biometric systems provide access to only the final decision output by the system, fusion at the decision level is often the only viable option.

When the output of each biometric system is a subset of possible matches (i.e., identities) sorted in decreasing order of confidence, the fusion can be done at the *rank level*. This is relevant in an identification system where a rank may be assigned to the top matching identities. Ho et al., 1994 describe three methods to combine the ranks assigned by different matchers. In the highest rank method, each possible identity is assigned the best (minimum) of all ranks computed by different systems. Ties are broken randomly to arrive at a strict ranking order and the final decision is made based on the consolidated ranks. The Borda count method uses the sum of the ranks assigned by the individual systems to a particular identity in order to calculate the fused rank. The logistic regression method is a generalization of the Borda count method where a weighted sum of the individual ranks is used. The weights are determined using logistic regression.

2.7 Summary

Information and data fusion is an active research area spanning numerous fields and there are several applications that rely on effective evidence reconciliation schemes (Rao et al., 1996). In some applications, fusion may be viewed as a *problem* to be solved (e.g., robotics (Abidi and Gonzalez, 1992)) while in other applications, it may be viewed as a *solution* to a problem (e.g., forecasting (Clemen, 1989)). The role of multiple classifier systems in solving several pattern recognition problems has long been established (for an early example, see

Dasarathy and Sheela, 1979). Multiple classifier systems exploit the complementary strengths of participating experts (viz., classifiers) in order to enhance the performance of a pattern recognition application. In the context of multibiometrics, these experts represent different biometric sources (e.g., multiple biometric sensors, multiple traits, etc.) providing information at multiple levels (e.g., score-level, decision-level, etc.).

The design of a multibiometric system is governed by several different factors including the sources of information to be used, the acquisition and processing sequence to be adopted, the type of information to be combined and the fusion strategy to be employed. The development of robust human computer interfaces (HCIs) is necessary to permit the efficient acquisition of multibiometric data from individuals (see Sharma et al., 1998 and the references therein). A HCI that is easy to use can result in rapid user habituation and promote the acquisition of high quality biometric data. Indeed, the *user* is one of the key components in any biometric system and it is necessary that system designers take into account user-centric issues of the target population (such as age, gender and cultural considerations) whilst designing the HCI (Ashbourn, 2003). Acquiring and processing multibiometric information in a sequential fashion (i.e., cascaded logic) helps curtail the time required for generating a decision. The use of multiple modalities in the cascaded mode facilitates database indexing, where one modality can be used to narrow down the number of possible identities before invoking the next.

Information fusion in biometrics presents an elegant way to enhance the matching accuracy of a biometric system without resorting to non-biometric alternatives. Determining the sources of biometric information that would result in the best matching performance is not an easy task. Chang et al., 2005 describe a multibiometric system that utilizes the 2D and 3D face images of a user for recognition. In their experiments involving 198 subjects, they observe that multi-sensor fusion of 2D and 3D images results in better recognition performance compared to multi-sample fusion of 2D images alone (fusion was accomplished at the match score level in both cases). However, they state that increasing the number of 2D images in multi-sample fusion *may* result in the same recognition performance as multi-sensor fusion. Furthermore, employing alternate fusion strategies at other levels (besides the match score level) can lead to different conclusions. In view of this, it is difficult to predict the optimal sources of biometric information relevant for a particular application based on recognition performance alone. Factors such as cost, throughput time, user convenience, scalability, etc. play a large role in selecting the sources of biometric information and adopting a particular fusion strategy.

Chapter 3

LEVELS OF FUSION IN BIOMETRICS

3.1   Introduction

One of the most fundamental issues in an information fusion system is to determine the *type* of information that should be consolidated by the fusion module. As indicated earlier, there is information compression as one progresses along the various modules of a biometric system (Figure 3.1). The raw data (e.g., image or video) is the richest in information content and subsequent processing (e.g., feature extraction) compresses the amount of information that is available to the system. It must be noted, however, that a feature-level representation has certain advantages over the sensor-level (i.e, raw data-level) representation. The noise is suppressed in the former, and one may obtain an *invariant* representation of the biometric pattern under consideration. In a face recognition system, the raw data may correspond to a color image containing the frontal profile of an individual's face against a (possibly) cluttered background. The raw data not only contains the true biometric signal of an individual but is also corrupted by various types of noise (in this case the background clutter, shadows, etc.). After face localization and feature extraction, the available information reduces to tens or hundreds of data bytes. The effect of noise is expected to decrease after feature extraction since the extraction process typically engages enhancement operations to suppress the inherent noise. However, the enhancement procedure in itself may add spurious information to the original raw data. Thus, there is an interplay between the amount of useful information that is available at any stage in a biometric system and the degree of noise corrupting this information.

Biometric systems that integrate information at an early stage of processing are believed to be more effective than those systems which perform integration at a later stage. So, for example, since the feature set contains richer information

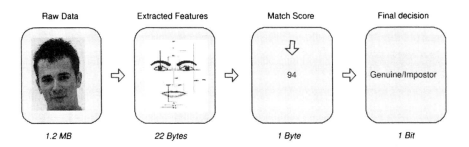

Figure 3.1. The amount of information available for fusion gets compressed as one progresses along the various processing modules of a biometric system. The raw data represents the richest source of information, while the final decision (in a verification scenario) contains just a single bit of information. However, the raw data is corrupted by noise and may have large intra-class variability which is expected to be reduced in the subsequent modules of the system.

about the input biometric pattern than the match score or the decision label, integration at this level is expected to provide better recognition results than the other two levels. However, in practice this is not always true since (i) the fusion process has to reckon with the presence of noise in constituent feature sets, and (ii) a new matching algorithm may be necessary to compare two fused feature sets. Developing efficient matching algorithms is often the most challenging aspect in the design of a biometric system and, thus, fusion at the sensor or feature levels introduces additional processing complexities.

In this chapter we discuss various strategies for fusion at the sensor level, feature level, rank level and decision level. Since fusion at the match score level has been extensively studied in the literature and is the dominant level of fusion in biometric systems, we examine it in detail in Chapters 4 and 5.

3.2   Sensor level fusion

Sensor level fusion entails the consolidation of evidence presented by multiple sources of raw data *before* they are subjected to feature extraction. In the image processing literature this is referred to as image level or pixel level fusion (Blum and Liu, 2006). The phrase sensor level fusion is used in order to accommodate other types of raw data also such as sound, video, text, symbols, etc.

Sensor level fusion can benefit multi-sample systems which capture multiple snapshots of the same biometric. For example, a small fingerprint sensor may capture two or more impressions of a person's fingerprint and create a composite fingerprint image that reveals more of the underlying ridge structure. This process, known as *mosaicing*, is particularly useful in sweep-sensors (Xia and O'Gorman, 2003) in which each image slice represents only a small portion of the fingerprint and, hence, an appropriate stitching algorithm is required to integrate the various slices. Two successive image slices are registered by determining the translational offset relating them. The sensor interface is designed in such a way as to avoid rotational offsets between the slices thus reducing the complexity associated with the image registration procedure.

Jain and Ross, 2002a discuss a mosaicing scheme that creates a composite fingerprint image from the evidence presented by multiple dab prints. The algorithm uses the minutiae points to first approximately register the two images using a simple affine transformation. The Iterative Closest Point (ICP) algorithm is then used to register the ridge information corresponding to the two images after applying a low-pass filter to the individual images and normalizing their histograms. The normalization ensures that the pixel intensities of the individual dab prints are comparable. Blending is accomplished by merely concatenating the two registered images (Figure 3.2). The performance using the mosaiced image templates was shown to exceed that of the individual dab print templates.

Ratha et al., 1998 describe a mosaicing scheme to integrate multiple snapshots of a fingerprint as the user *rolls* the finger on the surface of the sensor. Thus, a specific temporal order is imposed on the image frames when constructing the composite image. The authors investigate five different blending algorithms to construct a composite mosaiced image from the individual grayscale images. They evaluate the efficacy of these five schemes by observing the size of the mosaiced print and its quality (in terms of the number of valid minutiae points detected). Other approaches to fingerprint mosaicing have been discussed by Moon et al., 2004, Choi et al., 2005 and Zhang et al., 2005. Note that image mosaicing may not be possible when the component images are captured using different types of sensors.

Mosaicing has also been attempted by researchers in face recognition where multiple 2D images representing different poses are stitched to generate a single image. Yang et al., 2005 propose an algorithm to create panoramic face mosaics. Their acquisition system consists of five cameras that simultaneously obtain five different views of a subject's face. In order to determine the corresponding points in multiple face views, the authors place ten colored markers on the face. Based on these control points, their algorithm uses a sequence of fast linear transformations on component images to generate a face mosaic. Finally, a local smoothing process is carried out to smooth the mosaiced image. Two different schemes were used to represent the panoramic image: one in the spatial domain and the other in the frequency domain. The frequency domain representation resulted in an identification accuracy of 97.46% while the spatial domain representation provided 93.21% accuracy on a database of 12 individuals.

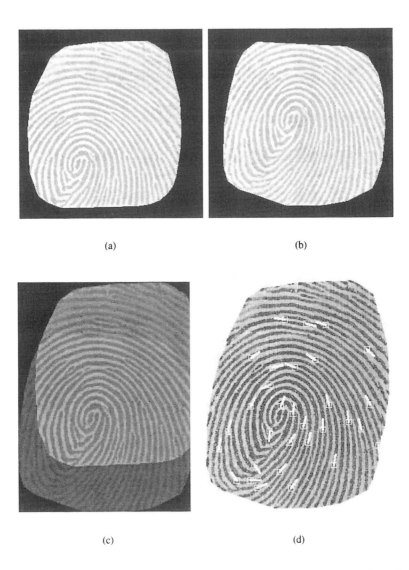

(a)   (b)

(c)   (d)

Figure 3.2. Constructing a fingerprint mosaic from multiple dab prints using the technique proposed by Jain and Ross, 2002a. (a) and (b) are dab impressions obtained after image segmentation and histogram normalization. The result of mosaicing is shown in (c). The minutiae points extracted from the composite print can be seen in (d). Typically, a larger number of minutiae and more ridge details are available in the composite print (compared to individual dab prints) thus enhancing the accuracy of a fingerprint matcher.

Liu and Chen, 2003 propose a face mosaicing technique that uses a statistical model to represent the mosaic. Given a sequence of face images captured under an orthographic camera model, each frame is unwrapped onto a certain portion of the surface of a sphere via a spherical projection. A minimization procedure using the Levenberg-Marquardt algorithm is employed to optimize the distance between an unwrapped image and the sphere. The representational (statistical) model comprises of a mean image and a number of eigen-images. The novelty of this technique is (a) the use of spherical projection, as opposed to cylindrical projection, which works better when there is head motion in both the horizontal and vertical directions, and (b) the computation of a representational model using both the mean image and the eigen-images rather than a single template image. Although the authors state that this method can be used for face recognition, no experimental results have been presented in the paper. In Liu and Chen, 2005, the authors propose another algorithm in which the human head is approximated with a 3D ellipsoidal model. The face, at a certain pose, is viewed as a 2D projection of this 3D ellipsoid. All 2D face images of a subject are projected onto this ellipsoid via geometrical mapping to form a texture map which is represented by an array of local patches. Matching is accomplished by adopting a probabilistic model to compute the distance of patches from an input face image. The authors report an identification accuracy of 90% on the CMU PIE database (Sim et al., 2003).

It is also possible to combine the 2D texture of a person's face with the corresponding 3D scan (i.e., the range image) in order to create a 3D texture. Two such 3D surfaces can be compared by first aligning them using landmark points, such as automatically detected high curvature points, and then comparing the texture associated with local patches. The local patches are usually defined using triangular meshes (Figure 3.3). Hsu, 2002 describes a face modeling algorithm that uses the 2D and 3D images of a person's face obtained during enrollment to modify a generic 3D face model and derive a user-specific 3D model. The generic 3D model is based on Waters' animation model (Parke and Waters, 1996) and contains 256 vertices and 441 triangular facets (for one-half of the face) that define various facial attributes. During the enrollment stage, the 2D and 3D images of a person's face are acquired using a Minolta Vivid 700 digitizer that generates a registered 200x200 range map and a 400x400 color image. A global alignment procedure is employed to approximately align the facial measurements of the user with the generic 3D model. A local alignment scheme is then invoked that perturbs features such as the eyes, nose, mouth, chin and face boundary of the generic 3D model so that they fit the actual facial measurements of the individual. Next, a combination of displacement propagation and 2.5D active contours is used to smooth the face model and to refine the local features present in the model resulting in a user-specific 3D representation of the face. The availability of this model permits the generation of new (previously unseen) 2D images of a person's face (e.g., at different poses, illumination, head-tilt, etc.) without actually employing a scanner to capture such images. Hsu, 2002 uses this approach to compare 2D images of a person's face acquired during authentication with the user-specific 3D model residing in the template database.

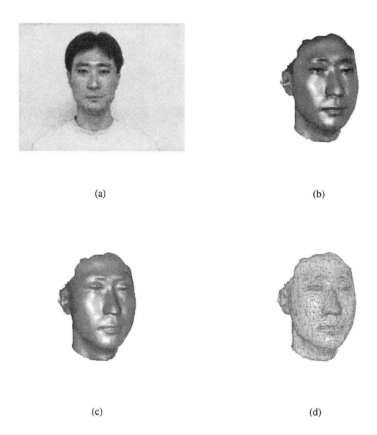

(a)   (b)

(c)   (d)

Figure 3.3.   Constructing a 3D face texture by combining the evidence presented by a 2D texture image and a 3D range image. (a) The 2D face texture of a person. (b) The corresponding 3D range (depth) image. (c) The 3D surface after mapping the 2D texture information from (a). (d) The local texture information available in the triangular meshes along with the high curvature points that define the shape of the face can be used for comparing two such face surfaces.

3.3   Feature level fusion

Feature level fusion involves consolidating the evidence presented by two biometric feature sets of the same individual. If the two feature sets originate from the same feature extraction algorithm (thus, a single modality is assumed) then feature level fusion can be used for template update or template improvement as discussed below.

1 **Template update**: The template in the database can be updated based on the evidence presented by the current feature set in order to reflect (possibly) permanent changes in a person's biometric. Hand geometry systems use this process to update the geometric measurements stored in the database in order to account for changes in an individual's hand over a period of time. A simple scheme would be to take the average of the two feature vectors corresponding to the two instances of the biometric signal and use the average feature vector as the new template (Figure 3.4).

2 **Template improvement**: In the case of fingerprints, the minutiae information available in two impressions can be combined by appropriately aligning the two prints and then removing duplicate minutia thereby generating a larger minutia set. This process known as template improvement can also be used to remove spurious minutiae points that may be present in a feature set. While template update is used to accommodate temporal changes in a person's biometric, the purpose of template improvement is to increase the number of features (*and* decrease the number of spurious features) whilst retaining its integrity.

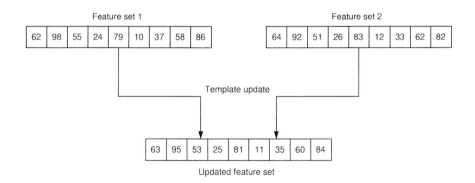

Figure 3.4. A template update procedure may be viewed as a feature fusion scheme. In this example, the nine-dimensional feature set of a user ('Feature Set 1') is updated based on the evidence presented by the current feature set ('Feature Set 2'), via the averaging scheme.

Several template improvement algorithms have been discussed in the literature for fingerprints. Jiang and Ser, 2002 propose a template improvement scheme where a reliability measure is associated with each extracted minutia point. This reliability measure is updated as minutiae evidence from newly acquired impressions is made available. The parameters of a minutia point (i.e., its x-y location and orientation) are updated via a weighted average scheme; even the 'type' of the minutiae (i.e., ridge-ending or ridge-bifurcation) is altered if necessary. Template improvement is applicable only when the new finger-print impression is accurately aligned with the stored one. The authors use the match score to determine if two impressions are accurately aligned. During the verification stage, only those minutia points whose reliability measure is above a certain threshold are used in the matching process. The authors show that their scheme results in (i) the elimination of spurious minutiae points, (ii) the addition of missed minutiae points, (iii) the relabeling of incorrect minutiae types and, consequently, (iv) a general improvement in matching performance. Other algorithms for minutiae template improvement have been discussed in Moon et al., 2004 and Yau et al., 2000.

How does one consolidate feature sets originating from different algorithms and modalities? Feature level fusion is difficult to achieve in such cases because of the following reasons:

1 The relationship between the feature spaces of different biometric systems may not be known.

2 The feature sets of multiple modalities may be incompatible. For exam-ple, the minutiae set of fingerprints and the eigen-coefficients of face are irreconcilable. One is a variable length feature set (i.e., it varies across im-ages) whose individual values parameterize a minutia point; the other is a fixed length feature set (i.e., all images are represented by a fixed number of eigen-coefficients) whose individual values are scalar entities.

3 If the two feature sets are fixed length feature vectors, then one could con-sider augmenting them to generate a new feature set. However, concatenat-ing two feature vectors might lead to the curse-of-dimensionality problem (Jain and Chandrasekaran, 1982) where increasing the number of features might actually degrade the system performance especially in the presence of small number of training samples. Although the curse-of-dimensionality is a well known problem in pattern recognition, it is particularly pronounced in biometric applications because of the time, effort and cost required to collect large amounts of biometric (training) data.

4 Most commercial biometric systems do not provide access to the feature sets used in their products. Hence, very few biometric researchers have focused on integration at the feature level and most of them generally prefer fusion schemes that use match scores or decision labels.

If the length of each of the two feature vectors to be consolidated is fixed across all users, then a feature concatenation scheme followed by a dimension-ality reduction procedure may be adopted. Let $X = \{x_1, x_2, \ldots, x_m\}$ and

$Y = \{y_1, y_2, \ldots, y_n\}$ denote two feature vectors ($X \in R^m$ and $Y \in R^n$) representing the information extracted from two different biometric sources. The objective is to fuse these two feature sets in order to yield a new feature vector, Z, that would better represent an individual. The vector Z of dimensionality k, $k < (m + n)$, can be generated by first augmenting vectors X and Y, and then performing feature selection or feature transformation on the resultant feature vector in order to reduce its dimensionality. The key stages of such an approach are described below (also see Figure 3.5).

Feature Normalization: The individual feature values of vectors $X = \{x_1, x_2, \ldots, x_m\}$ and $Y = \{y_1, y_2, \ldots, y_n\}$ may exhibit significant differences in their range as well as form (i.e., distribution). Augmenting such diverse feature values will not be appropriate in many cases. For example, if the x_i's are in the range $[0, 100]$ while the y_i's are in the range $[0, 1]$, then the distance between two augmented feature vectors will be more sensitive to the x_i's than the y_i's. The goal of feature normalization is to modify the location (mean) and scale (variance) of the features values via a transformation function in order to map them into a common domain. Adopting an appropriate normalization scheme also helps address the problem of outliers in feature values. While a variety of normalization schemes can be used, two simple schemes are discussed here: the min-max and median normalization schemes.

Let x and x' denote a feature value before and after normalization, respectively. The min-max technique computes x' as

$$x' = \frac{x - \min(F_x)}{\max(F_x) - \min(F_x)}, \tag{3.1}$$

where F_x is the function which generates x, and $\min(F_x)$ and $\max(F_x)$ represent the minimum and maximum of all possible x values that will be observed, respectively. The min-max technique is effective when the minimum and the maximum values of the component feature values are known beforehand. In cases where such information is not available, an estimate of these parameters has to be obtained from the available set of training data. The estimate may be affected by the presence of outliers in the training data and this makes min-max normalization sensitive to outliers. The median normalization scheme, on the other hand, is relatively robust to the presence of noise in the training data. In this case, x' is computed as

$$x' = \frac{x - median(F_x)}{median(|\,(x - median(F_x))\,|)}. \tag{3.2}$$

The denominator is known as the Median Absolute Deviation (MAD) and is an estimate of the scale parameter of the feature value. Although, this normalization scheme is relatively insensitive to outliers, it has a low efficiency compared to the mean and standard deviation estimators (see Chapter 4). Normalizing the feature values via any of these techniques results in modified feature vectors $X' = \{x'_1, x'_2, \ldots x'_m\}$ and $Y' = \{y'_1, y'_2, \ldots y'_n\}$. Feature normalization may not be necessary in cases where the feature values pertaining to multiple sources are already comparable.

Feature Selection or Transformation: Augmenting the two feature vectors, X' and Y', results in a new feature vector, $Z' = \{x'_1, x'_2, \ldots x'_m, y'_1, y'_2, \ldots y'_n\}$, $Z' \in R^{m+n}$. The curse-of-dimensionality dictates that the augmented vector of dimensionality $(m + n)$ need not necessarily result in an improved matching performance compared to that obtained by X' and Y' alone. The feature selection process is a dimensionality reduction scheme that entails choosing a minimal feature set of size k, $k < (m + n)$, such that a criterion (objective) function applied to the training set of feature vectors is optimized. There are several feature selection algorithms in the literature, and any one of these could be used to reduce the dimensionality of the feature set Z'. Examples include sequential forward selection (SFS), sequential backward selection (SBS), sequential forward floating search (SFFS), sequential backward floating search (SBFS), "plus l take away r" and branch-and-bound search (see Pudil et al., 1994 and Jain and Zongker, 1997 for details). Feature selection techniques rely on an appropriately formulated criterion function to elicit the optimal subset of features from a larger feature set. In the case of a biometric system, this criterion function could be the Equal Error Rate (EER); the d-prime measure; the area of overlap between genuine and impostor training scores; or the average GAR at pre-determined FAR values in the ROC/DET curves corresponding to the training set (see Ross and Govindarajan, 2005).

Dimensionality reduction may also be accomplished using feature *transformation* methods where the vector Z' is subjected to a linear or a non-linear mapping that projects it to a lower dimensional subspace. Examples of such transformations include the use of principal component analysis (PCA), independent component analysis (ICA), multidimensional scaling (MDS), Kohonen Maps and neural networks (Jain et al., 2000a). The application of a feature selection or feature transformation procedure results in a new feature vector $Z = \{z_1, z_2, \ldots z_k\}$ which can now be used to represent the identity of an individual.

Examples of Feature Level Fusion: Ross and Govindarajan, 2005 discuss feature level fusion as applied to three different scenarios: (a) multi-algorithm, where two different face recognition algorithms based on Principal Component Analysis (PCA) and Linear Discriminant Analysis (LDA) are combined; (b) multi-sensor, where the three different color channels of a face image are independently subjected to LDA and then combined; and (c) multimodal, where the face and hand geometry feature vectors are combined. The general procedure adopted by Ross and Govindarajan, 2005 is summarized below.

1 Let $\{X_i, Y_i\}$ and $\{X_j, Y_j\}$ be the feature vectors obtained at two different time instances i and j. Here, X and Y represent the feature vectors derived from two different information sources. The corresponding fused feature vectors may be denoted as Z_i and Z_j, respectively.

2 Let s_X and s_Y be the normalized match scores generated by comparing X_i with X_j and Y_i with Y_j, respectively, and let $s_{match} = (s_X + s_Y)/2$ be the fused match score obtained using the simple sum rule.

3 A pair of fused feature vectors, Z_i and Z_j, are then compared using two different distance measures: the Euclidean distance (s_{euc}) and the Thresholded Absolute Distance or TAD (s_{tad}). Thus,

$$s_{euc} = \sum_{r=1}^{k} (z_{i,r} - z_{j,r})^2 \tag{3.3}$$

$$s_{tad} = \sum_{r=1}^{k} I(|z_{i,r} - z_{j,r}|, t). \tag{3.4}$$

Here, $I(u, t) = 1$, if $u > t$ (and 0, otherwise), t is a pre-specified threshold, and k is the dimensionality of the fused feature vector. The thresholded absolute distance measure determines the *number* of normalized feature values that differ by a magnitude greater than t. The s_{euc} and s_{tad} values are consolidated into one feature level score, s_{feat}, via the simple sum rule (Figure 3.5). This retains information both at the match score level (s_{match}) as well as the feature level (s_{feat}).

4 Finally, the simple sum rule is used to combine s_{match} and s_{feat} in order to obtain the final score s_{tot} (Figure 3.6).

The authors compare the matching performances obtained using s_{match} and s_{tot} in all three scenarios. Results indicate that feature level fusion is advantageous in some cases. The feature selection scheme ensures that redundant or correlated feature values are detected and removed before invoking the matcher. This is probably one of the key benefits of performing fusion at the feature level (Kumar and Zhang, 2005a). Therefore, it is important that vendors of biometric systems grant access to feature level information to permit the development of effective fusion strategies.

Chibelushi et al., 1997 discuss a scheme to combine the features associated with the voice (audio) and lip shape (video) of an individual in an identification system. 14 mel-frequency cepstral coefficients (MFCC) and 12 geometric

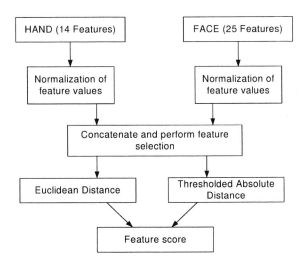

Figure 3.5. The procedure adopted by Ross and Govindarajan, 2005 to perform feature level fusion.

features are extracted from the audio and video streams to represent the voice and shape of the lips, respectively. The PCA and LDA transformations are used to reduce the dimensionality of the concatenated feature set. The authors demonstrate that the use of feature level fusion in their system is equivalent to increasing the signal-to-noise ratio (SNR) of the audio signal thereby justifying the use of lip shape in the fusion module. Other examples of feature level fusion can be found in Son and Lee, 2005 (face and iris) and Kumar et al., 2003 (hand geometry and palmprint).

3.4   Rank level fusion

When a biometric system operates in the identification mode, the output of the system can be viewed as a ranking of the enrolled identities. In this case, the output indicates the set of possible matching identities sorted in decreasing order of confidence. The goal of rank level fusion schemes is to consolidate the ranks output by the individual biometric subsystems in order to derive a consensus rank for each identity. Ranks provide more insight into the decision-making process of the matcher compared to just the identity of the best match, but they reveal less information than match scores. However, unlike match scores, the rankings output by multiple biometric systems are comparable. As a result, no normalization is needed and this makes the rank level fusion schemes simpler to implement compared to the score level fusion techniques.

Let us assume that there are M users enrolled in the database and let the number of matchers be R. Let $r_{j,k}$ be the rank assigned to user k by the jth

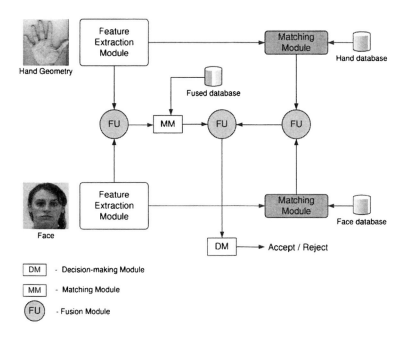

Figure 3.6. The flow of information when data from the feature level and match score level are combined in a multibiometric system (Ross and Govindarajan, 2005).

matcher, $j = 1, \ldots, R$ and $k = 1, \ldots, M$. Let s_k be a statistic computed for user k such that the user with the lowest value of s is assigned the highest consensus (or reordered) rank. Ho et al., 1994 describe the following three methods to compute the statistic s.

Highest Rank Method: In the highest rank method, each user is assigned the highest rank (minimum r value) as computed by different matchers, i.e., the statistic for user k is

$$s_k = \min_{j=1}^{R} r_{j,k}. \tag{3.5}$$

Ties are broken randomly to arrive at a strict ranking order. This method is useful only when the number of users is large compared to the number of matchers, which is usually the case in biometric identification systems. If this condition is not satisfied, most of the users will have ties rendering the final ranking uninformative. An advantage of the highest rank method is that it can utilize the strength of each matcher effectively. Even if only one matcher assigns a high rank to the correct user, it is still very likely that the correct user will receive a high rank after reordering.

Borda Count Method: The Borda count method uses the sum of the ranks assigned by the individual matchers to calculate the value of s, i.e., the statistic for user k is

$$s_k = \sum_{j=1}^{R} r_{j,k}. \tag{3.6}$$

The magnitude of the Borda count for each user is a measure of the degree of agreement among the different matchers on whether the input belongs to that user. The Borda count method assumes that the ranks assigned to the users by the matchers are statistically independent and all the matchers perform equally well.

Logistic Regression Method: The logistic regression method is a generalization of the Borda count method where a weighted sum of the individual ranks is calculated, i.e., the statistic for user k is

$$s_k = \sum_{j=1}^{R} w_j r_{j,k}. \tag{3.7}$$

The weight, w_j, to be assigned to the jth matcher, $j = 1, \ldots, R$, is determined by logistic regression (Agresti, 1996). The logistic regression method is useful when the different biometric matchers have significant differences in their accuracies. However, this method requires a training phase to determine the weights.

Figure 3.7 presents a simple example to illustrate the three rank level fusion techniques proposed by Ho et al., 1994. Two face recognition algorithms rank the four users in the database based on their similarity with the input face image. The fused score column in Figure 3.7 represents the value of s_k. When the highest rank method is used, we find that there is a tie for rank 1 between users "Alice" and "Bob". In this example, the reordered ranks were obtained by breaking the ties randomly. Since the highest rank and Borda count methods assume that both face matchers perform equally well, the reordered ranks tend to be a mixture of the ranks assigned individually by the two matchers. On the other hand, the logistic regression method assigns a higher weight to the ranks provided by the more accurate matcher. As a result, the reordered ranks can be expected to be similar to the ones provided by the matcher with a higher accuracy. In the example shown in Figure 3.7, the matcher 1 is more accurate than matcher 2. Therefore, a weight of 0.8 is assigned to it and due to this significant difference in the weights, the reordered ranks in the logistic regression case are exactly the same as the ranks assigned by the matcher 1.

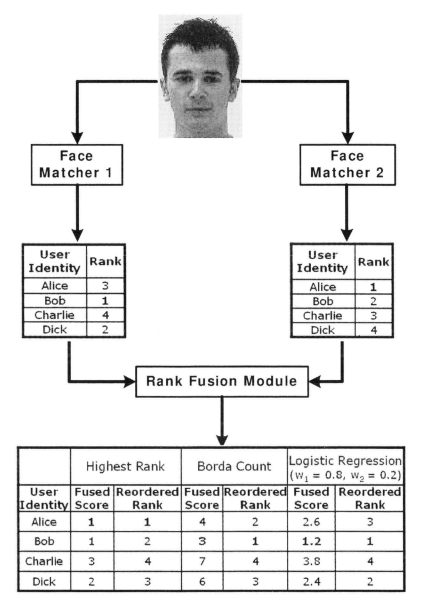

Figure 3.7. An illustration of rank level fusion as performed by the highest rank method, Borda count and logistic regression. In this example, the three schemes assign different consensus ranks to the individual identities.

3.5 Decision level fusion

In a multibiometric system, fusion is carried out at the *abstract* or *decision* level when only the decisions output by the individual biometric matchers are available. Many commercial off-the-shelf (COTS) biometric matchers provide access only to the final recognition decision. When such COTS matchers are used to build a multibiometric system, only decision level fusion is feasible. Methods proposed in the literature for decision level fusion include "AND" and "OR" rules (Daugman, 2000), majority voting (Lam and Suen, 1997), weighted majority voting (Kuncheva, 2004), Bayesian decision fusion (Xu et al., 1992), the Dempster-Shafer theory of evidence (Xu et al., 1992) and behavior knowledge space (Huang and Suen, 1995).

Let M denote the number of possible decisions (also known as *class labels* or simply *classes* in the pattern recognition literature; these three terms are used interchangeably in the following discussion) in a biometric system. Also, let $\omega_1, \omega_2, \ldots \omega_M$ indicate the classes associated with each of these decisions. In the verification mode, the decision rendered by a biometric matcher is either a "genuine user" or an "impostor" ($M = 2$). If the similarity between the input biometric sample and the template of the claimed identity is greater than a fixed threshold, the identity claim is declared as "genuine". A biometric matcher operating in the identification mode decides the identity of the user whose template best matches the given input (M is the number of users enrolled in the system). In some cases, a biometric identification system may also output a "reject" decision indicating that no stored template is sufficiently similar to the input.

"AND" and "OR" Rules: In a multibiometric verification system, the simplest method of combining decisions output by the different matchers is to use the "AND" and "OR" rules. The output of the "AND" rule is a "match" only when all the biometric matchers agree that the input sample matches with the template. On the contrary, the "OR" rule outputs a "match" decision as long as at least one matcher decides that the input sample matches with the template. The limitation of these two rules is their tendency to result in extreme operating points. When the "AND" rule is applied, the False Accept Rate (FAR) of the multibiometric system is extremely low (lower than the FAR of the individual matchers) while the False Reject Rate (FRR) is high (greater than the FRR of the individual matchers). Similarly, the "OR" rule leads to higher FAR and lower FRR than the individual matchers. When one biometric matcher has a substantially higher equal error rate compared to the other matcher, the combination of the two matchers using "AND" and "OR" rules may actually degrade the overall performance (Daugman, 2000). Due to this phenomenon, the "AND" and "OR" rules are rarely used in practical multibiometric systems.

Majority Voting: The most common approach for decision level fusion is majority voting where the input biometric sample is assigned to that identity on which a majority of the matchers agree. If there are R biometric matchers, the input sample is assigned an identity when at least k of the matchers agree on that identity, where

$$k = \begin{cases} \frac{R}{2} + 1 & \text{if } R \text{ is even,} \\ \\ \frac{R+1}{2} & \text{otherwise.} \end{cases} \tag{3.8}$$

When none of the identities is supported by k matchers, a "reject" decision is output by the system. The example shown in Figure 3.8 is a simple illustration of the majority voting scheme, where three face recognition algorithms are used. In the identification mode, two of the three matchers identify the user as "Bob". Therefore, the final identity decision after fusion is also "Bob". Similarly, in the verification mode, since two of the three matchers decide that the input face image matches with the template of the claimed identity, the final decision after fusion is a "match".

Majority voting assumes that all the matchers perform equally well. The advantages of majority voting are: (i) no apriori knowledge about the matchers is needed, and (ii) no training is required to come up with the final decision. A theoretical analysis of the majority voting fusion scheme was done by Kuncheva et al., 2003 who established limits on the accuracy of the majority vote rule based on the number of matchers, the individual accuracy of each matcher and the pairwise dependence between the matchers.

Weighted Majority Voting: When the matchers used in a multibiometric system are not of similar recognition accuracy (i.e, imbalanced matchers/classifiers), it is reasonable to assign higher weights to the decisions made by the more accurate matchers. In order to facilitate this weighting, the labels output by the individual matchers are converted into degrees of support for the M classes as follows.

$$s_{j,k} = \begin{cases} 1, & \text{if output of the } j^{th} \text{ matcher is class } \omega_k, \\ 0, & \text{otherwise,} \end{cases} \tag{3.9}$$

where $j = 1, \ldots, R$ and $k = 1, \ldots, M$. The discriminant function[1] for class ω_k computed using weighted voting is

$$g_k = \sum_{j=1}^{R} w_j s_{j,k}, \tag{3.10}$$

where w_j is the weight assigned to the jth matcher. A test sample is assigned to the class with the highest score (value of discriminant function).

Bayesian Decision Fusion: The Bayesian decision fusion scheme relies on transforming the discrete decision labels output by the individual matchers

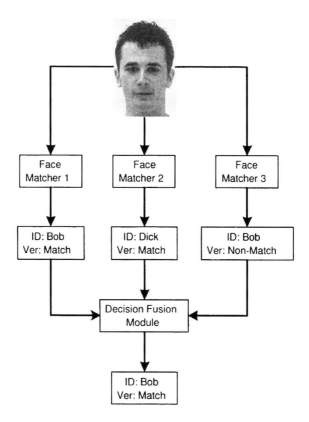

Figure 3.8. Flow of information when decisions provided by multiple biometric matchers are combined using the majority vote fusion scheme. Here "ID" and "Ver" represent the identification and verification modes of operation, respectively. For the verification mode, the claimed identity is Bob.

into continuous probability values. The first step in the transformation is the generation of the confusion matrix for each matcher by applying the matcher to a training set $\mathbf{D}$. Let CM^j be the $M \times M$ confusion matrix for the jth matcher. The (k, r)th element of the matrix CM^j (denoted as $cm_{k,r}^j$) is the number of instances in the training data set where a pattern whose true class label is ω_k is assigned to the class ω_r by the jth matcher. Let the total number of data instances in $\mathbf{D}$ be N and the number of elements that belong to class ω_k be N_k. Let c_j be the class label assigned to the test sample by the jth matcher. The value $cm_{k,c_j}^j / N_k$ can be considered as an estimate of the conditional probability $P(c_j|\omega_k)$ and N_k/N can be treated as an estimate of the prior probability of class ω_k. Given the vector of decisions made by R matchers $\mathbf{c} = [c_1, \ldots, c_R]$, we are interested in calculating the posterior probability of class ω_k, i.e., $P(\omega_k|\mathbf{c})$. According to the Bayes rule,

$$P\left(\omega_k|\mathbf{c}\right) = \frac{P\left(\mathbf{c}|\omega_k\right)P(\omega_k)}{P(\mathbf{x})}, \tag{3.11}$$

where $k = 1, \ldots, M$. The denominator in Equation 3.11 is independent of the class ω_k and can be ignored for the decision making purpose. Therefore, the discriminant function for class ω_k is

$$g_k = P\left(\mathbf{c}|\omega_k\right)P(\omega_k). \tag{3.12}$$

The Bayes decision fusion technique chooses that class which has the largest value of discriminant function calculated using equation 3.12. To simplify the computation of $P\left(\mathbf{c}|\omega_k\right)$, one can assume conditional independence between the different matchers, i.e., the matchers are mutually independent given a decision. Under this assumption, the decision rule is known as naive Bayes rule and $P\left(\mathbf{c}|\omega_k\right)$ is computed as

$$P\left(\mathbf{c}|\omega_k\right) = P\left(c_1, \ldots, c_R|\omega_k\right) = \prod_{j=1}^{R} P\left(c_j|\omega_k\right). \tag{3.13}$$

The accuracy of the naive Bayes decision fusion rule has been found to be fairly robust even when the matchers are not independent (Domingos and Pazzani, 1997). The naive Bayes combination rule can be illustrated using the following example. Let Alice, Bob, Charlie be three users enrolled in a face-based biometric system. Let two face recognition algorithms be deployed for identity determination. Suppose that 300 face images (100 from each user) are available to train the fusion algorithm in the multibiometric system. These images are presented to the two face matchers and the following two 3×3 confusion matrices, one for each matcher, are obtained.

$$CM^1 = \begin{bmatrix} 65 & 9 & 26 \\ 50 & 37 & 13 \\ 32 & 32 & 36 \end{bmatrix}$$

and

$$CM^2 = \begin{bmatrix} 49 & 21 & 30 \\ 10 & 66 & 24 \\ 10 & 19 & 71 \end{bmatrix}.$$

Note that the (k, r)th element of the matrix CM^j denotes the number of face images from user ω_k that are identified as user ω_r by the jth matcher. For example, matcher 1 correctly identifies only 65 out of the 100 face images from Alice. The remaining 35 images were wrongly identified as either Bob (9 out of 100) or Charlie (26 out of 100). Similarly, matcher 2 correctly identifies 49 out of the 100 face images from Alice, while the remaining 51 images were wrongly identified as either Bob (21 out of 100) or Charlie (30 out of 100).

Assume that for a test image, the outputs of the two matchers are c_1 =Alice and c_2 =Bob. The following conditional probabilities $P(c_j|\omega_k)$ can be estimated from the observed confusion matrices: $P(c_1 = \text{Alice}|\omega = \text{Alice}) = 65/100$, $P(c_2 = \text{Bob}|\omega = \text{Alice}) = 21/100$, $P(c_1 = \text{Alice}|\omega = \text{Bob}) = 50/100$, $P(c_2 = \text{Bob}|\omega = \text{Bob}) = 66/100$, $P(c_1 = \text{Alice}|\omega = \text{Charlie}) = 32/100$ and $P(c_2 = \text{Bob}|\omega = \text{Charlie}) = 19/100$. Since each user had 100 face images in the training set, the prior probability for each user is $100/300$. Therefore, the discriminant functions for the three users based on equations 3.12 and 3.13 are

$$g_{Alice} = \left(\frac{65}{100} \times \frac{21}{100} \right) \times \frac{100}{300} = 0.05,$$

$$g_{Bob} = \left(\frac{50}{100} \times \frac{66}{100} \right) \times \frac{100}{300} = 0.11,$$

$$g_{Charlie} = \left(\frac{32}{100} \times \frac{19}{100} \right) \times \frac{100}{300} = 0.02. \qquad (3.14)$$

Since g_{Bob} is the highest of the three values, the naive Bayes fusion rule will assign the identity Bob to the test face image.

Now, let us analyze the naive Bayes decision rule for the special case of a biometric verification system where each matcher individually decides whether the user's identity claim is "genuine" or the user is an "impostor". Let c_j be the decision of the jth matcher for an input pattern, where $c_j \in \{genuine, impostor\}$. By changing the matching threshold λ_j for the jth biometric matcher, it is possible to vary the false accept ($P(c_j = genuine|\omega = impostor)$) and false reject ($P(c_j = impostor|\omega = genuine)$) rates of that specific matcher. However, in a multibiometric system we are interested only in minimizing the global error rate (the overall error rate of the multibiometric system after the fusion of decisions from the individual biometric matchers). Therefore, we must find an optimal solution for the local thresholds $\{\lambda_1, \ldots, \lambda_R\}$ such that the global error rate is minimized. Veeramachaneni et al., 2005 propose an evolutionary algorithm, called the particle swarm optimization, to solve for the local thresholds in a multibiometric system.

Dempster-Shafer Theory of Evidence: The Dempster-Shafer theory of evidence is based on the concept of assigning degrees of belief for uncertain events. Note that the degree of belief for an event is different from the probability of the event. This subtle difference is explained in the following example. Suppose we know that a biometric matcher has a reliability of 0.95, i.e., the output of the matcher is reliable 95% of the time and unreliable 5% of the time. Suppose that the matcher outputs a "match" decision. We can assign a 0.95 degree of belief to the "match" decision and a zero degree of belief to the "non-match" decision. The zero belief does not rule out the "non-match" decision completely, unlike a zero probability. Instead, the zero belief indicates that there is no reason to believe that the input does not match successfully against the template. Hence, we can view belief theory as a generalization of probability theory. Indeed, belief functions are more flexible than probabilities when our knowledge about the problem is incomplete.

Rogova, 1994 and Kuncheva et al., 2001 propose the following methodology to compute the belief functions and to accumulate the belief functions according to the Dempster's rule. For a given input pattern, the decisions made by R classifiers for a M-class problem is represented using a $R \times M$ matrix known as a decision profile (DP) (Kuncheva et al., 2001) which is given by,

$$
DP = \begin{bmatrix}
s_{1,1} & \cdots & s_{1,k} & \cdots & s_{1,M} \\
\cdots & & & & \\
s_{j,1} & \cdots & s_{j,k} & \cdots & s_{j,M} \\
\cdots & & & & \\
s_{R,1} & \cdots & s_{R,k} & \cdots & s_{R,M}
\end{bmatrix},
$$

where $s_{j,k}$ is the degree of support provided by the jth matcher to the kth class. At the decision level, the degree of support is expressed as

$$
s_{j,k} = \begin{cases} 1, & \text{if output of the } j^{th} \text{ matcher is class } \omega_k, \\ 0, & \text{otherwise,} \end{cases} \tag{3.15}
$$

where $j = 1, \ldots, R$ and $k = 1, \ldots, M$. The decision template (DT^k) of each class ω_k is the average decision profile for all the training instances that belong to the class ω_k. When the degrees of support defined in Equation 3.15 are used, one can easily see that the elements of the decision template DT^k are related to the elements of the confusion matrices of the R matchers in the following manner.

$$
DT_{j,r}^k = \frac{CM_{k,r}^j}{N_k}, \tag{3.16}
$$

where N_k is the number of instances in the training set **D** that belong to class ω_k, $j = 1, \ldots, R$ and $k, r = 1, \ldots, M$. For a given test pattern X^t, the decision profile DP^t is computed after the decisions of the R matchers are obtained. The similarity between DP^t and the decision templates for the various classes is calculated as follows.

$$\Phi_{j,k} = \frac{\left(1 + \left(||DT_j^k - DP_j^t||\right)^2\right)^{-1}}{\sum_{r=1}^{M}\left(\left(1 + \left(||DT_j^r - DP_j^t||\right)^2\right)^{-1}\right)}, \tag{3.17}$$

where DT_j^k represents the jth row of DT^k belonging to class ω_k, DP_j^t represents the jth row of DP^t belonging to the test pattern X^t, and $||.||$ denotes the matrix norm. For every class $k = 1, \ldots, M$ and for every matcher $j = 1, \ldots, R$, we can compute the degree of belief as

$$b_{j,k} = \frac{\Phi_{j,k}\left[\prod_{r=1,r\neq k}^{M}\left(1 - \Phi_{j,r}\right)\right]}{1 - \Phi_{j,k}\left[\prod_{r=1,r\neq k}^{M}\left(1 - \Phi_{j,r}\right)\right]}. \tag{3.18}$$

The accumulated degree of belief for each class $k = 1, \ldots, M$ based on the outputs of R matchers is then obtained using the Dempster's rule as

$$g_k = \prod_{j=1}^{R} b_{j,k}. \tag{3.19}$$

The test pattern X^t is assigned to the class having the highest degree of belief g_k.

To get a better understanding of the Dempster-Shafer fusion rule, let us consider the same example that was used for the illustration of the naive Bayes decision fusion technique. From the confusion matrices CM^1 and CM^2 used in that example, we can derive the following decision templates for the three classes using Equation 3.16. Note that the number of training instances is 100 for each of the three classes.

$$DT^1 = \begin{bmatrix} 0.65 & 0.09 & 0.26 \\ 0.49 & 0.21 & 0.30 \end{bmatrix},$$

$$DT^2 = \begin{bmatrix} 0.50 & 0.37 & 0.13 \\ 0.10 & 0.66 & 0.24 \end{bmatrix},$$

and

$$DT^3 = \begin{bmatrix} 0.32 & 0.32 & 0.36 \\ 0.10 & 0.19 & 0.71 \end{bmatrix}.$$

Suppose that for the test image, the outputs of the two matchers are $c_1 = $ Alice and $c_2 = $ Bob. This results in the following decision profile DP^t.

$$DP^t = \begin{bmatrix} 1 & 0 & 0 \\ 0 & 1 & 0 \end{bmatrix}.$$

Using Equation 3.17, we can compute the matrix Φ representing the similarity between the decision profile DP^t and the decision templates DT^1, DT^2 and DT^3:

$$\Phi = \begin{bmatrix} 0.39 & 0.33 & 0.28 \\ 0.28 & 0.47 & 0.25 \end{bmatrix}. \tag{3.20}$$

Applying Equation 3.20 to Equation 3.18, we get

$$b = \begin{bmatrix} 0.23 & 0.17 & 0.13 \\ 0.13 & 0.34 & 0.11 \end{bmatrix}. \tag{3.21}$$

The discriminant functions for the three classes are obtained by substituting Equation 3.21 in Equation 3.19, which gives

$$\begin{aligned} g_{Alice} &= 0.23 \times 0.13 = 0.03 \\ g_{Bob} &= 0.17 \times 0.34 = 0.06 \\ g_{Charlie} &= 0.13 \times 0.11 = 0.01 \,. \end{aligned} \tag{3.22}$$

Since the user Bob has the highest belief value among the three users, the Dempster-Shafer fusion rule assigns Bob's identity to the test face image.

Behavior Knowledge Space: In the behavior-knowledge space (BKS) method, a lookup table that maps the decisions of the multiple matchers to a single decision is developed using the training data. Let c_j be the decision of the jth matcher, $j = 1, \ldots, R$. The vector of matcher decisions, $c = [c_1, \ldots, c_R]$, defines a point in the R-dimensional discrete space called the behavior-knowledge space. Each point in this space can be considered to be an index to a bin. For each bin, the decision with the highest proportion of samples is estimated during the training phase. During the verification phase, the given test pattern X^t is presented to the individual biometric matchers and the decision vector $c^t = [c_1^t, \ldots, c_R^t]$ is obtained. Next, the corresponding bin in BKS is identified. The BKS method assigns the pattern X^t to the best representative decision in that bin.

The operation of the BKS technique can be illustrated using the same example used for naive Bayes decision rule where two face matchers are used for identifying three users. A sample BKS table for this example is shown in Table 3.1. The first column in Table 3.1 is the list of all possible decision vectors that can be output by the two face matchers. The second column is a count of the number of training instances from each user that produced the corresponding decision vector. The third column represents the decision to be output when the corresponding decision vector is obtained for a test sequence. In this example, there are ties for the decision vectors [Alice, Charlie] and [Charlie, Bob]. Typically, the ties are broken arbitrarily. We also observe that there are no training

Table 3.1. A sample behavior knowledge space lookup table. Here, two face recognition algorithms are used for identifying three users. 100 face images from each user are used for constructing the BKS lookup table.

Possible decision vectors $[c_1, c_2]$	Number of training instances from each user	Decision label after fusion
Alice, Alice	30, 2, 4	Alice
Alice, Bob	12, 38, 5	Bob
Alice, Charlie	23, 10, 23	Alice, Charlie
Bob, Alice	0, 0, 0	Alice, Bob, Charlie
Bob, Bob	6, 25, 11	Bob
Bob, Charlie	3, 12, 21	Charlie
Charlie, Alice	19, 8, 6	Alice
Charlie, Bob	3, 3, 3	Alice, Bob, Charlie
Charlie, Charlie	4, 2, 27	Charlie

samples corresponding to the decision vector [Bob, Alice]. In such cases, the decision labels are assigned at random.

The advantage of the BKS method is that it takes into account the relative performance of the matchers and the correlation between the matchers. The limitation of this method is the large number of training samples required to train the behavior-knowledge space. This problem is especially pronounced in the case of a biometric system operating in the identification mode with a large number of enrolled users.

3.6 Summary

Information fusion in biometrics can be accomplished at several levels. In this chapter we examined fusion strategies pertaining to the sensor, feature set, rank and decision levels. Fusion at the match score level will be discussed in detail in Chapter 4.

Sensor level fusion reconciles information at the raw data level. Mosaicing multiple samples of the same biometric (e.g., multiple impressions of a finger) is an example of this type of fusion. Feature level fusion typically involves augmenting the feature vectors arising from multiple feature extractors and subjecting the fused feature vector to a feature transformation algorithm. This enables the system to compute discriminatory features that can enhance matching performance. Another application of feature level fusion is in template update (or improvement) where information from multiple feature sets (corresponding to a single biometric) is used to refine a biometric template. Rank level fusion is suitable for biometric systems operating in the identification mode. Decision level fusion is, perhaps, the simplest form of fusion that uses only the final outputs of individual sub-systems.

While the *availability* of multiple sources of biometric information (pertaining either to a single trait or to multiple traits) may present a compelling case for fusion, the *correlation* between the sources has to be examined before determining their suitability for fusion. Combining uncorrelated or negatively correlated sources is expected to result in a better improvement in matching performance than combining positively correlated sources. This has been demonstrated by Kuncheva et al., 2000 for fusion at the decision level using the majority vote scheme. Combining sources that make complementary errors is assumed to be beneficial. Kuncheva and Whitaker, 2003 discuss ten statistics that measure the diversity among binary classifiers: the Q-statistic, correlation coefficient, disagreement measure, double-fault measure, entropy of votes, difficulty index, Kohavi-Wolpert variance, inter-rater agreement, generalized diversity and coincident failure diversity. The authors state that there is a lack of definitive connection between these diversity measures and the *improvement* in matching performance obtained via decision fusion. In other words, it is difficult to formulate an efficient fusion rule based on the knowledge of these measures alone. Correlation between sources is not the only driving factor behind fusion - the performance disparity between individual sources of information also impacts the matching accuracy of the fusion scheme. If the performance disparity between component classifiers is large, then the performance of the "stronger" classifier *may* be diluted by the "weaker" one (Daugman, 2000). Defining a suitable diversity metric that would help predict the performance of a particular fusion scheme has been elusive thus far (Kuncheva, 2003).

There has been a proliferation of work discussing different fusion methodologies to combine multiple sources of biometric information. We conclude this chapter by presenting four tables that categorize some of the representative work in the multibiometric literature based on the sources of information used (see Tables 3.2, 3.3, 3.4, and 3.5). These tables also list the level of fusion and the fusion strategy employed to perform evidence reconciliation. It is immediately apparent, upon perusing these tables, that fusion at the match score level has received the most attention in the literature.

Table 3.2: Examples of multi-sensor systems.

Sensors Fused	Authors	Level of Fusion	Fusion Methodology
Optical and capacitive fingerprint sensors	Marcialis and Roli, 2004a	Match score	Sum and product rules; logistic regression
2D camera and range scanner for face	Chang et al., 2005	Match score	Weighted sum and product rules
	Lu and Jain, 2005	Match score	Weighted sum rule; hierarchical matching
2D camera and IR camera for face	Socolinsky et al., 2003	Match score	Weighted sum rule
	Chen et al., 2005a	Match score; rank	Sum rule; logistic regression
2D camera, range scanner and IR camera for face	Chang et al., 2004	Match score	Weighted sum rule
Red, Green, Blue channels for face	Kittler and Sadeghi, 2004	Match score	Sum and min rules
	Ross and Govindarajan, 2005	Feature; match score	Feature selection and concatenation; sum rule

Table 3.3: Examples of multi-algorithm systems.

Representations and/or Matchers Fused	Authors	Level of Fusion	Fusion Methodology
Fingerprint (minutiae and texture features)	Prabhakar and Jain, 2002	Match score	Likelihood ratio computed from non-parametric joint density estimates
	Ross et al., 2003	Match score	Weighted sum rule
	Marcialis and Roli, 2005	Match score	Sum and product rules; perceptron
Face (PCA, LDA, ICA)	Marcialis and Roli, 2004b	Match score	Sum rule; max rule; nearest neighbor
	Lu et al., 2003	Match score	Sum rule; RBF network
	Ross and Govindarajan, 2005	Feature; match score	Feature selection and concatenation; sum rule
Face (LDA, PM, HST)	Czyz et al., 2004	Match score	Sum, product, min, max and median rules; quadratic Bayes; Parzen; weighted sum rule
Face (global and local features)	Fang et al., 2002	Feature	ANFIS (Adaptive Neuro-Fuzzy Inference System); SVM
Face (two different sets of PCA-based features)	Yang et al., 2003	Feature	Feature concatenation; form a single feature vector in the complex space such that one feature set forms the real part and the other forms the imaginary part
Signature (global and local features)	Fierrez-Aguilar et al., 2005b	Match score	Sum and max rules (HMM for local features and Parzen window for global features)
	Fuentes et al., 2002	Match score	SVM (HMM for local features and neural network for global features)

Continued on next page

Representations and/or Matchers Fused	Authors	Level of Fusion	Fusion Methodology
Hand (geometry and texture features)	Kumar et al., 2003	Feature; match score	Feature concatenation; sum rule
Voice (SVM and GMM)	Campbell et al., 2004	Match score	Weighted sum rule; perceptron
Voice (spectral, phonetic, prosodic, lexical, conversational features)	Reynolds et al., 2003	Match score	Perceptron
Voice (spectral features - GMM and utterance verification - HMM)	Rodriguez-Linares et al., 2003	Match score	Sum, product, min, max and median rules; neural network
Voice (LPCC, MFCC, ARCSIN, FMT features)	Kinnunen et al., 2004	Feature; match score; decision	Feature concatenation; sum rule; majority voting
Voice (MFCC, CMS, MACV features)	Sanderson and Paliwal, 2001	Feature; match score	Feature concatenation; weighted sum rule
Palmprint (Gabor, line, appearance-based features)	Kumar and Zhang, 2005b	Match score; decision	Sum rule (for Gabor and line features) followed by product rule; SVM; neural network; AND rule
Palmprint (global geometry, global and local texture energy, fuzzy "interest" line)	You et al., 2004	Decision	Hierarchical (serial) matching

Table 3.4: Examples of multi-sample and multi-instance systems.

Modality	Authors	Level of Fusion	Fusion Methodology
Fingerprint (10 fingers)	Wilson et al., 2004	Match score	No details are available
Fingerprint (2 fingers)	Garris et al., 2004	Match score	Sum rule
Fingerprint (2 impressions, 2 fingers)	Prabhakar and Jain, 2002	Match score	Likelihood ratio computed from non-parametric joint density estimates
Fingerprint (2 impressions)	Jain and Ross, 2002a	Sensor; feature	Mosaicing of templates at the image level; mosaicing of minutiae sets
	Moon et al., 2004	Feature	Mosaicing of minutiae sets
Face (sequence of images from video)	Zhou et al., 2003	Match score	Temporal integration
	Li et al., 2003	Match score	Temporal integration through construction of identity surfaces
Voice (multiple utterances)	Cheung et al., 2004	Match score	Zero sum fusion after sorting of scores

Table 3.5: Examples of multimodal systems.

Modalities Fused	Authors	Level of Fusion	Fusion Methodology
Face and voice	Brunelli and Falavigna, 1995	Match score; rank	Geometric weighted average; HyperBF
	Kittler et al., 1998	Match score	Sum, product, min, max and median rules
	Ben-Yacoub et al., 1999	Match score	SVM; multilayer perceptron; C4.5 decision tree; Fisher's linear discriminant; Bayesian classifier
	Bigun et al., 1997	Match score	Statistical model based on Bayesian theory
Face, voice and lip movement	Frischholz and Dieckmann, 2000	Match score; decision	Weighted sum rule; majority voting
Face and fingerprint	Hong and Jain, 1998	Match score	Product rule
	Snelick et al., 2005	Match score	Sum rule, Weighted sum rule
Face, fingerprint and hand geometry	Ross and Jain, 2003	Match score	Sum rule; decision trees; linear discriminant function
Face, fingerprint and voice	Jain et al., 1999b	Match score	Likelihood ratio
Face and iris	Wang et al., 2003	Match score	Sum rule; weighted sum rule; Fisher's linear discriminant; neural network
Face and gait	Shakhnarovich et al., 2001	Match score	Sum rule
	Kale et al., 2004	Match score	Sum and product rules

Continued on next page

Modalities Fused	Authors	Level of Fusion	Fusion Methodology
Face and ear	Chang et al., 2003	Sensor	Concatenation of raw images
Face and palmprint	Feng et al., 2004	Feature	Feature concatenation
Fingerprint, hand geometry and voice	Toh et al., 2004	Match score	Weighted sum rule
Fingerprint and hand geometry	Toh et al., 2003	Match score	Reduced multivariate polynomial model
Fingerprint and voice	Toh and Yau, 2005	Match score	Functional link network
Fingerprint and signature	Fierrez-Aguilar et al., 2005c	Match score	SVM in which quality measures are incorporated
Voice and signature	Krawczyk and Jain, 2005	Match score	Weighted sum rule

Notes

1   The discriminant function is used to classify an input pattern. Typically, a
    discriminant function is defined for each pattern class and the input pattern
    is assigned to the class whose discriminant function gives the maximum
    response.

Chapter 4

SCORE LEVEL FUSION

4.1   Introduction

The match score is a measure of similarity between the input and template biometric feature vectors. When match scores output by different biometric matchers are consolidated in order to arrive at a final recognition decision, fusion is said to be done at the match score level. This is also known as fusion at the measurement level or confidence level. Apart from the raw data and feature vectors, the match scores contain the richest information about the input pattern. Also, it is relatively easy to access and combine the scores generated by different biometric matchers. Consequently, information fusion at the match score level is the most commonly used approach in multibiometric systems.

The general flow of information in a match score level fusion scheme is shown in Figure 4.1. It must be noted that the match scores generated by the individual matchers may not be homogeneous. For example, one matcher may output a distance or dissimilarity measure (a smaller distance indicates a better match) while another may output a similarity measure (a larger similarity value indicates a better match). Furthermore, the outputs of the individual matchers need not be on the same numerical scale (range). Finally, the match scores may follow different probability distributions. These three factors make match score level fusion a challenging problem. In this chapter, we will analyze some of the techniques to perform match score level fusion. We first present a mathematical framework that describes classifier combination from a pattern recognition perspective.

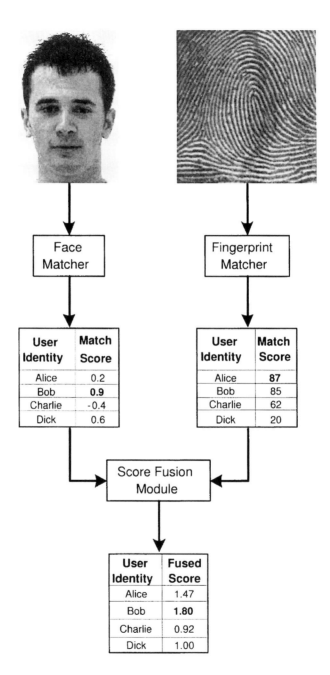

Figure 4.1. Flow of information in a match score level fusion scheme. In this example, the match scores have been combined using the sum of scores fusion rule after min-max normalization of each matcher's output. Note that the match scores generated by the face and fingerprint matchers are similarity measures. The range of match scores is assumed to be $[-1, +1]$ and $[0, 100]$ for the face and fingerprint matchers, respectively.

4.2 Classifier combination rules

In the context of statistical pattern recognition, Kittler et al., 1998 developed a theoretical framework for consolidating the evidence obtained from multiple classifiers, where each classifier makes use of a different representation derived from the same input pattern. Consider the problem of classifying an input pattern X into one of M possible classes $\{\omega_1, \omega_2, \ldots, \omega_M\}$ based on the evidence provided by R different classifiers. Let x_j be the feature vector (derived from the input pattern X) presented to the jth classifier. In general, each of the R classifiers can have its own multidimensional feature vector derived from the input pattern X. In the chosen feature space, each class ω_k can be modeled by a probability density function $p(x_j|\omega_k)$ and its prior probability of occurrence is denoted by $P(\omega_k)$.

According to the Bayesian decision theory (Duda et al., 2001), given the feature vectors $x_j, j = 1, \ldots, R$, the input pattern X should be assigned to the class ω_r that maximizes the posteriori probability, i.e.,

$$\text{Assign} \quad X \rightarrow \omega_r \quad \text{if}$$

$$P(\omega_r|x_1, \ldots, x_R) \geq P(\omega_k|x_1, \ldots, x_R), \tag{4.1}$$

where $k = 1, \ldots, M$. The Bayesian decision rule stated in Equation 4.1 is known as the minimum error-rate classification rule in the pattern recognition literature. This rule assumes a *zero-one* loss function which assigns no loss to a correct decision and assigns a unit loss to any misclassification error. The posterior probabilities in Equation 4.1 can be expressed in terms of the conditional joint probability densities of the feature vectors, $p(x_1, \ldots, x_R|\omega_k)$, by using the Bayes rule as follows:

$$P(\omega_k|x_1, \ldots, x_R) = \frac{p(x_1, \ldots, x_R|\omega_k)P(\omega_k)}{\sum_{l=1}^{M} p(x_1, \ldots, x_R|\omega_l)P(\omega_l)}. \tag{4.2}$$

Kittler et al., 1998 suggest many approximations to simplify the computation of the posterior probability in Equation 4.2 which lead to five classifier combination strategies. All the five strategies are based on the assumption of statistical independence of the R feature representations $x_1, \ldots, x_R$. Under this assumption, the conditional joint probability density $p(x_1, \ldots, x_R|\omega_k)$ can be expressed as the product of the marginal conditional densities, i.e.,

$$p(x_1, \ldots, x_R|\omega_k) = \prod_{j=1}^{R} p(x_j|\omega_k), \tag{4.3}$$

where $k = 1, \ldots, M$. In a multimodal biometric system, each one of the R classifiers uses features from a different biometric trait. Different biometric traits of an individual (e.g., face, fingerprint and hand geometry) generally tend to be mutually independent. Hence, the underlying assumption in Equation 4.3 is reasonable in most multimodal biometric systems. On the other hand, the independence assumption may not be true for a multi-sample biometric system (e.g., two impressions of the same finger) that uses the same representation scheme (e.g., minutiae) for each sample. This is because different samples of the same biometric trait usually tend to be correlated.

Product Rule: This rule is a direct implication of the assumption of statistical independence between the R feature representations $x_1, \ldots, x_R$. The product decision rule can be stated as

$$\text{Assign} \quad X \to \omega_r \quad \text{if}$$

$$P(\omega_r) \prod_{j=1}^{R} p(x_j | \omega_r) \geq P(\omega_k) \prod_{j=1}^{R} p(x_j | \omega_k), \tag{4.4}$$

where $k = 1, \ldots, M$. The product rule can also be expressed in terms of the product of the posteriori probabilities of the individual classifiers as follows.

$$\text{Assign} \quad X \to \omega_r \quad \text{if}$$

$$\frac{\prod_{j=1}^{R} P(\omega_r | x_j)}{(P(\omega_r))^{(R-1)}} \geq \frac{\prod_{j=1}^{R} P(\omega_k | x_j)}{(P(\omega_k))^{(R-1)}}, \tag{4.5}$$

where $k = 1, \ldots, M$. Further, in most practical biometric systems all classes (M users in the identification mode and "genuine" and "impostor" classes in the verification mode) are assigned equal prior probabilities. Under this assumption, the product rule can be simplified as

$$\text{Assign} \quad X \to \omega_r \quad \text{if}$$

$$\prod_{j=1}^{R} P(\omega_r | x_j) \geq \prod_{j=1}^{R} P(\omega_k | x_j). \tag{4.6}$$

One of the main limitations of the product rule is its sensitivity to errors in the estimation of the posteriori probabilities. Even if one of the classifiers outputs a probability close to zero, the product of the R posteriori probabilities is rather small and this often leads to an incorrect classification decision.

Sum Rule: The sum rule is more effective than the product rule when the input X tends to be noisy, leading to errors in the estimation of the posteriori probabilities. In such a scenario, we can assume that the posteriori probabilities do not deviate dramatically from the prior probabilities for each class, i.e.,

$$P(\omega_k | \boldsymbol{x}_j) = P(\omega_k)(1 + \delta_{j,k}), \tag{4.7}$$

where $\delta_{j,k}$ is a constant, $0 < \delta_{j,k} << 1$; $j = 1, \ldots, R$; $k = 1, \ldots, M$. Substituting Equation 4.7 for the posteriori probabilities in Equation 4.5, we get

$$\frac{\prod_{j=1}^{R} P(\omega_k | \boldsymbol{x}_j)}{(P(\omega_k))^{(R-1)}} = P(\omega_k) \prod_{j=1}^{R} (1 + \delta_{j,k}). \tag{4.8}$$

Expanding the product on the right hand side in Equation 4.8 and neglecting the higher order terms, we can approximate the product in terms of a summation as follows.

$$\prod_{j=1}^{R} (1 + \delta_{j,k}) \approx 1 + \sum_{j=1}^{R} \delta_{j,k}. \tag{4.9}$$

Further, by substituting for $\delta_{j,k}$ from Equation 4.7, we get

$$\sum_{j=1}^{R} \delta_{j,k} = \frac{\sum_{j=1}^{R} P(\omega_k | \boldsymbol{x}_j)}{P(\omega_k)} - R. \tag{4.10}$$

Finally, substituting Equations 4.9 and 4.10 into Equation 4.5 for the product rule, we obtain the sum decision rule which can be stated as follows:

$$\text{Assign} \quad X \to \omega_r \quad \text{if}$$

$$\left\{ (1 - R)P(\omega_r) + \sum_{j=1}^{R} P(\omega_r | \boldsymbol{x}_j) \right\} \geq \left\{ (1 - R)P(\omega_k) + \sum_{j=1}^{R} P(\omega_k | \boldsymbol{x}_j) \right\}, \tag{4.11}$$

where $k = 1, \ldots, M$. When the prior probabilities are equal, the sum rule can be expressed as follows.

$$\text{Assign} \quad X \to \omega_r \quad \text{if}$$

$$\sum_{j=1}^{R} P(\omega_r | \boldsymbol{x}_j) \geq \sum_{j=1}^{R} P(\omega_k | \boldsymbol{x}_j), \tag{4.12}$$

where $k = 1, \ldots, M$. The decision rule in Equation 4.12 is also known as the *mean* or *average* decision rule because it is equivalent to assigning the input pattern to the class that has the maximum average posteriori probability over all the R classifiers.

As mentioned earlier, the sum rule is primarily based on the assumption that the posteriori probabilities $P(\omega_k|\boldsymbol{x}_j)$ do not deviate much from the prior probabilities $P(\omega_k)$. In general, this assumption is unrealistic because the feature vectors $\boldsymbol{x}_1, \ldots, \boldsymbol{x}_R$ contain significant discriminatory information about the pattern class. However, Kittler et al., 1998 showed that the sum rule is robust to errors in the estimation of the posteriori probabilities. Therefore, the sum decision rule usually works quite well in practice and is commonly used in multibiometric systems.

Max Rule: The max rule approximates the mean of the posteriori probabilities by their maximum value, i.e.,

$$\frac{1}{R}\sum_{j=1}^{R} P(\omega_k|\boldsymbol{x}_j) \approx \max_{j=1}^{R} P(\omega_k|\boldsymbol{x}_j). \tag{4.13}$$

Hence, the max rule can be stated as follows:

Assign $X \rightarrow \omega_r$ if

$$\left\{(1-R)P(\omega_r) + R\max_{j=1}^{R} P(\omega_r|\boldsymbol{x}_j)\right\} \geq \left\{(1-R)P(\omega_k) + R\max_{j=1}^{R} P(\omega_k|\boldsymbol{x}_j)\right\}, \tag{4.14}$$

where $k = 1, \ldots, M$. Under the assumption of equal priors, the max rule can be simplified as

Assign $X \rightarrow \omega_r$ if

$$\max_{j=1}^{R} P(\omega_r|\boldsymbol{x}_j) \geq \max_{j=1}^{R} P(\omega_k|\boldsymbol{x}_j), \ k = 1, \ldots, M. \tag{4.15}$$

Min Rule: It is well known that the product of probabilities is always less than or equal to the minimum value of probability in the product. Hence,

$$\prod_{j=1}^{R} P(\omega_k|\boldsymbol{x}_j) \leq \min_{j=1}^{R} P(\omega_k|\boldsymbol{x}_j). \tag{4.16}$$

By substituting this upper bound in place of the product term in Equation 4.5, we obtain the min rule which can be stated as

$$\text{Assign} \quad X \to \omega_r \quad \text{if}$$

$$\frac{\min_{j=1}^{R} P(\omega_r|\boldsymbol{x}_j)}{(P(\omega_r))^{(R-1)}} \geq \frac{\min_{j=1}^{R} P(\omega_k|\boldsymbol{x}_j)}{(P(\omega_k))^{(R-1)}}, \ k = 1, \ldots, M. \qquad (4.17)$$

If the prior probabilities of all the classes are equal, the min rule reduces to

$$\text{Assign} \quad X \to \omega_r \quad \text{if}$$

$$\min_{j=1}^{R} P(\omega_r|\boldsymbol{x}_j) \geq \min_{j=1}^{R} P(\omega_k|\boldsymbol{x}_j), \ k = 1, \ldots, M. \qquad (4.18)$$

Median Rule: If we assume equal priors for all the classes, the sum rule in Equation 4.12 can be viewed as the mean rule. The mean rule assigns a pattern to the class that has the maximum average posteriori probability over all the classifiers. Since the average posteriori probability is sensitive to outliers, it is often replaced by the median value. The median decision rule can be stated as

$$\text{Assign} \quad X \to \omega_r \quad \text{if}$$

$$median_{j=1}^{R} P(\omega_r|\boldsymbol{x}_j) \geq median_{j=1}^{R} P(\omega_k|\boldsymbol{x}_j), \ k = 1, \ldots, M. \qquad (4.19)$$

The classifier combination rules developed by Kittler et al., 1998 can be used in a multibiometric system only if the output of each biometric matcher is of the form $P(\omega_k|\boldsymbol{x}_j)$ i.e., the posteriori probability of class ω_k given the features extracted by the jth modality from the input biometric sample X. In practice, most biometric matchers output only a match score $s_{j,k}$. Verlinde et al., 1999 proposed that the match score $s_{j,k}$ is related to $P(\omega_k|\boldsymbol{x}_j)$ as follows:

$$s_{j,k} = g\left(P(\omega_k|\boldsymbol{x}_j)\right) + \beta(\boldsymbol{x}_j), \qquad (4.20)$$

where g is a monotonic function and β is the error made by the biometric matcher that depends on the input features. This error could be due to the noise introduced by the sensor during the acquisition of the biometric signal, and the errors made by the feature extraction and matching processes. If we assume that β is zero, it is reasonable to approximate $P(\omega_k|\boldsymbol{x}_j)$ by $P(\omega_k|s_{j,k})$. In this scenario, the classifier combination rules can be applied for fusion of match scores from different biometric matchers. On the other hand, if we assume that the value of β is non-zero, $P(\omega_k|s_{j,k})$ may not be a good estimate of $P(\omega_k|\boldsymbol{x}_j)$. Hence, it is not possible to directly apply the classifier combination rules in such a scenario.

4.3   Score fusion techniques

Let us consider a multibiometric system operating in the verification mode where the output of each biometric matcher is a match score (the formulation presented below can be trivially extended to the identification scenario also). Since the goal of the multibiometric system is to determine whether the input biometric sample X belongs to a "genuine" user or an "impostor", the number of classes (M) is now reduced to two. The minimum error-rate decision rule in Equation 4.1 is based on the assumption that all types of errors (misclassifying a sample from class ω_k as $\omega_{k'}$, $\forall k$, $k' = 1, \ldots, M$, $k \neq k'$) are equally costly. Most practical verification systems assign different costs to the false accept and false reject errors. Let λ_1 and λ_2 be the cost (or loss) associated with the false accept and false reject errors, respectively, and let $\eta = \lambda_1/\lambda_2$ be the ratio of the two cost values. Therefore, when a biometric system operating in the verification mode has different costs for the false accept and false reject errors, the modified Bayesian decision rule is

$$\text{Assign} \quad X \to genuine \quad \text{if}$$

$$\frac{P(genuine|\boldsymbol{x}_1, \ldots, \boldsymbol{x}_R)}{P(impostor|\boldsymbol{x}_1, \ldots, \boldsymbol{x}_R)} \geq \eta. \tag{4.21}$$

In score level fusion, it is assumed that the feature representations of the R biometric matchers $\boldsymbol{x}_1, \ldots, \boldsymbol{x}_R$ are not available. Hence, the posteriori probabilities $P(genuine \mid \boldsymbol{x}_1, \ldots, \boldsymbol{x}_R)$ and $P(impostor|\boldsymbol{x}_1, \ldots, \boldsymbol{x}_R)$ must be estimated from the vector of match scores $\boldsymbol{s} = [s_1, s_2, \ldots, s_R]$, where s_j is the match score provided by the jth matcher, $j = 1, \ldots, R$ (note that since the class is fixed as either "genuine" or "impostor", we drop the subscript k that represents the class information). Techniques that have been proposed for estimating these posteriori probabilities can be divided into three broad categories listed below.

1 The first approach assumes that the posteriori probabilities $P(genuine|\boldsymbol{x}_1,$ $\ldots, \boldsymbol{x}_R)$ and $P(impostor|\boldsymbol{x}_1, \ldots, \boldsymbol{x}_R)$ can be approximated by $P(genuine|$ $\boldsymbol{s} = [s_1, s_2, \ldots, s_R])$ and $P(impostor|\boldsymbol{s} = [s_1, s_2, \ldots, s_R])$, respectively. Conversion of the vector of scores, $\boldsymbol{s}$, into the probabilities $P(genuine|\boldsymbol{s})$ and $P(impostor|\boldsymbol{s})$ requires explicit estimation of the underlying conditional densities $p(\boldsymbol{s}|genuine)$ and $p(\boldsymbol{s}|impostor)$. Hence, this approach is referred to as *density-based score fusion*. After estimating the densities, the probabilities $P(genuine|\boldsymbol{s})$ and $P(impostor|\boldsymbol{s})$ are computed, and the Bayesian decision rule in Equation 4.21 can be used to make a decision.

2 Accurate estimation of the class conditional densities $p(\boldsymbol{s}|genuine)$ and $p(\boldsymbol{s}|impostor)$ is possible only when the number of match scores available

for training the fusion module is large. Also, the assumption that the posteriori probabilities $P(genuine|x_1, \ldots, x_R)$ and $P(impostor|x_1, \ldots, x_R)$ can be approximated by $P(genuine|s)$ and $P(impostor|s)$ is valid only when the value of β in Equation 4.20 is zero. Hence, in cases where the number of training match scores is limited and/or β's are non-zero, an alternative approach is to transform the match scores obtained from the different matchers into a common domain in order to make them compatible. This transformation is known as score normalization and the resulting fusion approach is known as *transformation based score fusion*. In the transformed domain, the sum, max and min classifier combination rules can be directly applied. In general, the normalized scores do not have any probabilistic interpretation. Therefore, the product rule given by Equation 4.6 cannot be applied.

3 The third approach is *classifier based score fusion* where the relationship between the vector of match scores $[s_1, s_2, \ldots, s_R]$ and the posteriori probabilities, $P(genuine|s_1, s_2, \ldots, s_R)$ and $P(impostor|s_1, s_2, \ldots, s_R)$, is indirectly learned using a pattern classifier.

It must be emphasized that these three methodologies are essentially different approaches to solving the same problem, namely, deciding whether the input pattern X belongs to the "genuine" or the "impostor" class based on the match score vector $[s_1, s_2, \ldots, s_R]$ generated by the R different biometric matchers. Each method has its own advantages and limitations. Further, each method requires estimation of some parameters from the training data and exhibits different levels of sensitivity to problems like lack of sufficient training data and noisy training samples. Finally, none of these three methods is guaranteed to provide optimum performance under all scenarios. In the following sections, we will describe these three approaches in detail.

4.4 Density-based score fusion

Let S_{gen} and S_{imp} be the random variables denoting the genuine and impostor match scores, respectively. Let $F_{gen}(s)$ be the distribution function of S_{gen} and $f_{gen}(s)$ be the corresponding density, i.e.,

$$P(S_{gen} \leq s) = F_{gen}(s) = \int_{-\infty}^{s} f_{gen}(v)dv. \qquad (4.22)$$

Similarly, let $F_{imp}(s)$ be the distribution function of S_{imp} and $f_{imp}(s)$ be the corresponding density, i.e.,

$$P(S_{imp} \leq s) = F_{imp}(s) = \int_{-\infty}^{s} f_{imp}(v)dv. \qquad (4.23)$$

The densities $f_{gen}(s)$ and $f_{imp}(s)$ are known as the class conditional densities because they represent the probability density functions of the match score given that the score comes from the genuine or impostor class ($p(s|genuine)$ and $p(s|impostor)$), respectively. The densities $f_{gen}(s)$ and $f_{imp}(s)$ are usually not known and have to be estimated from a set of training scores from the genuine and impostor classes.

Density estimation can be done either by parametric or non-parametric methods (Duda et al., 2001). In parametric density estimation techniques, the form of the density function is assumed to be known and only the parameters of this density function are estimated from the training data. For example, if we assume a Gaussian (normal) density function, only the mean and the standard deviation parameters that characterize this density are estimated during training. On the other hand, non-parametric techniques do not assume any standard form for the density function and are essentially data-driven. The Parzen window and K-NN density estimation schemes fall in this category. In the context of multibiometric systems, it is very difficult to choose a specific parametric form for the density of genuine and impostor scores. It is well known that the commonly assumed Gaussian density approximation is usually not appropriate for genuine and impostor scores of a biometric matcher. The match score distributions generally have a large tail and may have more than one mode (see Figure 4.2). However, the Gaussian distribution is unimodal and does not capture the information contained in the tails of the distribution very well, making it inappropriate for modeling genuine and impostor score distributions. Another major problem that biometric researchers are facing is that they do not have access to large amounts of training data (especially genuine match scores) to reliably estimate the genuine and impostor densities. For example, if a multibiometric database has n users and if each user provides m biometric samples, then the maximum number of genuine scores, N_{gen}, that can be obtained from this database is $nm(m-1)/2$. On the other hand, $n(n-1)m^2$ impostor matches, N_{imp}, can be performed using the same database. Suppose that $n = 100$ and $m = 4$, the number of genuine scores available is only 600 while the number of impostor scores is $158,400$. Due to the limited availability of training data, especially genuine scores, the density estimation method must be chosen carefully.

Snelick et al., 2003 adopt a parametric approach to estimate the conditional densities of the match scores. They assume a normal distribution for the conditional densities of the match scores, i.e.,

$$p(s_j|genuine) \sim \mathcal{N}(\mu_{j,gen}, \sigma_{j,gen}) \qquad (4.24)$$

and

$$p(s_j|impostor) \sim \mathcal{N}(\mu_{j,imp}, \sigma_{j,imp}), \qquad (4.25)$$

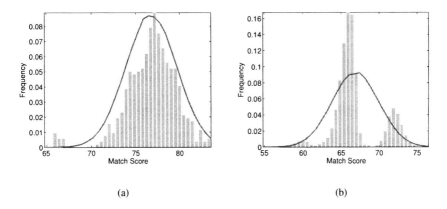

Figure 4.2. Histograms of match scores and the corresponding Gaussian density estimates for the Face-G matcher in the NIST BSSR1 database. (a) Genuine and (b) Impostor. Note that the Gaussian density does not account well for the tail in the genuine score distribution and the multiple modes in the impostor score distribution.

where $\mu_{j,gen}$ ($\mu_{j,imp}$) and $\sigma_{j,gen}$ ($\sigma_{j,imp}$) are the mean and standard deviation of the genuine (impostor) match scores of the jth matcher, respectively. Based on the training data containing N_{gen} genuine scores and N_{imp} impostor scores for each matcher, the maximum likelihood estimates of the parameters $\mu_{j,gen}$, $\sigma_{j,gen}$, $\mu_{j,imp}$, and $\sigma_{j,imp}$ are obtained as follows.

$$\hat{\mu}_{j,gen} = \frac{1}{N_{gen}} \sum_{i=1}^{N_{gen}} s^i_{j,gen}, \tag{4.26}$$

$$\hat{\mu}_{j,imp} = \frac{1}{N_{imp}} \sum_{i=1}^{N_{imp}} s^i_{j,imp}, \tag{4.27}$$

$$\hat{\sigma}_{j,gen} = \frac{1}{N_{gen}} \sum_{i=1}^{N_{gen}} \left(s^i_{j,gen} - \hat{\mu}_{j,gen}\right)^2, \tag{4.28}$$

$$\hat{\sigma}_{j,imp} = \frac{1}{N_{imp}} \sum_{i=1}^{N_{imp}} \left(s^i_{j,imp} - \hat{\mu}_{j,imp}\right)^2, \tag{4.29}$$

where $s^i_{j,gen}$ ($s^i_{j,imp}$) represents the ith genuine (impostor) training score of the jth matcher, $i = 1, \ldots, N_{gen}$ for the genuine class and $i = 1, \ldots, N_{imp}$ for the impostor class.

Given a test match score s_j^t for the jth matcher, the posteriori probabilities of the score belonging to a genuine user and an impostor are computed as follows.

$$P(genuine|s_j^t) = \frac{p(s_j^t|genuine)P(genuine)}{p(s_j^t)} \qquad (4.30)$$

and

$$P(impostor|s_j^t) = \frac{p(s_j^t|impostor)P(impostor)}{p(s_j^t)}, \qquad (4.31)$$

where $p(s_j^t) = (p(s_j^t|genuine)P(genuine) + p(s_j^t|impostor)P(impostor))$ and $P(genuine)$ and $P(impostor)$ are the prior probabilities of a genuine user and an impostor, respectively. Snelick et al., 2003 assumed that prior probabilities of the genuine and impostor classes are equal and the matchers are conditional independent. Hence, the posteriori probabilities based on the scores from the different matchers can be computed as follows.

$$P(genuine|s_1^t, \ldots, s_R^t) = \prod_{j=1}^{R} P(genuine|s_j^t) \qquad (4.32)$$

and

$$P(impostor|s_1^t, \ldots, s_R^t) = \prod_{j=1}^{R} P(impostor|s_j^t). \qquad (4.33)$$

The final accept/reject decision is based on the Bayesian decision rule in Equation 4.21 which can be stated as follows.

$$\text{Assign} \quad X^t \rightarrow genuine \quad \text{if}$$

$$\frac{P(genuine|s_1^t, \ldots, s_R^t)}{P(impostor|s_1^t, \ldots, s_R^t)} \geq \eta, \qquad (4.34)$$

where X^t is the given test sample and η is the decision threshold which is a tradeoff between the false accept and false reject error rates. When the goal is to minimize the total error rate (sum of the false accept and the false reject rates), the value of η should be set to 1. As pointed out earlier, the assumption of a normal distribution for the scores is generally not true for biometric match scores.

Jain et al., 2005 propose the use of the Parzen window based non-parametric density estimation method (Duda et al., 2001) to estimate the conditional density of the genuine and impostor scores. After estimating the conditional densities, equations 4.30 through 4.34 can be applied to make a decision. Although the Parzen window density estimation technique is appropriate for estimating the conditional densities $p(s_j|genuine)$ and $p(s_j|impostor)$, especially when the densities are non-Gaussian, the resulting density estimates may still have inaccuracies due to the finite training set and the problems in choosing the optimum window width during the density estimation process.

Both Snelick et al., 2003 and Jain et al., 2005 estimate only the marginal densities of the individual matchers in a multibiometric system. The combination of these marginal densities is achieved using the framework developed by Kittler et al., 1998 based on the assumption of statistical independence of the feature vectors (or the biometric matchers). Prabhakar and Jain, 2002 argue that the assumption of statistical independence of the matchers may not be true in a multi-algorithm biometric system that uses different feature representations and different matching algorithms on the same biometric trait. Hence, they propose a scheme based on non-parametric estimation of the joint multivariate density. Using the genuine and impostor match scores from the R matchers that were available for training, they directly estimate the R-variate densities $p(s_1, \ldots, s_R|genuine)$ and $p(s_1, \ldots, s_R|impostor)$. But estimating the joint multivariate densities requires a larger number of training samples than estimating the univariate (marginal) densities. Hence, this approach is applicable only when a very large amount of training data is available to estimate the joint densities. Based on the joint densities, the posteriori probabilities can be computed using the Bayes rule as follows.

$$P(genuine|s_1, \ldots, s_R) = \frac{p(s_1, \ldots, s_R|genuine)P(genuine)}{p(s_1, \ldots, s_R)} \quad (4.35)$$

and

$$P(impostor|s_1, \ldots, s_R) = \frac{p(s_1, \ldots, s_R|impostor)P(impostor)}{p(s_1, \ldots, s_R)}, \quad (4.36)$$

where

$$p(s_1, \ldots, s_R) = p(s_1, \ldots, s_R|genuine)P(genuine) + p(s_1, \ldots, s_R|impostor)P(impostor).$$

Hence, the ratio of the posteriori probabilities is given by

$$\frac{P(genuine|s_1, \ldots, s_R)}{P(impostor|s_1, \ldots, s_R)} = \frac{p(s_1, \ldots, s_R|genuine)P(genuine)}{p(s_1, \ldots, s_R|impostor)P(impostor)}. \quad (4.37)$$

When the prior probabilities of the genuine and impostor classes are equal, the ratio of the posteriori probabilities is

$$\frac{P(genuine|s_1,\ldots,s_R)}{P(impostor|s_1,\ldots,s_R)} = \frac{p(s_1,\ldots,s_R|genuine)}{p(s_1,\ldots,s_R|impostor)}. \tag{4.38}$$

The terms $p(s_1,\ldots,s_R|genuine)$ and $p(s_1,\ldots,s_R|impostor)$ are also referred to as the likelihood of the genuine and impostor class with respect to $[s_1,\ldots,s_R]$. Hence, the ratio on the right hand side in Equation 4.38 is known as the likelihood ratio. The Neyman-Pearson theorem (Lehmann and Romano, 2005) states that when the prior probabilities of the classes are equal (or not known), the *optimal* test for deciding whether a match score vector $s = [s_1,\ldots,s_R]$ corresponds to a genuine or impostor match is the likelihood ratio test. The Neyman-Pearson decision rule is optimal in the sense that if we assume that the false accept rate (FAR) is given, the likelihood ratio test will minimize the false reject rate (FRR) for the fixed FAR and no other decision rule will give a lower FRR. The decision rule based on the likelihood ratio test can be stated as follows.

$$\text{Assign} \quad X \rightarrow genuine \quad \text{if}$$

$$\frac{p(s_1,\ldots,s_R|genuine)}{p(s_1,\ldots,s_R|impostor)} \geq \eta, \tag{4.39}$$

where η is the threshold value that achieves the specified value of FAR. The likelihood ratio test is optimal only when the underlying densities are either known or can be estimated very accurately. Hence, given a set of genuine and impostor match scores, it is important to be able to estimate the conditional densities $f_{gen}(s)$ and $f_{imp}(s)$ without incurring large errors in the estimation process.

Another important consideration is that the distribution of genuine and impostor scores of some biometric matchers may exhibit discrete components. This happens because most biometric matching algorithms apply certain thresholds at various stages in the matching process. When the required threshold conditions are not met, pre-determined match scores are output by the matcher (e.g., some fingerprint matchers produce a match score of zero if the number of extracted minutiae is less than a threshold, irrespective of how many minutiae actually match between the query and the template). This leads to discrete components in the match score distribution that cannot be modeled accurately using a continuous density function. Thus, discrete components need to be detected and the discrete and continuous portions of the density must be modeled separately to avoid large errors in estimating $f_{gen}(s)$ and $f_{imp}(s)$. To address this problem, Dass et al., 2005 propose a framework for combining the match scores from multiple matchers based on generalized densities estimated from the genuine and impostor match scores. The generalized densities are a mixture of discrete and continuous components and a brief description of the methodology used for computing the generalized densities is presented below.

4.4.1 Generalized densities

The following methodology models a distribution based on a generic set of observed scores (the same formulation can be used for both genuine and impostor scores from any biometric matcher). Let S denote a generic match score with distribution function F and density $f(s)$, i.e.,

$$P(S \leq s) = F(s) = \int_{-\infty}^{s} f(v)dv. \qquad (4.40)$$

For a fixed threshold T, the discrete values are identified as those values s_0 with $P(S = s_0) > T$, where T is a threshold, $0 \leq T \leq 1$. Since the underlying match score distribution is unknown, the probability $P(S = s_0)$ can be estimated by $N(s_0)/N$, where $N(s_0)$ is the number of observations in the data set that equals s_0 and N is the total number of observations. Let the subset of all discrete components for a match score distribution be denoted by

$$\mathcal{D} \equiv \left\{ s_0 : \frac{N(s_0)}{N} > T \right\}. \qquad (4.41)$$

The discrete components constitute a proportion $p_D \equiv \sum_{s_0 \in \mathcal{D}} \frac{N(s_0)}{N}$ out of the total of N available observations. The subset $\mathcal{C}$ of observations can be obtained by removing all discrete components from the available data set. The scores in $\mathcal{C}$ constitute a proportion $p_C \equiv 1 - p_D$ of the entire data set, and they are used to estimate the continuous component of the distribution ($F_C(s)$) and the corresponding density ($f_c(s)$). A non-parametric kernel density estimate of $f_c(s)$ is obtained from $\mathcal{C}$ as follows. The empirical distribution function for the observations in $\mathcal{C}$ is computed as

$$\hat{F}_C(s) = \frac{1}{N_C} \sum_{v \in \mathcal{C}} I\{v \leq s\}, \qquad (4.42)$$

where N_C is the number of observations in $\mathcal{C}$ and

$$I\{v \leq s\} = \begin{cases} 1, & \text{if } v \leq s, \\ 0, & \text{otherwise;} \end{cases} \qquad (4.43)$$

also, $N_C \equiv N p_C$. Note that $\hat{F}_C(s) = 0 \; \forall \; s < s_{min}$ and $\hat{F}_C(s) = 1 \; \forall \; s \geq s_{max}$, where s_{min} and s_{max}, respectively, are the minimum and maximum values of the observations in $\mathcal{C}$. For values of $s, s_{min} < s < s_{max}$, not contained in $\mathcal{C}$, $\hat{F}_C(s)$, is obtained by linear interpolation. Next, B samples are simulated from $\hat{F}_C(s)$, and the density estimate of $f_C(s)$, $\hat{f}_C(s)$, is obtained from the simulated samples using a Gaussian kernel density estimator. The optimal bandwidth, h, of the kernel is obtained using the "solve-the-equation" bandwidth estimator (Wand and Jones, 1995), which is an automatic bandwidth selector that prevents oversmoothing and preserves important properties of the distribution of match scores. The generalized density is defined as

$$f(s) = p_C\,\hat{f}_C(s) + \sum_{s_0 \in \mathcal{D}} \frac{N(s_0)}{N} \cdot I\{s = s_0\}, \qquad (4.44)$$

where

$$I\{s = s_0\} = \left\{ \begin{array}{ll} 1, & \text{if } s = s_0, \\ 0, & \text{otherwise.} \end{array} \right. \qquad (4.45)$$

The distribution function corresponding to the generalized density is defined as

$$F(s) = p_C \int_{-\infty}^{s} \hat{f}_C(v)\, dv + \sum_{s_0 \in \mathcal{D},\, s_0 \leq s} \frac{N(s_0)}{N}. \qquad (4.46)$$

For a multibiometric system with R matchers, the generalized densities and distributions estimated for the genuine (impostor) scores for the jth matcher will be denoted by $f_{j,gen}(s)$ and $F_{j,gen}(s)$ ($f_{j,imp}(s)$ and $F_{j,imp}(s)$), respectively, for $j = 1, 2, \ldots, R$. Figures 4.3 (a)-(f) give the plots of $f_{j,gen}(x)$ and $f_{j,imp}(x)$ ($j = 1, \ldots, R$) for the distributions of observed genuine and impostor match scores for $R = 3$ modalities of the MSU-Multimodal database (Jain et al., 2005). Figures 4.3 (a)-(f) also give the histograms of the genuine and impostor match scores for the three modalities. The "spikes" (see Figures 4.3 (d) and (e)) represent the detected discrete components whose individual heights are greater than the threshold $T = 0.02$. Note that the individual "spikes" cannot be represented by a continuous density function. Forcing a continuous density estimate for these values will result in gross density estimation errors and yield suboptimal performance of the multibiometric system.

The above procedure only estimates the marginal score distributions of each of the R matchers in the multibiometric system instead of estimating the joint distribution. The simplest approach to estimate the joint distribution is to assume statistical independence between the R matchers and estimate the joint distribution as the product of the R marginal distributions. In this case, the fused likelihood ratio (referred to as the product fusion score, $PFS(s)$) is the product of the likelihood ratios of the R matchers. Given the vector of match scores $s = [s_1, \ldots, s_R]$, $PFS(s)$ is given by

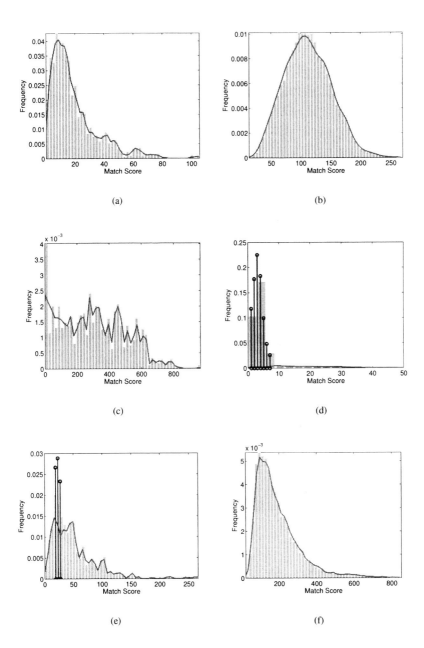

Figure 4.3. Histograms of match scores and corresponding generalized density estimates for MSU-Multimodal database. First Row: Histograms of match scores for face modality (a) genuine and (b) impostor. Second Row: Histograms of match scores for fingerprint modality (c) genuine and (d) impostor. Third Row: Histograms of match scores for hand geometry modality (e) genuine and (f) impostor. The solid line is the estimated density using the kernel density estimator, and the spikes in (d) and (e) correspond to the detected discrete components. Note that no score normalization needs to be performed before density estimation.

$$PFS(\boldsymbol{s}) = \frac{p(s_1, \ldots, s_R | genuine)}{p(s_1, \ldots, s_R | impostor)} = \prod_{j=1}^{R} \frac{f_{j,gen}(s_j)}{f_{j,imp}(s_j)}, \qquad (4.47)$$

where $f_{j,gen}(\cdot)$ and $f_{j,imp}(\cdot)$ are the estimates of generalized densities of the genuine and impostor scores of the jth biometric matcher. Hence, the decision rule can be stated as follows.

Assign $X \rightarrow genuine$ if

$$PFS(\boldsymbol{s}) \geq \eta, \qquad (4.48)$$

where η is the decision threshold.

However, a more appropriate procedure to estimate the joint density is to incorporate the correlation (if it exists) among the R matchers. One way to incorporate the correlation between the matchers is by using the copula models (Nelsen, 1999). Let $F_1, F_2, \ldots, F_R$ be R continuous distribution functions on the real line and F be a R-dimensional distribution function with the jth marginal given by $F_j, j = 1, 2, \ldots, R$. According to Sklar's Theorem (Nelsen, 1999), there exists a unique function $C(u_1, u_2, \ldots, u_R)$ from $[0, 1]^R \rightarrow [0, 1]$ satisfying

$$F(s_1, s_2, \ldots, s_R) = C(F_1(s_1), F_2(s_2), \ldots, F_R(s_R)), \qquad (4.49)$$

where $s_1, s_2, \ldots, s_R$ are R real numbers. The function C is known as a R-copula function that "couples" the one-dimensional distribution functions $F_1, F_2, \ldots, F_R$ to obtain the R-variate function F. Equation 4.49 can also be used to construct R-dimensional distribution function F whose marginals are the distributions $F_1, F_2, \ldots, F_R$.

Copula functions are effective in modeling a joint distribution whose marginal distributions are non-normal and do not have a parametric form (as is usually the case for biometric match scores). The family of copulas considered in Dass et al., 2005 is the R-dimensional multivariate Gaussian copulas (Cherubini et al., 2004). These functions can represent a variety of dependence structures among the R matchers using a $R \times R$ correlation matrix Σ_ρ. Note that multivariate Gaussian copulas do not assume that the joint or marginal distributions are Gaussian. They simply incorporate the second-order dependence in the form of a $R \times R$ correlation matrix. The R-dimensional Gaussian copula function with correlation matrix Σ_ρ is given by

$$C_{\Sigma_\rho}^R(u_1, \ldots, u_R) = \Phi_{\Sigma_\rho}^R(\Phi^{-1}(u_1), \ldots, \Phi^{-1}(u_R)), \qquad (4.50)$$

where each $u_j \in [0, 1]$ for $j = 1, \ldots, R$, $\Phi(\cdot)$ is the distribution function of the standard normal, $\Phi^{-1}(\cdot)$ is its inverse, and $\Phi_{\Sigma_\rho}^R$ is the R-dimensional distribution function of a random vector $\mathcal{Z} = (Z_1, \ldots, Z_R)^T$ with component means and variances given by 0 and 1, respectively. The density of $C_{\Sigma_\rho}^R$, denoted by $c_{\Sigma_\rho}^R$, is given by

$$
\begin{aligned}
c_{\Sigma_\rho}^R (u_1, \ldots, u_R) &\equiv \frac{\partial C_{\Sigma_\rho}^R (u_1, \ldots, u_R)}{\partial u_1 \ldots \partial u_R} \\
&= \frac{\phi_{\Sigma_\rho}^R (\Phi^{-1}(u_1), \ldots, \Phi^{-1}(u_R))}{\prod_{j=1}^R \phi(\Phi^{-1}(u_j))},
\end{aligned}
\tag{4.51}
$$

where $\phi_{\Sigma_\rho}^R (v_1, \ldots, v_R)$ is the joint probability density function of the R-variate normal distribution with mean 0 and covariance matrix Σ_ρ, and $\phi(x)$ is the standard normal density function.

The (m, n)-th entry of Σ_ρ, ρ_{mn}, measures the degree of correlation between the scores of the m-th and n-th matchers for $m, n = 1, \ldots, R$. In practice, the correlation matrix Σ_ρ is unknown. We can estimate Σ_ρ using the product moment correlation of normal quantiles corresponding to the observed scores from the R matchers as follows. Suppose there are N training score vectors available for density estimation. Let $s^i = [s_1^i, \ldots, s_R^i]$ denote the ith score vector, $i = 1, \ldots, N$. The normal quantile of score s_j^i is given by

$$
z_j^i = \Phi^{-1} \left(F_j \left(s_j^i \right) \right),
\tag{4.52}
$$

where $F_j(\cdot)$ denotes the jth marginal distribution, $j = 1, \ldots, R$ and $i = 1, \ldots, N$. Thus, the ith score vector $s^i = [s_1^i, \ldots, s_R^i]$ is transformed to $z^i = [z_1^i, \ldots, z_R^i]$, $i = 1, \ldots, N$. The covariance matrix of the N vectors, $z^1, \ldots, z^N$, is estimated as follows.

$$
\hat{\Sigma} = \frac{1}{N} \sum_{i=1}^N (z^i - \bar{z})^T (z^i - \bar{z}),
\tag{4.53}
$$

where

$$
\bar{z} = \frac{1}{N} \sum_{i=1}^N z^i.
\tag{4.54}
$$

The estimate of the (m, n)-th entry of Σ_ρ, $\hat{\rho}_{mn}$, is given by

$$
\hat{\rho}_{mn} = \frac{\hat{\sigma}_{mn}}{\sqrt{\hat{\sigma}_{mm} \hat{\sigma}_{nn}}},
\tag{4.55}
$$

where $\hat{\sigma}_{mn}$ is the (m, n)-th entry of $\hat{\Sigma}$.

The joint density function of genuine (impostor) match scores for R matchers, f_{gen}^R (f_{imp}^R) for some correlation matrix $\Sigma_{\rho,gen}$ ($\Sigma_{\rho,imp}$) is given by

$$f_{gen}^R(s_1,\ldots,s_R) = \left(\prod_{j=1}^{R} f_{j,gen}(s_j)\right) c_{\Sigma_{\rho,gen}}^R(F_{1,gen}(s_1),\ldots,F_{R,gen}(s_R))$$

(4.56)

and

$$f_{imp}^R(s_1,\ldots,s_R) = \left(\prod_{j=1}^{R} f_{j,imp}(s_j)\right) c_{\Sigma_{\rho,imp}}^R(F_{1,imp}(s_1),\ldots,F_{R,imp}(s_R)).$$

(4.57)

Given the vector of match scores $s = [s_1,\ldots,s_R]$, the likelihood ratio of the joint densities known as the copula fusion score $CFS(s)$, is given by

$$
\begin{aligned}
CFS(s) &= \frac{f_{gen}^R(s_1,\ldots,s_R)}{f_{imp}^R(s_1,\ldots,s_R)} \\
&= PFS(s)\frac{c_{\Sigma_{\rho,gen}}^R(F_{1,gen}(s_1),\ldots,F_{R,gen}(s_R))}{c_{\Sigma_{\rho,imp}}^R(F_{1,imp}(s_1),\ldots,F_{R,imp}(s_R))}, \quad (4.58)
\end{aligned}
$$

where $F_{j,gen}(s_j)$ and $F_{j,imp}(s_j)$ are, respectively, the estimates of generalized distribution functions for the jth biometric component, and $c_{\Sigma_\rho}^R$ is the density of $C_{\Sigma_\rho}^R$ as defined in Equation 4.51. The decision rule is given by

$$\text{Assign} \quad X \to genuine \quad \text{if}$$

$$CFS(s) \geq \eta,$$

(4.59)

where η is the decision threshold.

Dass et al., 2005 demonstrated that fusion based on the generalized density estimates gives better performance over fusion based on continuous density estimates. The MSU-Multimodal database (Jain et al., 2005) collected from 100 users, with each user providing 5 face, fingerprint and hand geometry samples is used in this study. Fingerprint matching is done using the minutiae features (Jain et al., 1997b) and the output of the fingerprint matcher is a similarity score. Eigenface coefficients are used to represent features of the face image (Turk and Pentland, 1991). The Euclidean distance between the eigenface coefficients of the face template and that of the input face is used as the matching score. The hand geometry images are represented by a 14-dimensional feature vector (Jain et al., 1999d) and the matching score is computed as the Euclidean distance between the input feature vector and the template feature vector. The histograms of the genuine and impostor scores of the three modalities in the MSU-Multimodal database are shown in Figure 4.3.

Figure 4.4 shows the ROC curves for the product and copula fusion rules (given by equations 4.48 and 4.59, respectively) and the ROC curves based on the match scores of the individual modalities for the MSU-Multimodal database. Figure 4.4(a) shows the recognition performance when the genuine and impostor score distributions of the three modalities are modeled purely by continuous densities, while Figure 4.4(b) gives the ROCs for generalized densities. Substantial performance improvement is obtained by modeling the match score distributions as a mixture of discrete and continuous components (generalized densities); for example, at a False Accept Rate (FAR) of 0.1%, the corresponding values of Genuine Accept Rate (GAR) for the continuous and generalized densities are 90.0% and 99.26%, respectively. Further, we can observe that although both the product and copula fusion rules give significantly better matching performance compared to the best individual modality, there is not much difference between the product and copula fusion rules. Dass et al., 2005 argue that this is due to the fact that the best modality in the MSU-Multimodal database is approximately independent (low correlation) of the other modalities, so the copula fusion involving more parameters than product fusion was not needed. The estimates of the correlation of the best single modality (fingerprint) with the other two modalities (face and hand geometry) were -0.01 and -0.11 for the genuine scores, and -0.05 and -0.04 for the impostor scores.

Dass et al., 2005 also applied the product and copula fusion rules on the match scores in the first partition of the Biometric Scores Set - Release I (BSSR1) released by NIST (see Appendix A.3 for more details). The ROC curves for the product and copula fusion rules on the NIST BSSR1 database are shown in Figure 4.5. In the NIST BSSR1 database, the correlation estimates of the best single modality (finger 2) with the other three modalities (face1, face2, and finger1 modalities, respectively) are -0.02, -0.06, and 0.43 for the genuine cases and 0.04, 0.02, and 0.14 for the impostor cases. Since the fusion is driven mostly by the best modality, the fact that this modality is approximately independent of the others means that the performances of product and copula fusion rules should be comparable to each other as reflected by the ROC curves in Figure 4.5.

4.5   Transformation-based score fusion

In practical multibiometric systems, the number of match scores available for training the fusion module is small due to the time, effort and cost involved in collecting multibiometric data. Due to the limited availability of training data, accurate estimation of the joint conditional densities $p(s =$

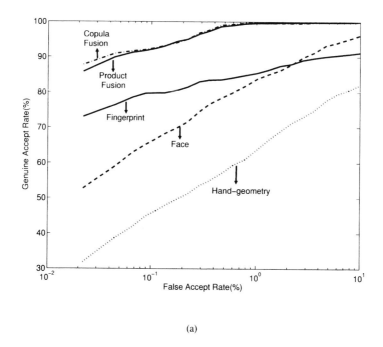

(a)

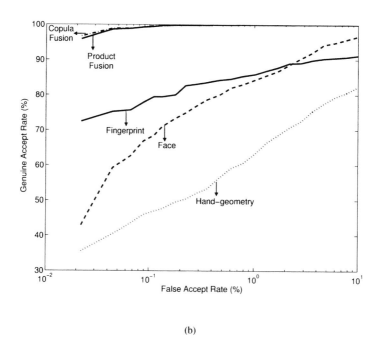

(b)

Figure 4.4. Performance of product and copula fusion on the MSU-Multimodal database based on (a) continuous and (b) generalized density estimates.

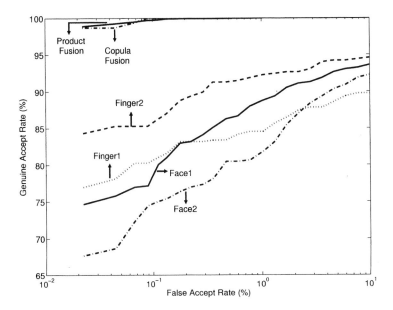

Figure 4.5. Performance of product and copula fusion on the NIST BSSR1 database.

$[s_1, \ldots, s_R]|genuine)$ and $p(s = [s_1, \ldots, s_R]|impostor)$ is not always possible. In such situations, a more appropriate fusion method is to directly combine the match scores provided by different matchers without converting them into posteriori probabilities. However, the combination of match scores is meaningful only when the scores of the individual matchers are comparable. Hence, a transformation known as score normalization is applied to transform the match scores obtained from the different matchers into a common domain. The sum, max and min classifier combination rules developed by Kittler et al., 1998 (as discussed earlier in Section 4.2) can be applied to obtain the fused match scores from the normalized match scores. Since the normalized match scores do not have any probabilistic interpretation, the sum, max and min rules are referred to as sum of scores, max score and min score fusion rules, respectively. The max score and min score fusion rules are referred to as order statistics. The combined match score can also be computed as a weighted sum of the match scores of the individual matchers (Ross and Jain, 2003; Wang et al., 2003), which is known as the weighted sum of scores rule (or simply, weighted sum rule).

Figures 4.3(a)-(f) show the conditional distributions of the face, fingerprint and hand geometry match scores of the MSU-Multimodal database used in experiments by Jain et al., 2005. The scores obtained from the face and hand geometry matchers are distance scores whereas those obtained from the fingerprint matcher are similarity scores. One can also observe the non-homogeneity (differences in the numerical scale and statistical distributions) in these scores demonstrating the need for score normalization prior to any meaningful combination.

4.5.1 Score Normalization

Score normalization refers to changing the location and scale parameters of the match score distributions at the outputs of the individual matchers, so that the match scores of different matchers are transformed into a common domain. When the parameters used for normalization are determined using a fixed training set, it is referred to as *fixed score normalization* (Brunelli and Falavigna, 1995). In such a case, the set of match scores available for training the fusion module of a multibiometric system is examined and a suitable statistical model is chosen to fit to the data. Based on the model, the score normalization parameters are determined. In *adaptive score normalization*, the normalization parameters are estimated based on the match score of the current test sample. This approach has the ability to adapt to variations in the input data such as the changes in the duration of the speech signals in speaker recognition systems.

For a good normalization scheme, the estimates of the location and scale parameters of the match score distribution must be *robust* and *efficient*. *Robustness* refers to insensitivity to the presence of outliers whereas *efficiency* refers to the proximity of the obtained estimates to the optimal estimates when the distribution of the data is known. Huber, 1981 explains the concepts of robustness and efficiency of statistical procedures and emphasizes the need for statistical procedures that have both these desirable characteristics. Although many techniques can be used for score normalization, the challenge lies in identifying a technique that is both robust and efficient.

The simplest normalization technique is the *min-max* normalization. Min-max normalization is best suited for the case where the bounds (maximum and minimum values) of the scores produced by a matcher are known. In this case, we can easily transform the minimum and maximum scores to 0 and 1, respectively. However, even if the match scores are not bounded, we can estimate the minimum and maximum values for the given set of training match scores and then apply the min-max normalization. Let s_j^i denote the ith match score output by the jth matcher, $i = 1, 2, \ldots, N; j = 1, 2, \ldots, R$ (R is the number of matchers and N is the number of match scores available in the training set). The min-max normalized score, ns_j^t, for the test score s_j^t is given by

$$ns_j^t = \frac{s_j^t - \min_{i=1}^N s_j^i}{\max_{i=1}^N s_j^i - \min_{i=1}^N s_j^i}. \tag{4.60}$$

When the minimum and maximum values are estimated from the given set of match scores, this method is not robust (i.e., the method is sensitive to outliers in the data used for estimation). Min-max normalization retains the original distribution of scores except for a scaling factor and transforms all the scores into a common range $[0, 1]$. Distance scores can be transformed into similarity scores by subtracting the normalized score from 1.

Decimal scaling can be applied when the scores of different matchers are on a logarithmic scale. For example, if one matcher has scores in the range $[0, 10]$ and the other has scores in the range $[0, 1000]$, the following normalization could be applied to transform the scores of both the matchers to the common $[0, 1]$ range.

$$ns_j^t = \frac{s_j^t}{10^{n_j}}, \tag{4.61}$$

where $n_j = \log_{10} \max_{i=1}^N s_j^i$. In the example with two matchers where the score ranges are $[0, 10]$ and $[0, 1000]$, the values of n would be 1 and 3, respectively. The problems with this approach are the lack of robustness and the implicit assumption that the scores of different matchers vary by a logarithmic factor.

The most commonly used score normalization technique is the *z-score* normalization that uses the arithmetic mean and standard deviation of the training data. This scheme can be expected to perform well if the average and the variance of the score distributions of the matchers are available. If we do not know the values of these two parameters, then we need to estimate them based on the given training set. The z-score normalized score is given by

$$ns_j^t = \frac{s_j^t - \mu_j}{\sigma_j}, \tag{4.62}$$

where μ_j is the arithmetic mean and σ_j is the standard deviation for the jth matcher. However, both mean and standard deviation are sensitive to outliers and hence, this method is not robust. Z-score normalization does not guarantee a common numerical range for the normalized scores of the different matchers. If the distribution of the scores is not Gaussian, z-score normalization does not preserve the distribution of the given set of scores. This is due to the fact that mean and standard deviation are the optimal location and scale parameters only for a Gaussian distribution. While mean and standard deviation are reasonable estimates of location and scale, respectively, they are not optimal for an arbitrary match score distribution.

The *median* and *median absolute deviation* (MAD) statistics are insensitive to outliers as well as points in the extreme tails of the distribution. Hence, a normalization scheme using median and MAD would be robust and is given by

$$ns_j^t = \frac{s_j^t - med_j}{MAD_j}, \qquad (4.63)$$

where $med_j = median_{i=1}^{N} s_j^i$ and $MAD_j = median_{i=1}^{N} |s_j^i - med_j|$. However, the median and the MAD estimators have a low efficiency compared to the mean and the standard deviation estimators, i.e., when the score distribution is not Gaussian, median and MAD are poor estimates of the location and scale parameters. Therefore, this normalization technique does not preserve the input score distribution and does not transform the scores into a common numerical range.

Cappelli et al., 2000 use a *double sigmoid function* for score normalization in a multibiometric system that combines different fingerprint matchers. The normalized score is given by

$$ns_j^t = \begin{cases} \dfrac{1}{1+\exp\left(-2\left(\frac{s_j^t - \tau}{\alpha_1}\right)\right)} & \text{if } s_j^t < \tau, \\[4mm] \dfrac{1}{1+\exp\left(-2\left(\frac{s_j^t - \tau}{\alpha_2}\right)\right)} & \text{otherwise,} \end{cases} \qquad (4.64)$$

where τ is the reference operating point and α_1 and α_2 denote the left and right edges of the region in which the function is linear. The double sigmoid function exhibits linear characteristics in the interval $(\tau - \alpha_1, \tau - \alpha_2)$. Figure 4.6 shows an example of the double sigmoid normalization, where the scores in the $[0, 300]$ range are mapped to the $[0, 1]$ range using $\tau = 200$, $\alpha_1 = 20$ and $\alpha_2 = 30$.

While the double sigmoid normalization scheme transforms the scores into the $[0, 1]$ interval, it requires careful tuning of the parameters τ, α_1 and α_2 to obtain good efficiency. Generally, τ is chosen to be some value falling in the region of overlap between the genuine and impostor score distributions, and α_1 and α_2 are set so that they correspond to the extent of overlap between the two distributions toward the left and right of τ, respectively. This normalization scheme provides a linear transformation of the scores in the region of overlap, while the scores outside this region are transformed non-linearly. The double sigmoid normalization is very similar to the min-max normalization followed by the application of a two-quadrics (QQ) or a logistic (LG) function as suggested by Snelick et al., 2005. When the values of α_1 and α_2 are large, the double sigmoid normalization closely resembles the QQ-min-max normalization. On

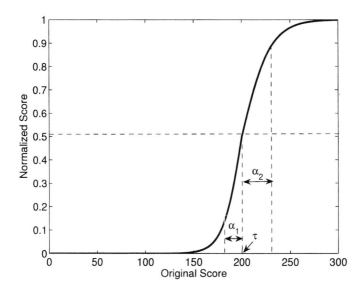

Figure 4.6. Double sigmoid normalization with $\tau = 200$, $\alpha_1 = 20$, and $\alpha_2 = 30$.

the other hand, we can make the double sigmoid normalization approach toward LG-min-max normalization by assigning small values to α_1 and α_2.

The *tanh-estimators* introduced by Hampel et al., 1986 are robust and highly efficient. The tanh normalization is given by

$$
ns_j^t = \frac{1}{2} \left\{ \tanh \left(0.01 \left(\frac{s_j^t - \mu_{GH}}{\sigma_{GH}} \right) \right) + 1 \right\},
\tag{4.65}
$$

where μ_{GH} and σ_{GH} are the mean and standard deviation estimates, respectively, of the genuine score distribution as given by Hampel estimators. Hampel estimators are based on the following influence (ψ)-function:

$$
\psi(u) = \begin{cases}
u & 0 \leq |u| < a, \\
a * sign(u) & a \leq |u| < b, \\
a * sign(u) * \left(\frac{c - |u|}{c - b} \right) & b \leq |u| < c, \\
0 & |u| \geq c,
\end{cases}
\tag{4.66}
$$

where

$$
sign\{u\} = \begin{cases}
+1, & \text{if } u \geq 0, \\
-1, & \text{otherwise.}
\end{cases}
\tag{4.67}
$$

A plot of the Hampel influence function is shown in Figure 4.7. The Hampel influence function reduces the influence of the scores at the tails of the distribution (identified by a, b, and c) during the estimation of the location and scale parameters. Hence, this method is not sensitive to outliers. If many of the points that constitute the tail of the distributions are discarded, the estimate is robust but not efficient (optimal). On the other hand, if all the points that constitute the tail of the distributions are considered, the estimate is not robust but its efficiency increases. Therefore, the parameters a, b, and c must be carefully chosen depending on the amount of robustness required which in turn depends on the amount of noise in the available training data.

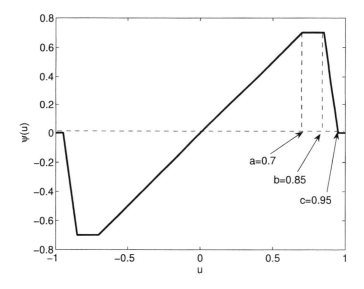

Figure 4.7.   Hampel influence function with $a = 0.7$, $b = 0.85$, and $c = 0.95$.

Mosteller and Tukey, 1977 introduce the biweight location and scale estimators that are robust and efficient. But, the *biweight estimators* are iterative in nature (initial estimates of the biweight location and scale parameters are chosen, and these estimates are updated based on the training scores), and are applicable only for Gaussian data. A summary of the characteristics of the different normalization techniques discussed here is shown in Table 4.1. The min-max, decimal scaling and z-score normalization schemes are efficient, but are not robust to outliers. On the other hand, the median normalization scheme is robust but inefficient. Only the double sigmoid and tanh-estimators have both the desired characteristics, namely, robustness and efficiency.

Table 4.1. Summary of score normalization techniques.

Normalization Technique	Robustness	Efficiency
Min-max	No	High
Decimal scaling	No	High
Z-score	No	High
Median and MAD	Yes	Moderate
Double sigmoid	Yes	High
Tanh-estimators	Yes	High

4.5.2   Evaluation of normalization techniques

It must be noted that no normalization scheme has been shown to be optimal for all kinds of match score data. Hence, a number of score normalization techniques are admissible, i.e., they may work better than other normalization techniques depending on the fusion problem at hand. In practice, it is recommended that a number of normalization techniques be evaluated to determine the one that gives the best performance on the given data. Jain et al., 2005 studied the performance of a multimodal biometric system comprising of face, fingerprint and hand geometry modalities under different normalization and fusion techniques. They used the MSU-Multimodal database for these experiments. The simple sum of scores, the max-score, and the min-score fusion methods were applied on the normalized scores. The normalized scores were obtained by using the following techniques: simple distance-to-similarity transformation with no change in scale (STrans), min-max normalization (Minmax), z-score normalization (ZScore), median-MAD normalization (Median), double sigmoid normalization (Sigmoid), tanh normalization (Tanh), and Parzen normalization (Parzen). Note that the conversion of match scores into posteriori probabilities by the Parzen window density estimation method is really not a normalization technique. It actually falls under the density-based match score fusion approach. However, Jain et al., 2005 treat the ratio of the posteriori probabilities of the genuine and impostor classes as a normalized match score and hence, they refer to this method as Parzen normalization.

The recognition performance of the face, fingerprint, and hand geometry modalities in the MSU-Multimodal database is shown in Figure 4.8. We observe that the fingerprint modality gives the best performance followed by the face and hand geometry modalities in that order. At a False Accept Rate (FAR) of 0.1%, the Genuine Accept Rates (GAR) are 83.6%, 67.7% and 46.8% for the fingerprint, face and hand geometry modalities, respectively.

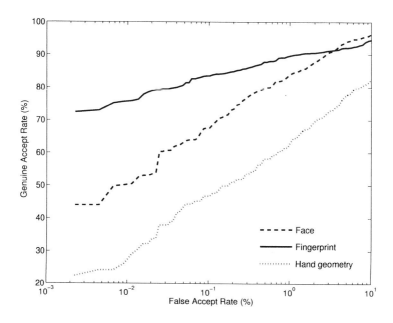

Figure 4.8. ROC curves for the individual modalities in the MSU-Multimodal database.

To evaluate the performance after fusion, the set of match scores obtained from the MSU-Multimodal database was randomly partitioned into training (60% of the scores were used for estimating the normalization parameters) and test (the remaining 40% of the scores were used for evaluating the performance of the multibiometric system) sets. This random splitting of the database into training and test sets was repeated 40 times resulting in 40 trials. Table 4.2 summarizes the average (over the 40 trials) Genuine Accept Rate (GAR) of the multimodal system along with the standard deviation of the GAR (shown in parentheses) for different normalization and fusion schemes, at a False Accept Rate (FAR) of 0.1%. From Table 4.2, it is apparent that the sum of scores method provides better recognition performance than the max-score and min-score methods. Hence, we compare the different normalization techniques only for the sum of scores fusion method.

Figure 4.9 shows the recognition performance of the multimodal system when the scores that are normalized using various techniques described above, are combined using the sum of scores method. We observe that a multimodal system employing the sum of scores method provides better performance than the best unimodal system (fingerprint in this case) for all normalization techniques except median-MAD normalization. For example, at a FAR of 0.1%, the GAR of the fingerprint module is about 83.6%, while that of the multimodal

Table 4.2. Genuine Accept Rate (GAR) (%) of different normalization and fusion techniques at the 0.1% False Accept Rate (FAR) for the MSU-Multimodal database. At 0.1% FAR, the GAR of the unimodal systems are 83.6%, 67.7% and 46.8% for the fingerprint, face and hand geometry modalities, respectively. Note that the values in the table represent average GAR, and the values indicated in parentheses correspond to the standard deviation of GAR computed over the 40 trials of randomly splitting the available data into training and test sets.

Normalization	Fusion Technique		
Technique	Sum of scores	Max-score	Min-score
STrans	98.3 (0.4)	46.7 (2.3)	83.9 (1.6)
Minmax	97.8 (0.6)	67.0 (2.5)	83.9 (1.6)
Zscore	98.6 (0.4)	92.1 (1.1)	84.8 (1.6)
Median	84.5 (1.3)	83.7 (1.6)	68.8 (2.2)
Sigmoid	96.5 (1.3)	83.7 (1.6)	83.1 (1.8)
Tanh	98.5 (0.4)	86.9 (1.8)	85.6 (1.5)
Parzen	95.7 (0.9)	93.6 (2.0)	83.9 (1.9)

system is 98.6% when z-score normalization is used. The performance of the multimodal biometric system is a significant improvement over the best unimodal system and it underscores the benefit of deploying multimodal systems.

Among the various normalization techniques on this dataset, we observe that the tanh and min-max normalization techniques outperform other techniques at low FARs. At higher FARs, z-score normalization provides slightly better performance than tanh and min-max normalization. In the multimodal system based on the MSU-Multimodal database, the combined score of test pattern, s^t_{fus}, after sum of scores fusion is just a linear transformation of the score vector $s^t = [s^t_1, s^t_2, s^t_3]$, i.e., $s^t_{fus} = (a_1 s^t_1 - b_1) + (a_2 s^t_2 - b_2) + (a_3 s^t_3 - b_3)$, where s^t_1, s^t_2, and s^t_3 correspond to the match scores for the test pattern obtained from the face, fingerprint and hand geometry matchers, respectively. The effect of different normalization techniques is to determine the weights a_1, a_2, and a_3, and the biases b_1, b_2, and b_3. Since the value of the MAD statistic for the fingerprint scores is very small compared to that of face and hand geometry scores, the median-MAD normalization assigns a much larger weight to the fingerprint score ($a_2 \gg a_1$ and $a_2 \gg a_3$). This is a direct consequence of the moderate efficiency of the median-MAD estimator. Since the distribution of the fingerprint scores (see Figures 4.3(c) and (d)) deviates drastically from the Gaussian assumption, the median and MAD statistics are not the correct measures of location and scale, respectively. In this case, the combined score is approximately equal to the fingerprint score and the performance of the multimodal system is close to that of the fingerprint module. On the

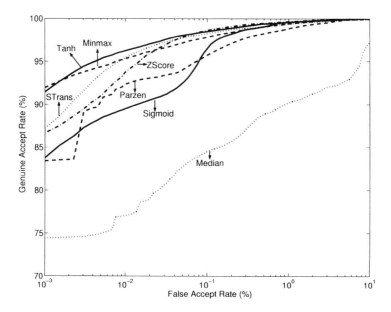

Figure 4.9. ROC curves for sum of scores fusion method under different normalization schemes on the MSU-Multimodal database.

other hand, min-max normalization, z-score normalization, tanh and distance-to-similarity transformation assign more reasonable weights to the scores of the three modalities. Therefore, the recognition performance of the multimodal system applying one of these four normalization techniques (min-max, z-score, tanh and distance-to-similarity transformation) along with the sum of scores fusion method is significantly better than that of the fingerprint matcher. The difference in performance between the min-max, z-score, tanh and distance-to-similarity transformation is relatively small. However, it should be noted that the raw scores of the three modalities used in the experiments are comparable and, hence, a simple distance-to-similarity conversion works reasonably well here. If the match scores of the three modalities were significantly different, then the distance-to-similarity transformation method would not work as well.

For sum of scores fusion, we observe that the performance of a robust normalization technique like tanh is almost the same as that of the non-robust techniques like min-max and z-score normalization. However, the performance of such non-robust techniques is highly dependent on the accuracy of the estimates of the location and scale parameters. The scores produced by the matchers used by Jain et al., 2005 are unbounded and, hence, can theoretically produce any value in the interval $(0, \infty)$. Also, the statistics of the scores (e.g., average or deviation from the average) produced by these three matchers will not be known. Therefore, parameters like the average and standard deviation of scores (needed for z-score normalization) have to be estimated from the available data. The particular data set used in these experiments did not contain any outliers and, hence, the performance resulting from the use of non-robust normalization techniques was not degraded.

In order to demonstrate the sensitivity of the min-max and z-score normalization techniques in the presence of outliers, Jain et al., 2005 artificially introduced outliers in the fingerprint scores. For min-max normalization, a single outlier whose value is 75%, 125%, 150%, 175% or 200% of the maximum score (in the training set) is introduced. Figure 4.10 shows the recognition performance of the multimodal system after the introduction of the outlier. We observe that the performance is sensitive to the maximum score. A single outlier that is twice the original maximum score can reduce the recognition rate of the multimodal system by 3-5% depending on the operating point of the system. The performance degradation is more severe at lower values of FAR.

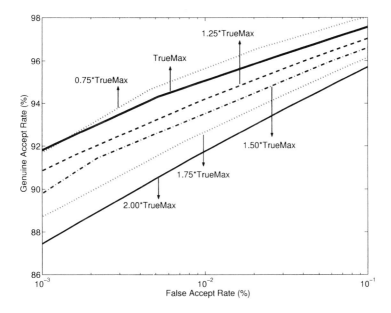

Figure 4.10. Robustness analysis of min-max normalization. Note that TrueMax represents the maximum fingerprint match score in the training set. The different ROC curves are obtained by replacing the maximum fingerprint score in the training set with an outlier score whose value is 75%, 125%, 150%, 175% or 200% of TrueMax.

In the case of z-score normalization, several outliers were introduced in the fingerprint match scores so that the standard deviation of the fingerprint score is increased by 125%, 150%, 175% or 200% of the original standard deviation. In one trial, some large match scores were reduced to decrease the standard deviation of the scores to 75% of the original value. In the case of an increase in standard deviation, the performance improves after the introduction of outliers as indicated in Figure 4.11. Since the original standard deviation was small, fingerprint scores were assigned a higher weight compared to the other modalities. As the standard deviation is increased, the dominance of the fingerprint modality was reduced and this resulted in improved recognition rates. However, the goal of this experiment was to show the sensitivity of the system to those estimated parameters that can be easily affected by outliers. A similar experiment was done for tanh normalization technique and, as shown in Figure 4.12, there is no significant variation in the performance of the tanh normalization method after the introduction of outliers. This result highlights the robustness of the tanh normalization method.

In many cases, the maximum and minimum score output by a matcher will be known in advance. Therefore, the min-max normalization scheme *may* not require an explicit estimation procedure based on the training data.

4.6   Classifier-based score fusion

In classifier-based score fusion, a pattern classifier (Duda et al., 2001) is used to indirectly learn the relationship between the vector of match scores $[s_1, s_2, \ldots, s_R]$ provided by the R biometric matchers and the posteriori probabilities of the genuine and impostor classes, namely, $P(genuine|s_1, s_2, \ldots, s_R)$ and $P(impostor|s_1, s_2, \ldots, s_R)$. In this approach, the vector of match scores $[s_1, s_2, \ldots, s_R]$ is treated as a feature vector which is then classified into one of two classes: "genuine user" or "impostor". Based on the training set of match scores from the genuine and impostor classes, the classifier learns a decision boundary between the two classes. Figure 4.13 shows an example of a linear decision boundary learned by a classifier based on the genuine and impostor match scores from two different matchers. During verification, any match score vector that falls in the genuine region (to the right of the decision boundary in Figure 4.13) is classified as "genuine". In general, the decision boundary can be quite complex depending on the nature of the classifier. However, the classifier is capable of learning the decision boundary irrespective of how the feature vectors are generated. Hence, the output scores of the different matchers can be non-homogeneous (distance or similarity metric, different numerical ranges, etc.) and no processing is required prior to designing the classifier. A limitation of the classifier-based score fusion approach is that it is not easy to fix one type of error (say FAR) and then compute the FRR at the specified FAR.

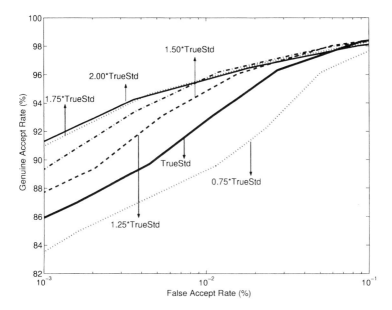

Figure 4.11. Robustness analysis of z-score normalization. Note that TrueStd represents the standard deviation of the fingerprint match scores in the training set. The different ROC curves are obtained by introducing outlier scores in the training set so that the standard deviation of the fingerprint match scores is changed to 75%, 125%, 150%, 175% or 200% of TrueStd.

Several classifiers have been used to consolidate the match scores of multiple matchers and arrive at a decision. Brunelli and Falavigna, 1995 use a HyperBF network to combine matchers based on voice and face features. The speaker recognition subsystem was based on vector quantization of the acoustic parameter space and included an adaptation phase of the codebooks to the test environment. Face identification was achieved by analyzing three facial components, namely, eyes, nose, and mouth. The basic template matching technique was applied for face matching. While the rank-one recognition rates of the voice and face matchers were 88% and 91%, respectively, the fusion of these two matchers achieved a rank-one recognition rate of 98%.

Verlinde and Cholet, 1999 compare the relative performance of three different classifiers, namely, the k-Nearest Neighbor classifier using vector quantization, the decision tree classifier, and the classifier based on logistic regression model when used for the fusion of match scores from three biometric matchers. The three matchers were based on profile face image, frontal face image, and voice. Experiments by Verlinde and Cholet, 1999 on the multimodal M2VTS database (Pigeon and Vandendrope, 1996) show that the total error rate (sum of the

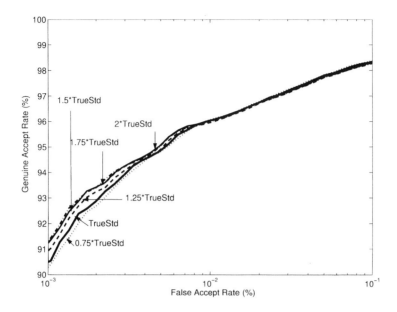

Figure 4.12. Robustness analysis of tanh normalization. Note that TrueStd represents the standard deviation of the fingerprint match scores in the training set. The different ROC curves are obtained by introducing outlier scores in the training set so that the standard deviation of the fingerprint match scores is changed to 75%, 125%, 150%, 175% or 200% of TrueStd.

false accept and false reject rates) of the multimodal system was an order of magnitude less than that of the individual modalities. While the total error rates of the individual modalities were 8.9% for profile face, 8.7% for frontal face, and 3.7% for speaker verification, the total error rate of the multimodal system was found to be 0.1% when the classifier based on logistic regression model was employed.

Chatzis et al., 1999 use classical k-means clustering, fuzzy clustering and median radial basis function (MRBF) algorithms for fusion at the match score level. Five biometric matchers that were based on the grey-level and shape information of face image and voice features were employed. Each matcher provided a match score and a quality metric that measures the reliability of the match score, and these values were concatenated to form a ten-dimensional vector. Clustering algorithms were applied on this ten-dimensional feature vector to form two clusters, namely, genuine and impostor.

Ben-Yacoub et al., 1999 evaluate a number of classification schemes for fusion of match scores from multiple modalities, including support vector machine (SVM) with polynomial kernels, SVM with Gaussian kernels, C4.5 decision

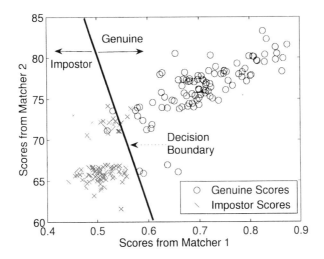

Figure 4.13. Example of a linear decision boundary learned by a classifier in a 2-dimensional ($R = 2$) feature space. During verification, any match score vector that falls in the region marked as 'Genuine' (to the right of the decision boundary) is classified as "genuine user". On the other hand, any match score vector that falls in the region marked as 'Impostor' (to the left of the decision boundary) is classified as "impostor".

trees, multilayer perceptron, Fisher linear discriminant, and Bayesian classifier. This evaluation is conducted on the XM2VTS database (Messer et al., 1999) consisting of 295 subjects. The database includes four recordings of each person obtained at one month intervals. During each session, two recordings were made: a speech shot and a head rotation shot. The speech shot was composed of the frontal face recording of each subject during the dialogue. Face recognition was performed by using elastic graph matching (EGM) (Lades et al., 1993). Two different approaches were used for speaker verification. A sphericity measure (Bimbot et al., 1995) was used for text-independent speaker verification. Hidden Markov models (HMM) were used for text-dependent speaker verification. The total error rate of 0.6% achieved by the Bayesian classifier was significantly lower than the total error rate of 1.48% achieved by the HMM based speaker recognition system, which was the best individual modality in terms of total error rate.

Bigun et al., 1997 propose a new algorithm based on the Bayesian classifier for fusion in a multibiometric system. Their model takes into account the estimated accuracy of the individual classifiers during the fusion process. Sanderson and Paliwal, 2002 use a support vector machine (SVM) to combine the scores of face and speech experts. They show that the performance of such a classifier deteriorates under noisy input conditions. To overcome this problem, they implement structurally noise-resistant classifiers like piece-wise linear classifier and modified Bayesian classifier. Wang et al., 2003 consider the match scores resulting from face and iris recognition modules as a two-dimensional feature vector and use Fisher's discriminant analysis and a neural network classifier with radial basis function to classify the 2-dimensional match score vector into "genuine" and "impostor" classes. Ross and Jain, 2003 use decision tree and linear discriminant classifiers for combining the match scores of face, fingerprint and hand geometry modalities. Random forest algorithm was used by Ma et al., 2005 for the classification of 3-dimensional match score vectors described in Ross and Jain, 2003 into "genuine" and "impostor" classes.

4.7   Comparison of score fusion techniques

The existence of a large number of score fusion techniques makes it difficult for the designer of a multibiometric system to select an appropriate fusion method for the problem at hand. Most of these score fusion techniques have not been tested on benchmark databases. Recently, the National Institute of Standards and Technology (NIST) released a true multimodal match score database known as the Biometric Score Set Release-1 (National Institute of Standards and Technology, 2004) containing the face and fingerprint matching scores of 517 individuals (see Appendix for more details). Also, a benchmark match score database based on the XM2VTS multimodal dataset (face and voice modalities) has been released by IDIAP (Poh and Bengio, 2005a). The emergence of these benchmark databases is likely to result in a more careful and thorough evaluation of score fusion techniques. In this section, we briefly compare some of the score fusion techniques based on the NIST BSSR1 database. In order to clearly illustrate the differences in recognition performance of the various fusion schemes, we consider the match scores corresponding to only two biometric matchers in this database: the Face-G matcher and the fingerprint matcher corresponding to the right index fingerprint. Henceforth, we refer to these two matchers simply as face and fingerprint matchers, respectively.

Firstly, we compare the recognition performance of the various classifier combination rules (Kittler et al., 1998) described in Section 4.2. As pointed out earlier in Section 4.3, we assume that the feature representations of the two biometric matchers x_1 and x_2 are not available. Hence, the posteriori probabilities $P(genuine|x_1, x_2)$ and $P(impostor|x_1, x_2)$ are estimated from the vector of match scores $s = [s_1, s_2]$, where s_1 and s_2 are the match scores provided by the face and fingerprint matchers, respectively. Further, we adopt the density-based score fusion approach and estimate the conditional densities $p(s_1|genuine)$, $p(s_1|impostor)$, $p(s_2|genuine)$ and $p(s_2|impostor)$ using a non-parametric density estimation technique. Specifically, we use a Gaussian kernel density estimator and the bandwidth of the kernel is obtained using the "solve-the-equation" bandwidth estimator (Wand and Jones, 1995). We also assume that the prior probabilities of the genuine and impostor classes are equal. 80% of the genuine and impostor scores are used for estimating the conditional densities and the remaining 20% are used for evaluating the fusion performance. Five-fold cross validation is performed and the reported results correspond to the average over the five trials.

Figure 4.14 shows the ROC curves for the face and fingerprint unibiometric systems as well as the ROC curves for the multibiometric system, when fusion is performed using the product, sum, max and min rules. We can clearly see that the fingerprint matcher is more accurate than the face matcher. For the selected face and fingerprint matchers in the NIST BSSR1 database, we also observe that fusion using the product rule gives the best recognition performance. It must be noted that the only assumption in deriving the product rule is the independence between the biometric matchers. The sum, max and min rules are derived by introducing other constraints to the product rule. This explains the relatively good performance of the product rule compared to the other fusion rules. In general, the sum rule has been shown to perform well because it is less sensitive to errors in the probability estimates (Kittler et al., 1998). However, the sum rule is derived based on the strong assumption that genuine and impostor classes are highly ambiguous, and that the observed match scores enhance the prior class probabilities marginally. This assumption is not valid for the match scores in the NIST BSSR1 database because the genuine and impostor score distributions have only a small region of overlap. Therefore, the sum rule does not provide any improvement in recognition performance over the best unimodal biometric system (fingerprint in this case).

Secondly, we compare some of the transformation-based score fusion techniques discussed in Section 4.5. Specifically, the match scores provided by the face and fingerprint matchers are first normalized using five different normalization techniques, viz., min-max, z-score, median-MAD, double sigmoid and tanh techniques. The normalized match scores are then combined using the sum of scores method. Again, five-fold cross validation is performed using 80% of the genuine and impostor scores for estimating the normalization parameters, and the remaining 20% for evaluating the performance of the fusion technique. Figure 4.15 summarizes the matching performance of the multimodal biometric system when the normalized scores are combined using the sum of scores method. We observe that the multimodal system results in better performance than the best unimodal system (fingerprint in this case). Among the various normalization schemes, the min-max and tanh normalization techniques result in the best performance on the NIST BSSR1 database.

Finally, we evaluate the performance of a classifier-based score fusion scheme on the same data set. As indicated earlier, the classifier-based approach assigns a two-dimensional match score vector to one of the two classes, namely, genuine and impostor. A Support Vector Machine (SVM) with a radial basis

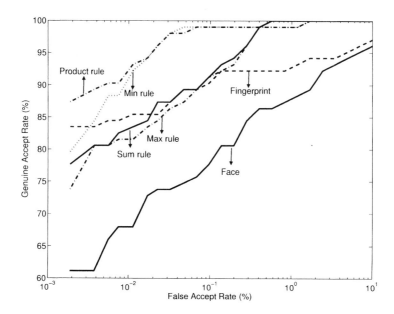

Figure 4.14. Comparison of recognition performance of the classifier combination rules proposed by Kittler et al., 1998 on the NIST BSSR1 database. In this experiment, the match scores are converted into probabilities using a non-parametric density estimation technique.

function kernel is used for the classification and a five-fold cross-validation is performed. The SVM classifier has an average FAR of 0.01% (standard deviation of 0.008%) and an average GAR of 95.1% (standard deviation of 3.4%). The performance of the SVM classifier is shown in Figure 4.16. Note that the operating point (FAR and the corresponding GAR) of a classifier-based score fusion scheme can be changed by tuning the parameters of the classifier. However, it is not always possible to fix the FAR and then compute the corresponding GAR in classifier-based score fusion.

Figure 4.16 compares the performance of the best transformation-based score fusion technique (tanh normalization followed by sum of scores fusion) and the best density-based score fusion approach (product rule). We see that fusion based on the product rule has a lower recognition rate than the sum of scores fusion method (after tanh normalization) at small values of False Accept Rate (FAR). For example, at a FAR of 0.01%, the average Genuine Accept Rate (GAR) of the product rule is 92.4% while the sum of scores fusion has an average GAR of 96.5%. This may be due to the limited availability of genuine match scores for estimating the conditional densities $p(s_1|genuine)$ and $p(s_2|genuine)$, where s_1 and s_2 are the match scores provided by the face

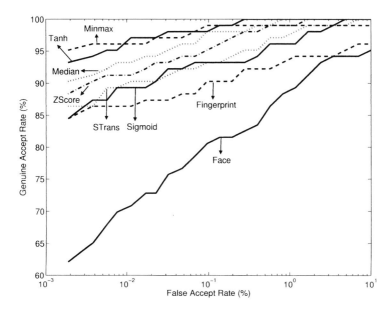

Figure 4.15. ROC curves for sum of scores fusion method under different normalization schemes on NIST BSSR1 dataset.

and fingerprint matchers, respectively. Since there are only 517 genuine match scores for each matcher in the NIST BSSR1 database, the density estimates of the genuine scores are not very reliable.

4.8 User-specific score fusion

It is possible to further enhance the performance of multibiometric systems by adopting user-specific matching thresholds and user-specific weights. Matching thresholds are used by biometric matchers to classify a certain match score as being genuine or impostor. Weights, on the other hand, are used to indicate the importance of individual biometric matchers in a multibiometric framework. In the multibiometric systems described so far, we implicitly assumed that each biometric sub-system provides the same discriminatory information across all users. In practice, the performance of a particular sub-system will vary across users.

Users of a biometric system are prone to different types of errors. The False Reject Rate (FRR) of users with large intra-class variations will be high. Similarly, the False Accept Rate (FAR) amongst users having small inter-class variations will be high. Thus, a "strict" threshold will be appropriate to distinguish users exhibiting a high FAR, while a "loose" threshold may be necessary for

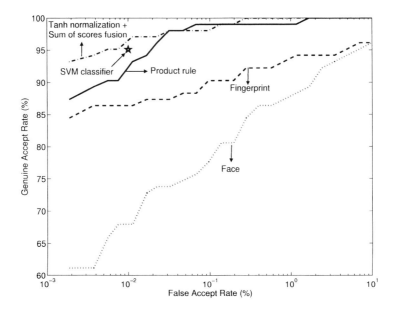

Figure 4.16. Comparison of recognition performance of the density-based, transformation-based and classifier-based score fusion approaches on the NIST BSSR1 database.

users having a high FRR. Furthermore, in a multimodal system, it is instructive to assign different degrees of importance to the various traits on a user-by-user basis. This is especially significant when the biometric traits of a user cannot be reliably acquired. For example, users with persistently dry fingers may not be able to provide good quality fingerprints. Such users can experience higher false rejects when interacting with a fingerprint system. By reducing the weight of the fingerprint trait of such users and increasing the weights associated with the other traits, the FRR of these users can be reduced.

A multibiometric system can be trained to invoke a specific set of threshold and weight parameters based on the claimed identity, I. Automatic learning and update of user-specific thresholds and weights can help reduce the error rates associated with a specific user, thereby improving the overall recognition accuracy of the system (Jain and Ross, 2002b). This will appeal to that segment of the population averse to interacting with a system that constantly requests them to provide multiple readings of the same biometric due to the poor quality of the acquired data.

Toh et al., 2004 identify the following four paradigms in the context of learning user-specific weights and thresholds:

1 Learn globally, decide globally (GG): In this scheme, the multibiometric system learns a common set of weights for the different matchers irrespective of the user and uses a common (global) decision threshold for all users.

2 Learn globally, decide locally (GL): The system learns a common set of weights for the different matchers irrespective of the user but uses user-specific decision thresholds.

3 Learn locally, decide globally (LG): The system learns user-specific weights and a common decision threshold

4 Learn locally, decide locally (LL): The system learns user-specific weights and uses user-specific thresholds.

In these four paradigms, the system either makes use of user-dependent parameters (thresholds and weights) for all users or the parameters are independent of the user. Fierrez-Aguilar et al., 2005a propose a new adaptive learning strategy that offers a trade-off between the user-specific and user-independent approaches.

4.8.1 User-specific matching thresholds

Jain and Ross, 2002b compute the matching thresholds for each user using the cumulative histogram of impostor scores corresponding to that user. Since a sufficient number of user-specific genuine scores would not be available when the user begins to use the system, only the impostor scores are used initially to learn the user-specific thresholds. The impostor scores are generated by comparing the feature sets of a user with feature sets of other users or with feature sets available in a predetermined impostor database. Suppose that the match scores have been quantized into 100 bins. The cumulative histogram at a value x_i, $i = 1, 2, \ldots 100$, is the sum of all those impostor scores less than or equal to x_i. The user-specific matching thresholds are computed as follows.

1 For the ith user in the database, let $t_i(\gamma)$ correspond to the threshold in the cumulative histogram that retains γ fraction of scores, $0 \leq \gamma \leq 1$.

2 Using $\{t_i(\gamma)\}$ as the matching threshold, compute $\{FAR_i(\gamma), GAR_i(\gamma)\}$, where GAR is the Genuine Accept Rate.

3 Compute the total FAR and GAR as

$$FAR(\gamma) = \sum_i FAR_i(\gamma)$$

$$GAR(\gamma) = \sum_i GAR_i(\gamma). \tag{4.68}$$

4 Use $\{FAR(\gamma), GAR(\gamma)\}$ to generate the ROC curve.

Figure 4.17 shows that the choice of the threshold relies on the distribution of impostor scores for each user. This is in contrast to traditional methods where the threshold is established by pooling together the impostor scores associated with all the users. When the multibiometric system is deployed, the γ corresponding to a specified FAR is used to invoke the set of user-specific thresholds, $\{t_i(\gamma)\}$. Table 4.3 shows the user-specific thresholds (corresponding to a FAR of 1%) associated with the 10 users whose data was collected over a period of two months. The ROC curves indicating the improved performance as a result of using user-specific thresholds are shown in Figure 4.18.

User-specific thresholds may also be derived via user-specific score normalization schemes that have been widely used in the speaker recognition community (see Poh and Bengio, 2005b and the references therein). The primary idea here is to shift and scale the genuine and/or impostor score distributions for each user so that their location coincides with a predetermined value. The amount of shift that is necessary determines the user-specific matching threshold.

Table 4.3. User-specific thresholds for the biometric traits of 10 users at a FAR of 1%.

User #	Fingerprint	Face	Hand Geometry
1	14	91	94
2	17	91	95
3	15	92	95
4	12	94	95
5	11	91	90
6	11	90	92
7	16	95	94
8	19	92	97
9	11	90	96
10	19	94	93

4.8.2   User-specific weights

Each biometric matcher provides a match score based on the input feature set and the template against which it is compared. These scores can be weighted according to the biometric trait used, in order to reduce the importance of less reliable biometric traits (and increase the influence of more reliable traits). The weights can be determined in several ways, three of which are described below.

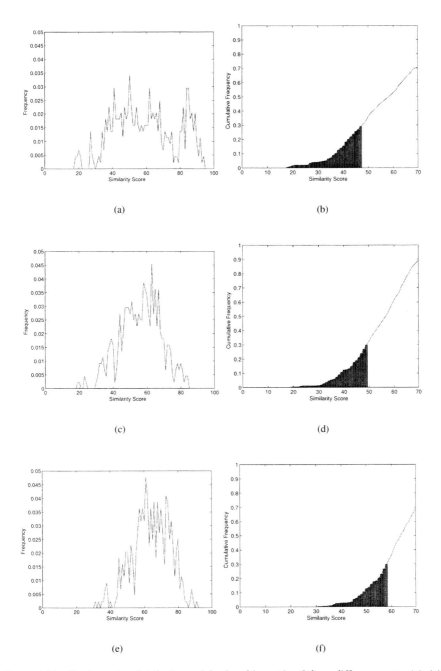

Figure 4.17. The impostor distributions of the face biometric of three different users. (a), (c) and (e) are the histograms of impostor scores associated with the three users. (b), (d) and (f) are the corresponding cumulative histograms. For $\gamma = 0.3$, it is observed that the thresholds for each of the three users are different.

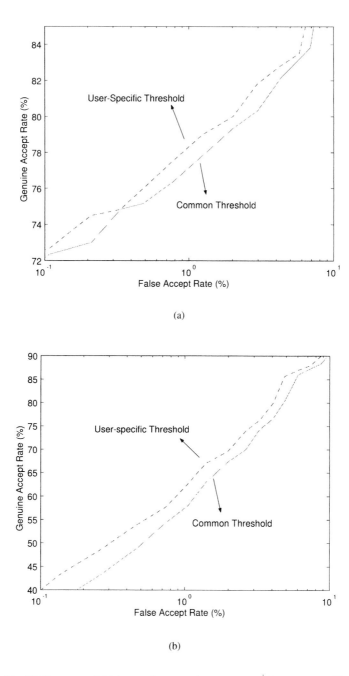

(a)

(b)

Figure 4.18. ROC curves exhibiting performance improvement when user-specific thresholds are utilized to verify a claimed identity. (a) Fingerprint and (b) Face.

1 Equal weights may be assigned to all the modalities, and the fused score obtained as

$$s_{fus} = \frac{1}{n} \sum_{j=1}^{n} s_j, \qquad (4.69)$$

where n represents the number of modalities considered. This technique assumes that the performance of the component classifiers are comparable (i.e., balanced classifiers), and that there is no reason to favor one modality over another.

2 Different weights may be assigned to each modality based on their individual performance as summarized by the ROC curve or the EER. Wang et al., 2003 use the following expression to compute the weights in a bimodal system utilizing the face and iris traits.

$$w_i = \frac{1 - (FAR_i + FRR_i)}{2 - (FAR_j + FRR_j + FAR_i + FRR_i)}, \qquad (4.70)$$

where $i = 1, 2, j = 1, 2$ and $i \neq j$. The values for FAR and FRR in the above equation are threshold dependent. Thus, when the threshold is changed, the weights assigned to the individual modalities will be suitably modified. This technique is useful when the participating classifiers are imbalanced, i.e., when there is significant performance disparity between them. However, it must be noted that the use of order statistics (such as the min score, max score and median score fusion schemes) has been recommended when the classifiers are imbalanced and the optimal set of weights cannot be reliably estimated (Roli and Fumera, 2002; Tumer and Ghosh, 1999).

3 The set of weights can also be determined on a user-by-user basis. This process entails searching the space of weights $(w_{k,1}, w_{k,2}, \ldots, w_{k,n})$ for a user, k, such that the total error rate on a training set of fused scores corresponding to that user is minimized. The fused score is computed as

$$s_{fus} = \sum_{j=1}^{n} w_{k,j} s_j. \qquad (4.71)$$

Typically, the constraints $\sum_{j=1}^{n} w_{k,j} = 1$ and $w_{k,j} \geq 0$ are applied when searching for the optimal set of weights for user k. The total error rate is the region of overlap of the genuine and impostor score distributions (s_{fus}) corresponding to that user. This approach is beneficial when the performance of individual sub-systems varies significantly across users.

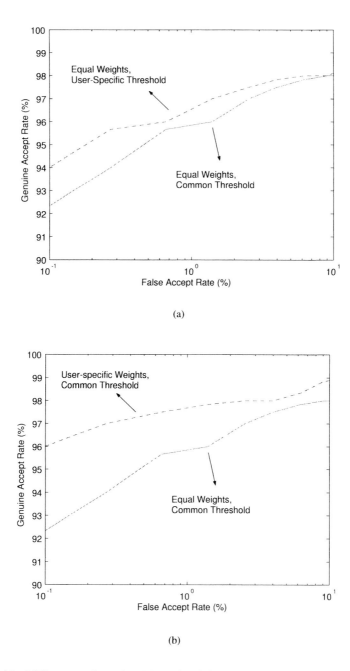

(a)

(b)

Figure 4.19. ROC curves when using (a) equal weights for the three traits and a user-specific matching threshold; and (b) user-specific weights for all the three traits and a common matching threshold (Jain and Ross, 2002b).

Table 4.4. Weights of different biometric modalities for 10 users (Jain and Ross, 2002b).

User #	Fingerprint (w_1)	Face (w_2)	Hand Geometry (w_3)
1	0.5	0.3	0.2
2	0.6	0.2	0.2
3	0.4	0.1	0.5
4	0.2	0.4	0.4
5	0.5	0.2	0.3
6	0.6	0.1	0.3
7	0.6	0.1	0.3
8	0.4	0.2	0.4
9	0.5	0.1	0.4
10	0.6	0.2	0.2

Jain and Ross, 2002b explore the use of a common matching threshold with user-specific weights. Table 4.4 lists the optimal weights (w_1 for fingerprint, w_2 for face and w_3 for hand geometry) computed for the set of 10 users listed in Table 4.3. From this table we observe that for user number 4, the weight assigned to the fingerprint modality is small ($w_1 = 0.2$). Upon examining the fingerprint images corresponding to this user (Figures 4.20(a) and 4.20(b)), it is apparent that the quality of the ridges is rather poor, therefore confounding both the minutiae extractor and matcher. Thus, the match scores in this instance will be unreliable. This demonstrates the importance of assigning user-specific weights to the individual biometric traits. Similarly, user number 3 has a small weight assigned to the face biometric, possibly due to changes in the pose of the face and ambient lighting during data acquisition (Figures 4.20(c), 4.20(d) and 4.20(e)). User number 2 has a small weight attached to hand geometry due to (repeated) incorrect placement of the hand and a slight curvature of the little finger (Figures 4.20(f) and 4.20(g)). The improvement in matching performance of the user-specific system is indicated by the ROC curves in Figure 4.19(b).

The utilization of user-specific matching thresholds and weights presupposes the availability of a large number of genuine and impostor scores pertaining to an individual. Since the number of biometric samples obtained from an individual during enrollment is very limited, user-specific schemes cannot be invoked at the time of system deployment. As more and more biometric samples of a user are made available over a period of time, user-specific parameters can be utilized to enhance recognition accuracy.

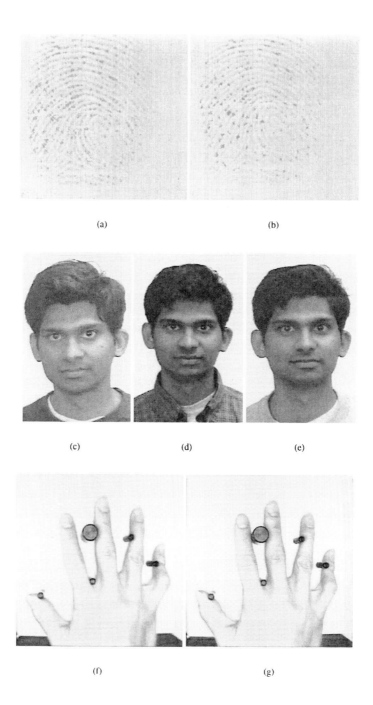

Figure 4.20. Examples of users with varying weights for the different modalities. (a) and (b) Fingerprint images of user number 4 whose ridge details are not very clear ($w_1 = 0.2$). (c), (d) and (e) Varying face poses of user number 3 ($w_2 = 0.1$). (f) and (g) Incorrect placement of hand and the curved finger of user number 2 ($w_3 = 0.2$).

4.9   Summary

In a multibiometric system, fusion at the score level offers the best tradeoff between information content and ease of fusion. Hence, score level fusion is typically adopted by most multibiometric systems. Although a wide variety of score level fusion techniques have been proposed in the literature, these can be grouped into three main categories, viz., density-based, transformation-based and classifier-based schemes. The performance of each scheme depends on the amount and quality of the available training data. If a large number of match scores is available for training the fusion module, then density-based approaches such as the likelihood ratio test can be used. Estimating the genuine and impostor distributions may not always be feasible due to the limited number of training samples that are available. In such cases, transformation-based schemes are a viable alternative. The non-homogeneity of the match scores presented by the different matchers raises a number of challenges. Suitable score normalization schemes are essential in order to transform these match scores into a comparable domain. The sum of scores fusion method with simple score normalization (such as z-score) represents a commonly used transformation-based scheme. Classification-based fusion schemes consolidate the outputs of different matchers into a single vector of scores which is then fed into a trained classifier. The classifier determines if this vector belongs to the "genuine" or "impostor" class.

User-specific fusion schemes can be invoked if sufficient training data is accumulated over a period of time for individual users. However, the following issues will have to be considered when deploying biometric systems with user-specific fusion schemes: (i) A malicious user may deliberately provide poor quality biometric data constantly (e.g., by touching the fingerprint sensor lightly), thereby forcing the system to reduce the weights associated with a specific biometric. The user may then claim that the biometric data belongs to someone else. Thus, the user can access a privilege and deny using it later. (ii) An intruder attempting to circumvent a biometric system might target enrolled users with known problems with their biometric data (e.g., users with calloused fingers or arthritis of the hand). Such users may have low weights associated with certain biometric traits and, therefore, the intruder will need to spoof only those traits with higher weights. Therefore, appropriate safeguards should be incorporated into multibiometric systems that employ user-specific fusion schemes.

As stated in the previous chapter, the gain in the matching performance of a multibiometric system is affected by the correlation between the match scores emitted by the different biometric matchers (Kuncheva et al., 2000; Prabhakar and Jain, 2002; Poh and Bengio, 2005d). In general, if the match scores are uncorrelated or negatively correlated, then the improvement in performance can be expected to be significant. Thus, combining two weak biometric matchers that are uncorrelated may result in a significant improvement in performance than combining two strong biometric matchers that are positively correlated (this means, when more than two biometric matchers are available, combining the two best matchers will not always result in the best matcher pair). In view of this, it is imperative that system integrators do not discard biometric matchers whose individual performances are poor without attempting to fuse them with other matchers.

Chapter 5

FUSION INCORPORATING ANCILLARY INFORMATION

5.1 Introduction

In some applications, ancillary information may be available to the multibiometric system apart from the match score or identity decision provided by the individual biometric matchers. Examples of such ancillary information include measures indicating the quality of the acquired biometric sample (e.g., fingerprint image quality) or certain additional information about the user (known as soft biometrics) like gender, ethnicity, height or weight. The quality measures are derived from the same biometric sample that is used for verifying or establishing the identity of the user. Hence, the biometric signal quality information is *intrinsic* to a matcher. On the other hand, the soft biometric features may be derived from sources other than the acquired biometric sample. Hence, soft biometric information can be *extrinsic* to a biometric matcher. The objective of this chapter is to introduce the reader to a few representative techniques that exploit either intrinsic or extrinsic information to improve the performance of a multibiometric system.

5.2 Quality-based fusion

The quality of acquired biometric data directly impacts the ability of the biometric matcher to perform the matching process effectively. Noise can be present in the acquired biometric data mainly due to defective or improperly maintained sensors. For example, accumulation of dirt or the residual remains on a fingerprint sensor can result in a noisy fingerprint image. When noisy fingerprint images are processed by a minutiae based fingerprint recognition algorithm, a number of false (spurious) minutia points are detected leading to incorrect matching results. Figures 5.1(c) and 5.1(d) show the minutiae extracted from good quality (see Figure 5.1(a)) and noisy fingerprint (see Figure

5.1(b)) images, respectively, using the minutiae extraction algorithm proposed by Jain et al., 1997a. We can observe that no false minutia is detected in the good quality fingerprint image shown in Figure 5.1(c). On the other hand, Figure 5.1(d) shows that several spurious minutia points are detected in the noisy fingerprint image. In practice, some true minutia points may not be detected in poor quality images. The presence of spurious minutiae will eventually lead to errors in the fingerprint matching process. Chen et al., 2005b show that the performance of a minutiae-based matcher is sensitive to the quality of the fingerprint images. Quality scores were assigned to the fingerprint images in the Fingerprint Verification Competition (FVC) 2002 (Maio et al., 2002) database 3 using a quality assessment algorithm that works in the frequency domain (see Section 5.2.1.1). The database was partitioned into five equal bins (the first bin corresponds to 20% of the fingerprint images in the database with the lowest quality and the fifth bin corresponds to 20% of the fingerprint images with the highest quality) based on the quality of the fingerprint images and five ROC curves were obtained (see Figure 5.2). The first ROC curve represents the performance of the matcher on the complete database and the other ROC curves represent the matching performance when the bins are successively pruned starting with the first (lowest quality) bin. From Figure 5.2, we can observe that the performance of the matcher improves as the poor quality images are excluded.

Another example of noisy biometric data is blurred face or iris images due to poor camera focus, motion blur and improper illumination. Figure 5.3(b) shows an iris image whose quality is severely degraded due to motion blur, non-uniform illumination and occlusion by the upper eyelid. The quality of an iris image generally affects both the iris segmentation process and the amount of texture information available in the segmented iris pattern. Figures 5.3(a) and 5.3(c) show a good quality iris image and the corresponding iris pattern obtained after segmentation and normalization using the algorithms proposed by Daugman, 1999. We can observe the rich texture information contained in the iris pattern shown in Figure 5.3(c). On the other hand, the iris pattern (see Figure 5.3(d)) corresponding to the poor quality iris image in Figure 5.3(b) is affected by occlusion on the left side and blurring on the right side. The iris patterns obtained from the poor quality iris images will result in incorrect iris matching results. The degradation of the iris matching performance due to poor quality iris images was demonstrated by Chen et al., 2006. They classified iris images from the CASIA1.0 iris database (Ma et al., 2003) into three quality classes, namely, poor, average and good, using a quality index based on wavelet transform (see Section 5.2.1.2). The performance of the iris matching algorithm proposed by Daugman, 1999 for each class of iris images was obtained (see Figure 5.4). Figure 5.4 clearly shows that poor quality iris images degrade the performance of an iris matching algorithm.

(a)

(b)

(c)

(d)

Figure 5.1. Minutiae extraction results for fingerprint images of varying quality. (a) A good quality fingerprint image. (b) A noisy fingerprint image (due to smearing, residual deposits, etc.). (c) Minutia points detected in the good quality fingerprint image by an automatic minutiae extraction algorithm (Jain et al., 1997a). (d) Minutia points detected in the noisy fingerprint image by the same automatic minutiae extraction algorithm (Jain et al., 1997a). The circles represent true minutia points while the squares represent false (spurious) minutiae. Note that the classification of minutia points into true and false minutiae is performed by a human expert. While no spurious minutia is detected in the good quality fingerprint image, several false minutia points are detected when the fingerprint image quality is poor.

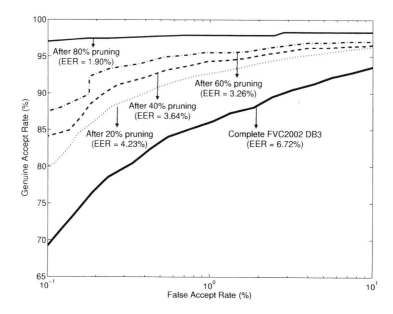

Figure 5.2. Improvement in the performance of a minutiae-based fingerprint matcher when poor quality fingerprint images are successively pruned from the database.

We have seen that the recognition accuracy of a biometric system is highly sensitive to the quality of the biometric input and noisy data can result in a significant reduction in the accuracy of the biometric system (Chen et al., 2005b; Chen et al., 2006). Estimating the quality of a biometric sample and predicting the performance of a biometric matcher based on the estimated quality can be very useful in building robust multibiometric systems. This can allow us to dynamically assign weights to the individual biometric matchers based on the quality of the input sample to be verified. For example, consider a bimodal biometric system with iris and fingerprint as the two modalities. Let us assume that during a particular access attempt by the user, the iris image is of poor quality (due to occlusion or loss of focus) but the fingerprint image quality is sufficiently good. In this case, we can assign a higher weight to the fingerprint matching result and a lower weight to the iris matching result. Even for the same biometric modality, different representations and matching algorithms may exhibit different levels of sensitivity to the quality of the biometric data. For example, a fingerprint image may not be of sufficient quality for the reliable extraction of minutiae. However, the texture features (Jain et al., 2000b) of the same fingerprint image may not be substantially affected by its poor quality. In this scenario, it would be prudent to give more emphasis to the matching

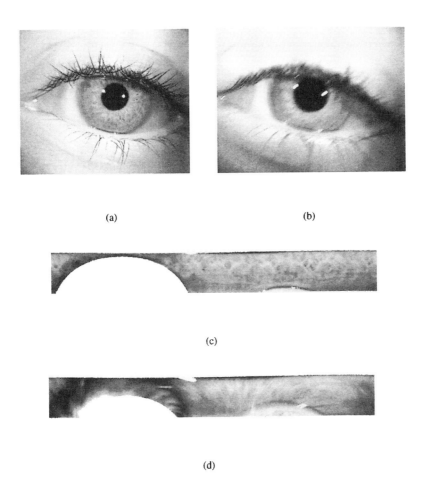

Figure 5.3. Feature extraction results for iris images of varying quality. (a) A good quality iris image. (b) A poor quality iris image (due to occlusion, motion blur and non-uniform illumination). (c) Normalized iris pattern of the good quality iris image extracted using the algorithm proposed by Daugman, 1999. (d) Normalized iris pattern of the poor quality iris image extracted using the algorithm proposed by Daugman, 1999. The iris pattern shown in (c) contains rich texture information. On the other hand, the left side of the iris pattern in (d) is occluded by the upper eyelid and the right side of the pattern is blurred.

result of a texture-based fingerprint matcher and less emphasis on the results of the minutiae-based matcher. The following sections describe techniques for automatic assessment of image quality for iris and fingerprint images and also present methods for incorporating the biometric signal quality into the fusion process.

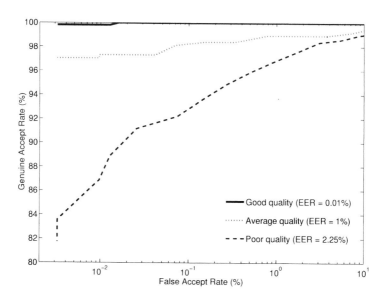

Figure 5.4. Performance of a iris matcher on iris images of varying quality.

5.2.1   Automatic quality assessment

One of the main requirements for developing a multibiometric system that performs quality-based fusion is the ability to automatically extract the quality information from the acquired biometric sample. A quality assessment algorithm must be able to accurately determine the quality of local regions in the biometric sample and also provide a metric to describe the overall (global) quality of the sample. Global measures of quality can be used to decide whether the feature extraction and matching processes can be performed satisfactorily on the given biometric sample. If the global quality of the input sample is very low, the sample is usually rejected leading to failure to enroll or failure to capture events. The local quality measures help in identifying regions in the sample that may be ignored or given less importance compared to other regions in the subsequent steps of processing. We will briefly discuss the techniques that have been proposed in the literature for determining the image quality in fingerprint and iris biometric systems.

5.2.1.1   Fingerprint image quality

Several methods have been proposed for estimating the quality of a fingerprint image. Within a small region of a fingerprint image, the orientation of ridges is almost constant. This is true in most of the fingerprint regions except in the neighborhood of the singular points. Note that singular points (core and delta points) are regions of high curvature in a fingerprint where the ridges change their directions abruptly. Hence, most of the local regions in a fingerprint image usually have a specific dominant direction. Figure 5.5 shows a good quality fingerprint image indicating the dominant ridge flow orientation in two local regions and the changes in the ridge directions near the core and delta points.

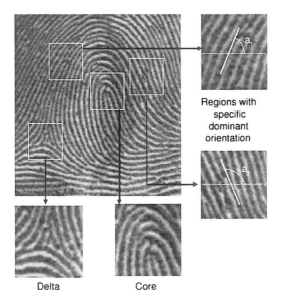

Figure 5.5. A fingerprint image showing two regions where the ridges have a fixed dominant orientation, and the core and delta regions where the orientation of the ridge changes abruptly.

Bolle et al., 1999 use the directional histogram to classify local regions of a fingerprint image as either directional or non-directional. They divide a fingerprint image into blocks and compute the histogram of pixel intensities in each block based on the direction of the ridge pixels within that block. The size of each block depends on the resolution of the fingerprint image and the typical block size for a 500 dpi fingerprint image is 7×7 pixels. If the maximum value of the histogram is greater than a fixed threshold, the block is labeled as directional. Further, a relative weight is assigned to each block based on its distance from the centroid of the fingerprint area in the image. Since the regions near the centroid of the fingerprint area are likely to provide more discriminatory information than the peripheral regions, higher weights are assigned to the blocks near the centroid. The weight, w_i, of the ith block centered at $l_i = [x_i, y_i]$ is computed as

$$w_i = \exp\left(\frac{-||l_i - l_c||^2}{2r^2}\right), \tag{5.1}$$

where $l_c = [x_c, y_c]$ is the location of the centroid of the fingerprint area and r is a normalization constant. The ratio of the total weight of the directional blocks to the total weight of all the blocks in the fingerprint is used as a measure of the overall (global) fingerprint image quality. In the same spirit, Hong et al., 1998 use Gabor filters instead of the directional histogram to determine if the local regions of a fingerprint image have a clear ridge-valley structure.

The directional nature of the ridges in a local fingerprint region can also be measured in terms of its coherence value. Consider a small rectangular block B of the fingerprint image of size $b \times b$ pixels. Let $\delta_i = (\delta_i^x, \delta_i^y)$ be the gradient vector of the gray level intensity at location $i \in B$. The covariance of all the gradient vectors in the block B is given by

$$\Sigma = \frac{1}{b^2} \sum_{i \in B} \delta_i^T \delta_i, \tag{5.2}$$

where δ_i^T denotes the transpose of the vector δ_i. Let α be the trace of the covariance matrix Σ and β be its determinant. The covariance matrix Σ is positive semi-definite and therefore, the two eigenvalues of Σ can be computed in terms of α and β as

$$
\begin{aligned}
\lambda_1 &= \frac{\alpha}{2} + \sqrt{\alpha^2 - 4\beta} \\
\lambda_2 &= \frac{\alpha}{2} - \sqrt{\alpha^2 - 4\beta}.
\end{aligned}
\tag{5.3}
$$

The coherence, γ, of the block B is defined in terms of λ_1 and λ_2 as

$$\gamma = \frac{(\lambda_1 - \lambda_2)^2}{(\lambda_1 + \lambda_2)^2}, \tag{5.4}$$

with $0 \leq \gamma \leq 1$. When the value of γ of a block B is close to 1 ($\lambda_1 \gg \lambda_2$), it indicates that the ridges in the fingerprint region have a specific orientation. On the other hand, a value of γ that is close to 0 ($\lambda_1 \approx \lambda_2$) indicates the ridges do not have a clear direction which is mostly due to the poor quality of the fingerprint image in that region. Chen et al., 2005b compute the global fingerprint image quality as the weighted average (weights are computed using Equation 5.1) of the block-wise coherence measures. The block size used by Chen et al., 2005b is 12×12 pixels. Tabassi et al., 2004 present a technique for assigning a quality label to a fingerprint image based on the discriminative ability of the extracted minutia features. This approach assumes that the feature extraction module is reliable and there is a strong correlation between the quality label assigned to the image and the performance of the fingerprint matcher.

Chen et al., 2005b also propose a global quality index for a fingerprint image that is computed in the frequency domain. Good quality fingerprint images have a clear ridge-valley structure and hence, most of the energy in the power spectrum of such images is concentrated in a narrow frequency band around the dominant ridge frequency. For example, consider the good quality fingerprint image shown in Figure 5.6(a). The power spectrum of this image shows that the energy is concentrated in a small frequency band (see the strong ring pattern in the power spectrum shown in Figure 5.6(c)) and hence, the energy distribution is highly peaked (see Figure 5.6(e)). In poor quality fingerprint images, the energy is more widely distributed in different frequency bands due to the lack of clear ridges and the non-uniformity of the inter-ridge spacing. This can be easily observed for the poor quality fingerprint image in Figure 5.6(b) which has a flat distribution of energy across the power spectrum (see Figures 5.6(d) and 5.6(f)). The entropy of the energy distribution in the power spectrum of a fingerprint image is used as the global quality measure by Chen et al., 2005b. The resulting quality measure Q is normalized linearly to lie in the range $[0, 1]$.

5.2.1.2 Iris image quality

The quality of the iris images is generally affected by one of the following four factors (see Figure 5.7): (i) occlusion caused by the eyelashes and eyelids, (ii) poor focus either due to the incorrect camera settings or due to the incorrect interaction of the user with the camera (e.g., motion of the eye during image capture), (iii) non-uniform illumination and (iv) large pupil area. Techniques for measuring the focus of the iris images were proposed by Daugman, 2001 and Zhang and Salganicoff, 1999. While Daugman, 2001 proposed the use of energy of the high frequency components in the Fourier power spectrum to determine the focus, Zhang and Salganicoff, 1999 analyzed the sharpness of the pupil/iris boundary for measuring the focus. Ma et al., 2003 utilize the values of energy in the low, moderate and high frequency bands of the 2-dimensional Fourier power spectrum to classify the iris images based on their quality. The four classes considered by Ma et al., 2003 are "clear", "defocused", "blurred" and "occluded". However, Chen et al., 2006 argue that since the Fourier transform does not localize well in the spatial domain, it is not appropriate for deriving local quality measures. Hence, they proposed a wavelet transform-based iris quality measurement algorithm.

The algorithm proposed by Chen et al., 2006 consists of the following steps. The given iris image is segmented into iris and non-iris regions in two stages. The first stage utilizes Canny edge detector and Hough transform (for detecting

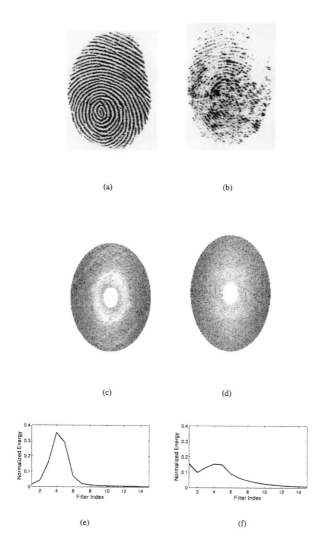

(a)   (b)

(c)   (d)

(e)   (f)

Figure 5.6. Computation of the global quality index of a fingerprint image in the frequency domain. (a) A good quality fingerprint image. (b) A poor quality fingerprint image. (c) Power spectrum of the good quality fingerprint image showing a distinct dominant frequency band. (d) Power spectrum of the poor quality fingerprint image. (e) Energy distribution of the good quality fingerprint image across concentric rings in the spatial frequency domain. (f) Energy distribution of the poor quality fingerprint image. It can be observed that the energy distribution is more peaked for the good quality fingerprint image. The resulting global quality measures for the fingerprint images in (a) and (b) are 0.92 and 0.05, respectively.

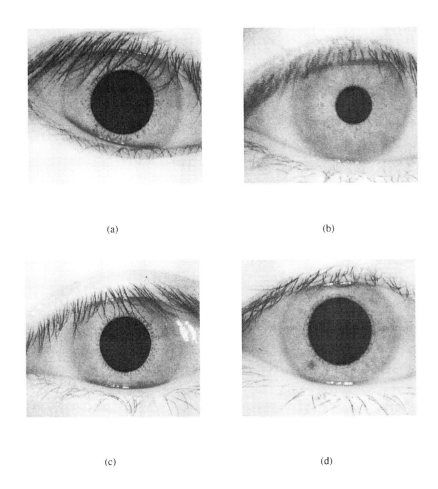

(a) (b)

(c) (d)

Figure 5.7. Poor quality of iris images caused by (a) occlusion, (b) poor focus and eye motion, (c) non-uniform illumination, and (d) large pupil area.

circles) to detect the inner and outer iris boundaries. In the second stage, the upper and lower eyelids are detected by using 2-dimensional wavelet decomposition, Canny edge detector, and parabolic curve fitting. The detected iris and eye-lid boundaries for a good quality iris image and a poor quality iris image are shown in Figures 5.8(a) and 5.8(b), respectively. An intensity thresholding is applied to remove the eyelashes. Figures 5.8(c) and 5.8(d) show the extracted iris patterns after the removal of eyelashes. Once the iris region has been localized, a 2-dimensional isotropic Mexican hat wavelet filter (Mallet, 1998) is applied to the extracted pattern. The Mexican hat filter is essentially a band-pass filter and this filter is applied at three different scales in order to capture features at different scales (frequency bands). The product of the responses at the three scales is treated as the overall response of the filter. The quality of the local regions in the iris image is obtained by partitioning the iris region into multiple concentric (at the pupil center) windows. The width of each circular window is 8 pixels. Let the total number of windows be T. The energy, E_t, of the tth window is defined as

$$E_t = \frac{1}{N_t} \sum_{i=1}^{N_t} |w_{t,i}^p|^2, \tag{5.5}$$

where $w_{t,i}^p$ is the ith wavelet response in the tth window (the superscript p indicates that the wavelet coefficient is the product of responses at three scales), N_t is the total number of wavelet coefficients in the tth window and $t = 1, 2, \ldots, T$. Chen et al., 2006 claim that the energy E_t is a good indicator of the quality of the iris features and hence, it is a reliable measure of the local iris quality (high values of E_t indicate good quality regions and vice versa). Figures 5.8(e) and 5.8(f) show the local quality measures based on the energy concentration in the individual windows. Note that brighter pixel intensities in Figures 5.8(e) and 5.8(f) indicate higher quality.

Chen et al., 2006 define the global quality Q of the iris image as a weighted average of the local quality measures. The global quality index Q is given by

$$Q = \frac{1}{T} \sum_{t=1}^{T} (m_t \times \log E_t), \tag{5.6}$$

where T is the total number of windows and m_t is the weight assigned to each window. The inner regions of the iris pattern which are close to the pupil contain richer texture information and are less occluded by eyelashes compared to the outer iris regions (Sung et al., 2004). Based on this observation, Chen et al., 2006 propose the following scheme for determining the weights m_t.

$$m_t = \exp\{-\frac{l^2}{2r^2}\}, \tag{5.7}$$

where l is the mean radius of the tth window from the pupil center, $t = 1, \ldots, T$ and r is a normalization constant. It must be noted that this method of determining the weights assigns higher weights to windows near the pupil center. To account for the variations in the pupil dilation, iris size and rotation, the rubber sheet model (Daugman, 2001) is used to normalize the iris texture and the local quality measures.

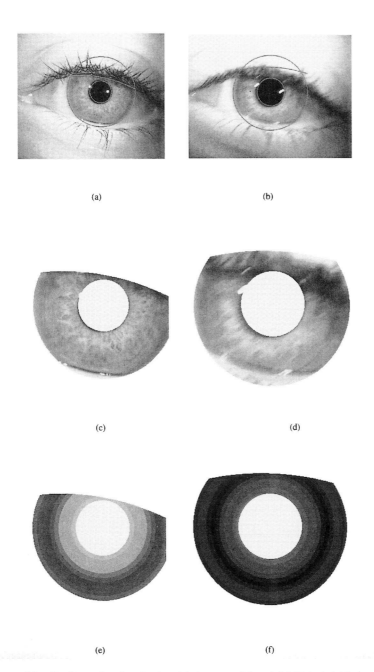

(a) (b)

(c) (d)

(e) (f)

Figure 5.8. Quality estimation for two iris images. (a) and (b) Detected iris boundaries and eyelids. (c) and (d) Extracted iris patterns after eyelash removal. (e) and (f) Local quality measures based on the energy concentration in the individual windows. The quality score for the good quality iris image on the left is 0.89, while the quality score for the poor quality iris image on the right is 0.58.

5.2.1.3   Margin-derived Quality

Poh and Bengio, 2005e propose another quality index that is independent of the characteristics of the underlying biometric modality (fingerprint, iris or face) but depends only on the match score provided by the biometric matcher. This quality index is derived from the "margin" which addresses the following question: "What is the risk associated with a decision made based on the given match score?" Under the assumption of equal prior probabilities for the "genuine" and "impostor" classes, the margin, $\mathcal{M}(s)$, for the given match score s is defined as

$$\mathcal{M}(s) = |FAR(s) - FRR(s)|, \qquad (5.8)$$

where $FAR(s)$ and $FRR(s)$ are the false accept rate and false reject rate of the biometric matcher, respectively, when the match score s is used as the decision threshold. Since both the false accept and false reject rates are cumulative distribution functions in the range $[0, 1]$, the margin is also bounded between 0 and 1. Let Δ_e be the decision threshold corresponding to the equal error rate (EER). If the match score s is close to Δ_e, the $FAR(s)$ and $FRR(s)$ are almost equal and the margin $\mathcal{M}(s)$ tends to zero. A zero value for the margin implies that a decision made based on the corresponding match score has 50% chance of being correct. On the other hand, when the match score s is further away from Δ_e, the margin tends to one. Higher the value of the margin, higher is the chance of making a correct decision. In this way, the margin reflects the quality of the match score provided by the biometric matcher. Note that the margin-based quality measure is specific to the biometric matcher being used and can be determined only after the matcher is invoked.

5.2.2   Quality-based fusion techniques

Biometric signal quality information can be utilized in any of the three match score fusion approaches, namely, density-based score fusion, transformation-based score fusion and classifier-based score fusion described in Chapter 4. This section describes two techniques for incorporating quality measures into the match score fusion scheme. The first technique uses classifier-based score fusion while the second technique uses transformation-based score fusion. Besides these two techniques, other methods to incorporate quality measures in match score fusion have also been proposed in the literature. For example, Baker and Maurer, 2005 adopt a hybrid (density-based and classifier-based) score fusion approach in a multi-instance biometric system that uses fingerprints from all 10 fingers of a person. The fingerprint images are divided into five quality levels and the genuine and impostor score densities are estimated at each quality level. Based on the quality-dependent density estimates, a Bayesian Belief

Network (BBN) classifier is used to decide whether the set of input fingerprints come from a "genuine user" or an "impostor".

5.2.2.1 Classifier-based fusion

Fierrez-Aguilar et al., 2005c propose the following methodology to incorporate the quality of the input biometric samples into a support vector machine (SVM) classifier that determines the decision boundary between the genuine and impostor classes. Let $s = [s_1, s_2, \ldots, s_R]^T$ be the vector of match scores output by R biometric matchers and $q = [q_1, q_2, \ldots, q_R]^T$ be the vector containing the corresponding quality measures of the biometric samples presented at the input of the R biometric matchers. Let us assume that we have N training samples of the form (s_i, q_i, y_i), where s_i and q_i represent the R-dimensional match score vector and the quality vector of the ith training sample, respectively, and $y_i \in \{-1, 1\}$ represents the corresponding class label (-1 if the sample belongs to the impostor class and $+1$ if the sample comes from the genuine class). The goal is to learn the fusion function $f_{sq}(s_t, q_t)$ that takes the match score and quality vectors (s_t and q_t, respectively) of the test sample as input and generates a fused score which helps in predicting the output label y_t as accurately as possible.

Support vector machines are commonly used to solve many binary classification problems (Burges, 1998). SVMs try to determine the decision boundary that has the largest separation from the samples of the genuine and impostor classes. Fierrez-Aguilar et al., 2005c use a SVM to determine an initial fusion function $f_s(s) = ws + w_0$ by solving the following optimization problem.

$$\min_{s, w_0} \left(\tfrac{1}{2}||w||^2 + \sum_{i=1}^{N} C_i \epsilon_i \right), \text{ such that} \tag{5.9}$$
$$y_i \left(ws_i + w_0 \right) \geq 1 - \epsilon_i,$$
$$\epsilon_i \geq 0, \forall i, \ i = 1, 2, \ldots, N.$$

In Equation 5.9, ϵ_i represents the training error (distance between an incorrectly classified training sample and the decision boundary) and C_i represents the cost assigned to the training error. In general, the cost C_i, $i = 1, \ldots, N$, is assigned a positive constant C and the value of C is a tradeoff between the training error rate and the generalization error rate (error rate on an unknown set of test samples). The weight vector $w = [w_1, w_2, \ldots, w_R]$ represents the weight assigned to each component of the match score vector s. In a multibiometric system, the weight vector represents the relative importance of the different biometric matchers, provided the scores of the matchers have been normalized. The above minimization problem is usually solved in its dual form using the kernel-trick approach (Aizerman et al., 1964).

The novelty in the scheme proposed by Fierrez-Aguilar et al., 2005c lies in the methodology used to assign costs to the training errors. The authors argue that if a biometric sample is of good quality, then the cost of misclassifying this sample during training must be relatively high and vice versa. Hence, the cost C_i for each training sample is made to be proportional to the biometric signal quality as follows.

$$C_i = C \left(\frac{\prod_{j=1}^{R} q_{ij}}{(Q_{max})^R} \right)^{\alpha_1}, \qquad (5.10)$$

where C and α_1 are positive constants and Q_{max} corresponds to the maximum quality score possible among all the R biometric matchers. Further, R different SVMs were trained by leaving out one component of vectors s_i at a time, i.e., f_s^j is trained using $s_i^j = \left[s_{i1}, \ldots, s_{i,(j-1)}, s_{i,(j+1)}, \ldots, s_{iR} \right]$.

During the authentication phase, the fused score provided by the SVM classifier is adaptively weighted based on the quality of each input biometric component. Let $q_t = [q_{t1}, q_{t2}, \ldots, q_{tR}]$ be the quality vector corresponding to the input test sample. The components of the quality vector q_t and the corresponding match score vector x_t are then re-ordered such that $q_{t1} \leq q_{t2} \leq \ldots \leq q_{tR}$. The quality-adapted fused score is then computed as,

$$f_{sq}(s_t, q_t) = \beta \left(\sum_{j=1}^{R-1} \frac{\gamma_j}{\sum_{k=1}^{R-1} \gamma_k} f_s^j(s_t^j) \right) + (1 - \beta) f_s(s_t), \qquad (5.11)$$

where $\gamma_j = \left(\frac{q_{tR} - q_{tj}}{Q_{max}} \right)^{\alpha_2}$, and α_2 and β are constants. The fused score computed using Equation 5.11 is a tradeoff between ignoring and using matchers or modalities in which the input sample is of low quality. Experiments conducted by Fierrez-Aguilar et al., 2005c on the MCYT database (Ortega-Garcia et al., 2003) containing fingerprint and online signature modalities show that the quality based fusion scheme results in a relative reduction of 20% in the Equal Error Rate (EER) over the case where no quality measures are used. In these experiments the quality scores are manually assigned to the fingerprint images while the quality of all the signature samples is assumed to be the same.

5.2.2.2   Weighted sum rule fusion

A quality-weighted sum rule for score level fusion was proposed by Fierrez-Aguilar et al., 2006. The scores from minutiae-based and ridge-based fingerprint matchers were combined using a weighted sum rule, where the weights were determined based on the sensitivity of the two matchers to the quality of the fingerprint image. When the fingerprint image is of low quality, the ridge-based matcher is assigned a higher weight because it was found to be less sensitive to image quality. On the other hand, when the fingerprint image is of good quality, the minutiae-based matcher was found to be more accurate and hence, assigned a higher weight.

Fierrez-Aguilar et al., 2006 used transformation-based match score fusion after appropriate score normalization. The match scores from the minutiae-based and ridge-based fingerprint matchers were normalized using tanh and double-sigmoid methods of normalization, respectively, transforming them into similarity scores in the range $[0, 1]$. It was observed that the ridge-based matcher was more robust to image quality degradation than the minutiae-based matcher. Hence, the following adaptive fusion rule was proposed.

$$s_q = \frac{Q}{2} s_m + \left(1 - \frac{Q}{2} \right) s_r, \tag{5.12}$$

where s_m and s_r are the normalized match scores from the minutiae- and ridge-based matchers, respectively, and Q is the global quality of the input fingerprint image computed using the algorithm proposed in Chen et al., 2005b. This fusion scheme relies more on the results of the ridge-based matcher when the quality of the fingerprint image is poor. On the other hand, the minutiae-based matcher is given more emphasis when the image quality is good. Experiments conducted on a subset of the MCYT database (Ortega-Garcia et al., 2003) containing 750 fingers with 10 impressions per finger, indicate that the combination of minutiae and texture-based matchers using the quality-weighted sum rule performs better than the two individual matchers and also the simple sum rule (without weights) as shown in Figure 5.9.

5.3 Soft biometrics

A multimodal biometric system that utilizes a combination of biometric identifiers like face, fingerprint, hand geometry and iris is more robust to noise and can alleviate problems such as non-universality and lack of distinctiveness, thereby reducing the error rates significantly. However, using multiple traits will increase the enrollment and verification times, cause more inconvenience to the users and increase the overall cost of the system. This motivated Jain et al., 2004a to propose another solution to reduce the error rates of the biometric system without causing any additional inconvenience to the user. Their solution was based on incorporating soft identifiers of human identity like gender, ethnicity, height, eye color, etc. into a (primary) biometric identification system. Figure 5.10 depicts a scenario where both primary (face) and soft (gender, ethnicity, height and eye color) biometric information can be automatically extracted and utilized to verify a user's identity. In this scenario, the height of the user can be estimated as he approaches the camera and his gender, ethnicity and eye color can be estimated from his face image. These additional attributes can be used along with the face biometric to accurately identify the person.

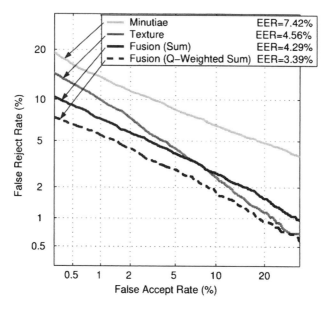

Figure 5.9. DET plot demonstrating the improvement in the verification performance due to the quality-weighted sum rule.

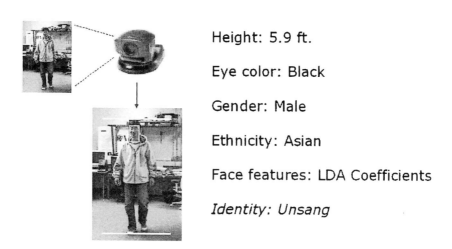

Height: 5.9 ft.

Eye color: Black

Gender: Male

Ethnicity: Asian

Face features: LDA Coefficients

Identity: Unsang

Figure 5.10. A scenario where the primary biometric identifier (face) and the soft biometric attributes (gender, ethnicity, eye color and height) are automatically extracted and utilized to verify a person's identity.

5.3.1 Motivation and challenges

Soft biometric information is utilized in Automated Fingerprint Identification Systems (AFIS) used in the forensic community. For example, the fingerprint card used by the Federal Bureau of Investigation (FBI) includes information on the gender, ethnicity, height, weight, eye color and hair color of the person along with the prints of all ten fingers (see Figure 5.11). However, in AFIS, the soft biometric information is determined manually and is not utilized during the automatic fingerprint matching phase.

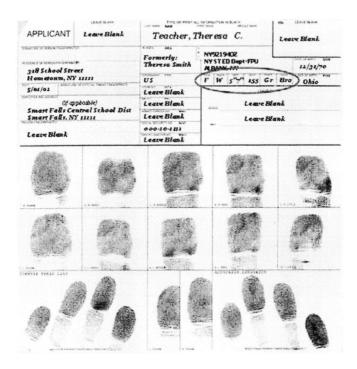

Figure 5.11. A sample FBI fingerprint card (http://www.highered.nysed.gov/tcert/ospra/samplefpcard.html). Information on the gender, ethnicity, height, weight, eye color and hair color of the person is included in the encircled region.

The usefulness of soft biometric traits in improving the performance of the primary biometric system can be illustrated by the following example. Consider three users A (1.8m tall, male), B (1.7m tall, female), and C (1.6m tall, male) who are enrolled in a fingerprint biometric system that works in the identification mode. Suppose user A presents his fingerprint sample X to the system. It is compared to the templates of all the three users stored in the database and the posteriori matching probabilities of all the three users given the sample X are calculated. Let us assume that the outputs of the fingerprint matcher are $P(A|X) = 0.42$, $P(B|X) = 0.43$, and $P(C|X) = 0.15$. In this case, user A will be falsely identified as user B based on the Bayesian decision rule. On the other hand, let us assume that as the user approaches the fingerprint sensor, there exists a secondary system that automatically identifies the gender of the user as male and measures the user's height as 1.78m. If we have this information in addition to the posteriori matching probabilities given by the fingerprint matcher, then a proper combination of these sources of information is likely to lead to a correct identification of the user as user A.

The first biometric system developed by Alphonse Bertillon in 1883 used anthropometric features such as the length and breadth of the head and the ear, length of the middle finger and foot, height, etc. along with attributes like eye color, scars, and tatoo marks for ascertaining a person's identity (Bertillon, 1896). These measurements were obtained manually by Bertillon. Although each individual measurement in the Bertillonage system may exhibit some (intra-class) variability, a combination of several quantized (or binned) measurements was sufficient to manually identify a person with reasonable accuracy. The Bertillon system was dropped in favor of the Henry's system of fingerprint identification over 100 years back due to three main reasons: (i) lack of persistence - the anthropometric features (e.g., height) can vary significantly for juveniles; (ii) lack of distinctiveness - features such as skin color or eye color cannot be used for distinguishing between individuals coming from a similar ethnic background; and (iii) the huge time, effort and training required to get reliable measurements.

Like the Bertillon system, Heckathorn et al., 2001 use attributes like gender, race, eye color, height, and other visible marks like scars and tattoos to recognize individuals for the purpose of welfare distribution. More recently, Aillisto et al., 2004 show that unobtrusive user identification can be performed in low security applications such as access to health clubs using a combination of "light" biometric identifiers like height, weight, and body fat percentage. While the biometric features used in the above mentioned systems provide some information about the identity of the user, they are not sufficient for accurately identifying the user. Hence, these attributes can be referred to as "soft biometric traits". The soft biometric information complements the identity information provided by traditional (primary) biometric identifiers such as fingerprint, iris, and voice. In other words, utilizing soft biometric traits can improve the recognition accuracy of primary biometric systems.

Wayman, 2000 proposed the use of soft biometric traits like gender and age, for filtering a large biometric database. Filtering refers to limiting the number of entries in a database to be searched, based on some characteristics of the user who needs to be identified. For example, if the user can somehow be identified as a middle-aged tall male, the search can be restricted only to the subjects with this profile enrolled in the database. Of course, the assumption is that the entries in the database are appropriately tagged with these attributes. Filtering greatly improves the speed or the search efficiency of the biometric system. In addition to filtering, the soft biometric traits can also be used for tuning the parameters of the biometric system. Several studies (Givens et al., 2004; Newham, 1995) show that factors such as age, gender, race, and occupation can affect the performance of a biometric system. For example, a young female Asian who works in a mine is considered as one of the most difficult subject for a fingerprint system (Newham, 1995) because the ridges in her fingerprints are worn-out. This provides the motivation for tuning the system parameters like threshold on the match score in a unimodal biometric system, and thresholds and weights of the different modalities in a multimodal biometric system to obtain the optimum performance for a particular user or a class of users. However, filtering and system parameter tuning require that highly accurate automatic soft biometric feature extractors are available.

Two key challenges need to be addressed in order to incorporate the soft biometric information into the traditional biometric framework. The first challenge is the automatic and reliable extraction of soft biometric information in a non-intrusive manner without causing any inconvenience to the users. It must be noted that the failure of Bertillon-like systems was caused by the unreliability and inconvenience in the manual extraction of these features. Once the soft biometric information about a user is available, the challenge is to optimally combine this information with the primary biometric identifier so that the overall recognition accuracy is enhanced. Jain et al., 2004a developed a Bayesian framework for integrating the primary and soft biometric features.

5.3.2 Automatic soft biometric feature extraction

Any trait that provides some information about the identity of a person, but does not provide sufficient evidence to precisely determine the identity can be referred to as soft biometric trait. Figure 5.12 shows some examples of soft biometric traits. Soft biometric traits are available and can be extracted in a number of practical biometric applications. For example, attributes like gender, ethnicity, age, eye color, skin color, and other distinguishing physical marks such as scars can be extracted with sufficient reliability from the face images. The pattern class of fingerprint images (right loop, left loop, whorl, arch, etc.) is another example of a soft trait. Gender (Parris and Carey, 1996), speech accent (Hansen and Arslan, 1995), and perceptual age (Minematsu et al., 2003) of the speaker can be inferred from the speech signal. Eye color can be estimated from iris images. However, automatic and reliable extraction of soft

Gender, Ethnicity

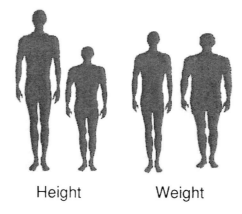

Height   Weight

Figure 5.12.   Examples of soft biometric traits.

biometric traits is a difficult task. In this section, we present a brief survey of the techniques that have been proposed in the literature for extracting soft biometric information and describe the system developed by Jain et al., 2004a for determining height, gender, ethnicity, and eye color.

Several researchers have attempted to derive gender, ethnicity, and pose information from the face images. Gutta et al., 2000 propose a mixture of experts consisting of ensembles of radial basis functions for the classification of gender, ethnic origin, and pose of human faces. Their gender classifier (male vs female) had an accuracy of 96%, while the ethnicity classifier (Caucasian, South Asian, East Asian, and African) had an accuracy of 92%. These results were reported on approximately 3000 good quality frontal face images corresponding to about 1000 subjects from the FERET database. Based on the same database, Moghaddam and Yang, 2002 show that the error rate for gender classification can be reduced to 3.4% by using non-linear support vector machines. Shakhnarovich et al., 2002 develop a demographic classification scheme that extracts faces from unconstrained video sequences and classifies them based on gender and ethnicity. The learning and feature selection modules uses a variant of the AdaBoost algorithm. Even under unconstrained environments, they show that a classification accuracy of more than 75% can be achieved for both gender and ethnicity (Asian vs non-Asian) classification on a database consisting of 30 subjects. For this database, the SVM classifier of Moghaddam and Yang also had a similar classification performance and there was also a noticeable bias toward males in the gender classification (females had an error rate of 28%). Balci and Atalay, 2002 report a classification accuracy of more than 86% for a gender classifier that uses PCA for feature extraction and multilayer perceptron for classification. Lu and Jain, 2004 propose a Linear Discriminant Analysis (LDA) based scheme to address the problem of ethnicity identification from facial images. The users are identified as either Asian or non-Asian by applying multiscale analysis to the input facial images. An ensemble framework based on the product rule is used for integrating the LDA analysis at different scales. This scheme had an accuracy of 96.3% on a database of 263 subjects (with approximately equal number of males and females).

Automatic age determination is a more difficult problem than gender and ethnicity classification. Kwon and Lobo, 1994 present an algorithm for age classification from facial images based on cranio-facial changes in feature-position ratios and skin wrinkle analysis. They attempted to classify users as "babies", "young adults", or "senior adults". However, they did not provide any classification accuracy. More recently, Lanitis et al., 2004 perform a quantitative evaluation of the performance of various classifiers developed for the task of automatic age estimation from face images. All the classifiers used eigenfaces obtained using Principal Component Analysis (PCA) as the input features. Quadratic classifier, minimum distance classifier, neural network classifier, and hierarchical classifier were used for estimating the age. The best age estimation algorithm had an average absolute error of 3.82 years which was comparable to the error made by humans (3.64 years) in performing the same task. Minematsu et al., 2003 show that the perceptual age of a speaker can be automatically estimated from voice samples. These results indicate that while automatic age estimation is possible from biometric traits, the current algorithms are not very reliable.

The weight of a user can be measured by asking him to stand on a weight sensor while he is providing his primary biometric. The height of a person can be estimated from a real-time sequence of images as the user approaches the biometric system. For example, Kim et al., 2002 use geometric features like vanishing points and vanishing lines to compute the height of an object. Jain et al., 2004a implemented a real-time vision system for automatic extraction of gender, ethnicity, height, and eye color. The system was designed to extract the soft biometric attributes as the person approaches the primary biometric system to present his primary biometric identifier (face and fingerprint). Their soft biometric system is equipped with two pan/tilt/zoom cameras. Camera I monitors the scene for any human presence based on the motion segmentation image. Once camera I detects an approaching person, it measures the height of the person and then guides camera II to focus on the person's face. It is reasonable to believe that the techniques for automatic soft biometric feature extraction would become more reliable and commonplace in the near future.

5.3.3   Fusion of primary and soft biometric information

A biometric system can operate either in identification mode or verification mode. Jain et al., 2004a present a Bayesian framework for fusion of soft and primary biometric information under both these modes of operation. The main advantage of this framework is that it does not require the soft biometric feature extractors to be perfect (100% accurate).

Identification mode: For a biometric system operating in the identification mode, the framework for integrating primary and soft biometric information is shown in Figure 5.13. Let us assume that the primary biometric system is based on R_p, $R_p \geq 1$ biometric identifiers like fingerprint, face, iris and hand geometry. Further, the soft biometric system is based on R_s, $R_s \geq 1$ attributes like age, gender, ethnicity, eye color and height. Let $\omega_1, \omega_2, \ldots, \omega_M$ represent the M users enrolled in the database. Let $x = [x_1, x_2, \ldots, x_{R_p}]$ be the collection of primary biometric feature vectors. Let $p(x_j | \omega_k)$ be the likelihood of observing the primary biometric feature vector x_j given the user is ω_k. If the output of each individual modality in the primary biometric system is a set of match scores, $s_k = [s_{1,k}, s_{2,k}, \ldots, s_{R_p,k}]$, one can approximate $p(x_j | \omega_k)$ by $p(s_j | \omega_k)$, provided the genuine match score distribution of each modality is known.

Let $y = [y_1, y_2, \ldots, y_{R_s}]$ be the soft biometric feature vector, where, for example, y_1 could be the gender, y_2 could be the eye color, etc. We require an estimate of the posteriori probability of user ω_k given both x and y. This posteriori probability can be calculated by applying the Bayes rule as follows:

$$P(\omega_k | x, y) = \frac{p(x, y | \omega_k) P(\omega_k)}{p(x, y)}. \tag{5.13}$$

If all the users are equally likely to access the system, then $P(\omega_k) = \frac{1}{M}$, $\forall\, k$. Further, if we assume that all the primary biometric feature vectors $x_1, \ldots, x_{R_p}$ and all the soft biometric variables $y_1, y_2, \ldots, y_{R_s}$ are statistically independent of each other given the user's identity ω_k, the posteriori probability in Equation 5.13 can be expressed in terms of the product of the likelihoods as follows.

$$P(\omega_k | x, y) = \prod_{j=1}^{R_p} p(x_j | \omega_k) \prod_{r=1}^{R_s} p(y_r | \omega_k). \tag{5.14}$$

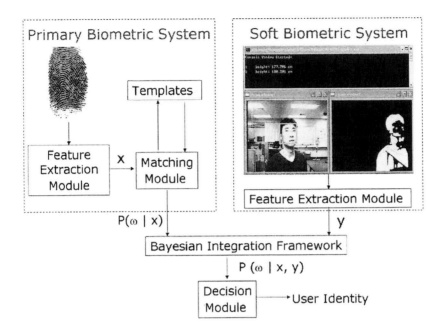

Figure 5.13. Framework for fusion of primary and soft biometric information. Here x is the primary (fingerprint) feature vector and y is the soft biometric feature vector.

The logarithm of the posteriori probability can be considered as the discriminant function, $g_k(x, y)$, for user ω_k, which is given by

$$g_k(x, y) = \sum_{j=1}^{R_p} \log p(x_j | \omega_k) + \sum_{r=1}^{R_s} \log p(y_r | \omega_k). \qquad (5.15)$$

During the identification phase, the input biometric sample is compared with the templates of all the M users enrolled in the database and the discriminant functions $g_1, \ldots, g_M$ are computed. The test user is identified as that user with the largest value of discriminant function among all the enrolled users.

Verification mode: A biometric system operating in the verification mode classifies each authentication attempt as either "genuine" or "impostor". In the case of verification, the Bayesian decision rule can be expressed as

$$\frac{P(genuine | x, y)}{P(impostor | x, y)} \geq \eta, \qquad (5.16)$$

where η is the decision threshold. Increasing η reduces the false accept rate and simultaneously increases the false reject rate and vice versa. If the prior probabilities of the genuine and impostor classes are equal, and if we assume that all the primary biometric feature vectors and all the soft biometric attributes are independent of each other, the ratio of the posteriori probabilities in Equation 5.16 can be expressed in terms of the product of the likelihood ratios as follows.

$$\frac{P(genuine|\boldsymbol{x}, \boldsymbol{y})}{P(impostor|\boldsymbol{x}, \boldsymbol{y})} = \prod_{j=1}^{R_p} \left(\frac{p(\boldsymbol{x}_j|genuine)}{p(\boldsymbol{x}_j|impostor)} \right) \prod_{r=1}^{R_s} \left(\frac{p(y_r|genuine)}{p(y_r|impostor)} \right).$$

(5.17)

The logarithm of the posteriori probability ratio can be considered as the discriminant function, $g(\boldsymbol{x}, \boldsymbol{y})$, which is given by

$$g(\boldsymbol{x}, \boldsymbol{y}) = \sum_{j=1}^{R_p} \log \left(\frac{p(\boldsymbol{x}_j|genuine)}{p(\boldsymbol{x}_j|impostor)} \right) + \sum_{r=1}^{R_s} \log \left(\frac{p(y_r|genuine)}{p(y_r|impostor)} \right).$$

(5.18)

The input biometric sample is assigned to the "genuine" class if $g(\boldsymbol{x}, \boldsymbol{y}) \geq \eta$. If the output of each individual modality in the primary biometric system is a set of match scores, $\boldsymbol{s} = [s_1, s_2, \ldots, s_{R_p}]$, one can approximate $p(\boldsymbol{x}_j|genuine)$ and $p(\boldsymbol{x}_j|impostor)$ by $p(s_j|genuine)$ and $p(s_j|impostor)$, respectively, provided the genuine and impostor match score distributions of each modality are known.

Computation of soft biometric likelihoods: A simple method for computing the soft biometric likelihoods $p(y_r|\omega_k), r = 1, 2, \ldots, R_s, k = 1, 2, \ldots, M$ is to estimate them based on the accuracy of the available soft biometric feature extractors. For example, if the accuracy of the gender classifier is α, we can estimate the likelihood for the gender attribute as

1 $P(\text{observed gender is male} \mid \text{true gender of the user is male}) = \alpha$,

2 $P(\text{observed gender is female} \mid \text{true gender of the user is female}) = \alpha$,

3 $P(\text{observed gender is male} \mid \text{true gender of the user is female}) = 1 - \alpha$,

4 $P(\text{observed gender is female} \mid \text{true gender of the user is male}) = 1 - \alpha$.

Similarly, if the average error made by the system in measuring the height of a person is μ_e and the standard deviation of the error is σ_e, then it is reasonable to assume that $p(\text{measured height}|\omega_k)$ follows a Gaussian distribution with mean $(h(\omega_k) + \mu_e)$ and standard deviation σ_e, where $h(\omega_k)$ is the true height of user ω_k. When the error in height measurement (characterized by the parameters μ_e and σ_e) is small, the distribution of the measured height of a person is highly peaked around the true height of the person. As a result, the measured height can provide better discrimination between the users enrolled in the database. On the other hand, if the standard deviation of the height measurement error, σ_e, is large, the measured height tends to follow a uniform distribution. Consequently, the measured height does not provide much discrimination between the enrolled users.

There is a potential problem when the likelihoods are estimated only based on the accuracy of the soft biometric feature extractors. The discriminant function in Equation 5.15 is dominated by the soft biometric terms due to the large dynamic range of the soft biometric log-likelihood values. For example, if the gender classifier is 98% accurate ($\alpha = 0.98$), the log-likelihood for the gender term in Equation 5.15 is -0.02 if the classification is correct and -3.91 in the case of a misclassification. This large difference in the log-likelihood values is due to the large variance of the soft biometric feature values compared to the primary biometric feature values. To offset this phenomenon, Jain et al., 2004a introduced a scaling factor β, $0 \leq \beta \leq 1$, to flatten the likelihood distribution of each soft biometric trait. If $q_{r,k}$ is an estimate of the likelihood $p(y_r|\omega_k)$ based on the accuracy of the feature extractor for the rth soft biometric trait, the weighted likelihood $\hat{p}(y_r|\omega_k)$ is computed as,

$$\hat{p}(y_r|\omega_k) = \frac{(q_{r,k})^{\beta_r}}{\sum_{Y_r}(q_{r,k})^{\beta_r}}, \tag{5.19}$$

where Y_r is the set of all possible values of the discrete soft biometric variable y_r and β_r is the weight assigned to the rth soft biometric trait. If the feature y_r is continuous with standard deviation σ_r, the likelihood can be scaled by replacing σ_r with σ_r/β_r. This weighted likelihood approach is commonly used in the speech recognition community in the context of estimating the word posterior probabilities using both acoustic and language models. In this scenario, weights are generally used to scale down the probabilities obtained from the acoustic model (Wessel et al., 2001).

The above method of likelihood computation also has other implicit advantages. An impostor can easily circumvent the soft biometric feature extraction because it is relatively easy to modify/hide one's soft biometric attributes by applying cosmetics and wearing other accessories (like mask, shoes with high heels, etc.). In this scenario, the scaling factor β_r can act as a measure of the reliability of the rth soft biometric feature and its value can be set depending on the environment in which the system operates. If the environment is hostile (where many users are trying to circumvent the system), the value of β_r can be set close to 0. Finally, the discriminant function given in equation 5.15 is optimal only if the assumption of independence between all the biometric traits is true. If there is any dependence between the features, the discriminant function is sub-optimal. In this case, appropriate selection of the weights β_r, $r = 1, \ldots, R_s$, during training can result in better recognition rates.

5.3.4   Performance gain using soft biometrics

Experiments by Jain et al., 2004a demonstrated the benefits of utilizing the gender, ethnicity, and height information of the user in addition to the face and fingerprint biometric identifiers. A subset of the Joint Multibiometric Database (JMD) collected at West Virginia University was used in their experiments. The selected database contained 4 face images and 4 impressions of the left index finger obtained from 263 users over a period of six months. The LDA-based classifier proposed in Lu and Jain, 2004 was used for gender and ethnicity classification of each user. The accuracy of the ethnicity classifier for the problem of classifying the users in the JMD as "Asian" and "Non-Asian" was 96.3%. The accuracy of the gender classifier on the JMD was 89.6%. When the reject rate was fixed at 25%, the accuracy of the ethnicity and gender classifiers were 99% and 98%, respectively. In cases where the ethnicity or the gender classifier made a reject decision on a user, the corresponding information is not utilized for updating the discriminant function, i.e., if the label assigned to the rth soft biometric trait is "reject", then the log-likelihood term corresponding to the rth feature in Equation 5.18 is set to zero. Further, during the collection of data in the JMD, the approximate height of each user was recorded during the first acquisition. However, no real-time height measurement was performed during subsequent biometric data acquisitions. Hence, Jain et al., 2004a simulated values for the measured height of user ω_k (at the verification time), $k = 1, \ldots, 263$ from a normal distribution with mean $h(\omega_k) + \mu_e$ and standard deviation σ_e, where $h(\omega_k)$ is the true height of user ω_k recorded during the database collection, $\mu_e = 2$ cm and $\sigma_e = 5$ cm. Here, μ_e and σ_e are the average and standard deviation of the height measurement error and the values of these two parameters were estimated based on the errors observed using the height measurement system developed by Jain et al., 2004a.

Figure 5.14(a) depicts the performance gain obtained when the soft biometric identifiers were used along with both face and fingerprint modalities in the identification mode. We can observe that the rank-one recognition rate of the multimodal biometric system based on face and fingerprint modalities is approximately 97% (rank-one error rate is 3%) and the addition of soft biometric information improves the rank-one accuracy by about 1% (rank-one error rate is now 2%). Although the absolute improvement in the rank-one accuracy due to the additional soft biometric information is small, it must be noted that the relative reduction in the rank-one error rate is about 33%, which is significant.

In the verification mode, the improvement in GAR after incorporating soft biometric information over the multimodal system is about 2% at 0.001% FAR (see Figure 5.14(b)). This improvement is quite significant given that the GAR

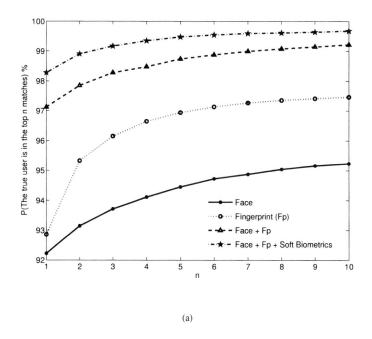

(a)

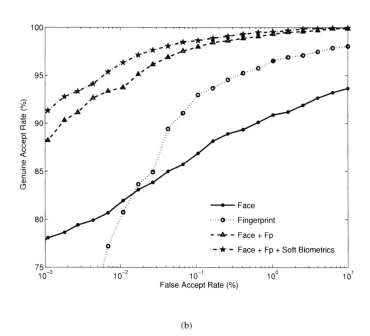

(b)

Figure 5.14. Improvement in the performance of a multimodal (face and fingerprint) system after addition of soft biometric traits. (a) Identification and (b) Verification mode.

of the multimodal (face and fingerprint) biometric system at this operating point is already very high (the false reject rate at this operating point is reduced from 11% to 9% which is a relative improvement of approximately 20%).

5.4   Summary

In addition to the match scores provided by the biometric matchers, ancillary information may also be available to a multibiometric system depending on the application scenario. Biometric signal quality and soft biometric information are two examples of such additional information that can be utilized to improve the accuracy of a multibiometric system. While biometric signal quality does not explicitly contain any information about the identity of the user, different biometric matchers exhibit different levels of sensitivity to the quality of the acquired biometric sample. This phenomenon can be exploited in a multibiometric system where the match scores or the identity decisions of the matchers can be appropriately weighted during fusion based on the quality of the input biometric sample. Soft biometric characteristics like gender, ethnicity, height and weight directly provide information about the identity of the user. Although the soft biometric information alone is not sufficient for accurate person recognition, they can be used to complement the information provided by the primary biometric identifiers like fingerprint, iris and face. Techniques for automatically extracting soft biometric information and estimating biometric signal quality have been incorporated into biometric systems only recently. Hence, fusion schemes that incorporate such ancillary information have not been thoroughly explored and there is plenty of scope for conducting more in-depth research in this area.

Appendix A
Evaluation of multibiometric systems

A.1   Biometric system evaluation

Evaluation of a complete biometric system is a complex and challenging task that requires experts from a variety of fields, including statistics, computer science, engineering, business, psychology and law enforcement. In order to gain a thorough understanding of the performance of a biometric system, one must address the following questions.

1 What is the error rate of the biometric system in a given application? (matching or technical performance)

2 What is the reliability, availability and maintainability of the system? (engineering performance)

3 What are the vulnerabilities of the biometric system? What level of security does the biometric system provide to the application in which it is embedded? (security of the biometric system)

4 What is the user acceptability of the system? How does the system address human factor issues like habituation and privacy concerns? (user concerns)

5 What is the cost and throughput of the biometric system and what tangible benefits can be derived from its deployment? (return on investment)

In order to fully evaluate a biometric system, one must also consider the existing security solutions in the application domain where the biometric system will be embedded. No existing biometric evaluation framework addresses all the above questions in a systematic manner. In this appendix, we focus only on the matching performance of a biometric system.

Phillips et al., 2000a have proposed a general framework for evaluating the matching performance of a biometric system. Ideally, the evaluation requires an independent third party to design, administer and analyze the test. Phillips et al., 2000a divide the matching performance evaluation of a biometric system into three stages:

1 **Technology evaluation**: Technology evaluation compares competing algorithms from a single technology on a standardized database. The Fingerprint Verification Competitions (FVC) (Maio et al., 2004), the Fingerprint Vendor Technology Evaluation (FpVTE) (Wilson et al., 2004), the Face Recognition Vendor Tests (FRVT) (Phillips et al., 2003), the Face Recognition Technology (FERET) program (Phillips et al., 2000b) and the NIST Speaker

Recognition Evaluations (SRE) (Przybocki and Martin, 2004) are examples of biometric technology evaluations. Since the database is fixed, the technology evaluation results are repeatable. However, characteristics of the database such as data collection environment, sample population and user habituation will affect the performance of the algorithms. Hence, care must be taken to ensure that the database is neither too hard nor too easy. If the database is too easy (i.e., it includes only good quality biometric samples with small intra-class variations), the error rates will be close to zero and it will be very difficult to distinguish between the competing systems. On the other hand, if the database is too challenging (i.e., it includes only poor quality biometric samples with large intra-class variations), the evaluation may be beyond the capabilities of existing technologies, thereby rendering the evaluation useless. Ideally, a database should include samples that are representative of the population and it must allow us to distinguish between the performance of competing algorithms and determine their strengths and limitations.

2 **Scenario evaluation**: In scenario evaluation, the testing of the prototype biometric systems is carried out in an environment that closely resembles the real-world application. Since each system will acquire its own biometric data, care must be taken to ensure uniformity in the environmental conditions and sample population across the different prototype systems.

3 **Operational evaluation**: Operational evaluation is used to ascertain the performance of a complete biometric system in a specific application environment with a specific target population.

Mansfield and Wayman, 2002 identify the best practices to be followed when evaluating the technical performance of a biometric system. They make recommendations on a number of testing issues, including size of the test, volunteer selection, factors that may affect the performance of a biometric system, data collection methodology, estimation of the performance metrics, estimating the uncertainty of performance metrics and reporting the performance results. They also note that since their recommendations are general in nature, it may not be possible to follow them completely in any practical biometric system evaluation. A sound evaluation of the technical performance of a biometric system must follow the best practices recommended by Mansfield and Wayman, 2002 as closely as possible and clearly explain any deviations from these recommendations that may be necessary.

A.2   Issues in multibiometric system evaluation

Evaluation of the matching performance of a multibiometric system is similar to the evaluation of a unibiometric system except for a few issues that are unique to a multibiometric system. One of the main differences between the evaluation of unimodal and multimodal biometric systems is the nature of the database used. The performance metrics of a biometric system such as accuracy, throughput, and scalability can be estimated with a high degree of confidence only when the system is tested on a large representative database. For example, face (Phillips et al., 2003) and fingerprint (Wilson et al., 2004) recognition systems have been evaluated on large databases (containing samples from more than $25,000$ individuals) obtained from a diverse population under a variety of environmental conditions. In contrast, current multimodal systems have been tested only on small databases containing fewer than $1,000$ individuals. This is mainly due to the absence of legacy multimodal databases and the cost and effort involved in collecting a large multimodal biometric database.

Multimodal biometric databases can be either true or virtual. In a true multimodal database (e.g., XM2VTS database (Messer et al., 1999)), different biometric cues are collected from the same individual. Virtual multimodal databases contain records which are created by consistently pairing a user from one unimodal database (e.g., face) with a user from another database (e.g., fingerprint). The creation of virtual users is based on the assumption that different biometric traits of the same person are independent. While this assumption of independence of the various modalities has not been thoroughly investigated, large virtual multimodal databases are easy to construct assuming that large unimodal databases are available. Indovina et al., 2003 attempt to validate the use of virtual subjects by randomly creating 1,000 sets of virtual users with face and fingerprint modalities. The performance of the multimodal biometric system for the 1,000 virtual user sets is shown in Figure A.1, which indicates that the variation in matching performance among these virtual user sets is not significant. The clustering of these ROC curves seems to support the independence assumption between the face and fingerprint modalities, thereby validating the use of virtual subjects. Garcia-Salicetti et al., 2005 also report similar results for experiments on a subset of the BIOMET multimodal database (Garcia-Salicetti et al., 2003). However, experiments by Poh and Bengio, 2005c seem to indicate that the recognition performance of a multimodal biometric system evaluated on a virtual multimodal database is significantly different from the results obtained on a true multimodal database. Hence, the issue of using virtual versus true multimodal databases to evaluate the performance of a multibiometric system needs further investigation.

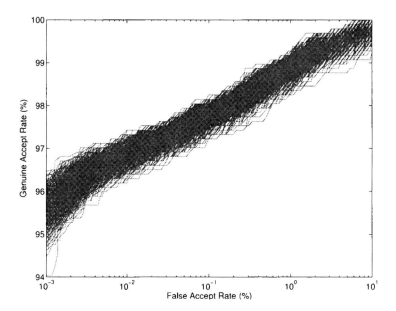

Figure A.1. ROC curves of the multimodal (face and fingerprint) biometric system for the 1,000 virtual user sets randomly created by Indovina et al., 2003. The variation in matching performance among these virtual user sets is not significant which seems to validate the use of virtual users.

Another issue unique to multibiometric system evaluation is the testing of a cascaded multi-biometric system, where multiple sources of biometric information are processed in a sequential order (see Chapter 2 for more details). The cascading scheme can improve user convenience as well as allow fast and efficient searches in large scale identification tasks. Further, a hierarchical processing architecture (mixture of cascade and parallel processing sequences) is also possible in a multibiometric system. Evaluation of cascaded or hierarchical multibiometric systems is more complex because of the trade-off between user convenience and security offered by such systems. Standard protocols are not available to evaluate cascaded or hierarchical multibiometric systems.

A.3   Multimodal biometric databases

A good multimodal biometric database must be representative of the population and each biometric trait must preferably exhibit realistic intra-class variations (achieved by collecting data over multiple sessions spread over a period of time and in different environmental conditions). One must also carefully decide which biometric traits and sensors to use and how many samples per user per trait needs to be collected. Further, due to the involvement of human subjects, legal and privacy issues must also be considered and approval of organizations like the Institutional Review Board (IRB) is mandatory in many countries (Penslar, 1993). This makes the collection of a true multimodal biometric database a time consuming and complicated process. In this section, we introduce some of the multimodal biometric databases that are available in the public domain. The following eight databases are true multimodal databases collected at various universities and research laboratories around the world.

1   **BT-DAVID (British Telecom Laboratories - Digital Audio-Visual Integrated Database)**: BT-DAVID (Mason et al., 1996) is a bimodal audio-visual database, which contains synchronized video and audio data obtained from more than 100 subjects. Of these 100 subjects, data from 30 subjects was recorded on five sessions spaced over several months. The video recordings include frontal and profile views of the subject's face with different illumination conditions and background scenes. The audio samples correspond to different utterances, including the English digit set, English alphabet E-set and vowel-consonant-vowel phrases. Portions of this database also include lip highlighting. Apart from its use in the development of biometric (audio-visual speaker recognition) algorithms, the BT-DAVID database can also be used to study a variety of research themes such as facial image segmentation in video, audio-visual speech recognition, speech-assisted video coding and synthesis of talking heads.

2   **M2VTS (Multi Modal Verification for Teleservices and Security applications) database**: The M2VTS database (Pigeon and Vandendrope, 1996) is another bimodal audio-visual database consisting of synchronized video and audio data of 37 subjects. This database contains five shots for each subject recorded at one week intervals in ideal conditions (good picture quality, indoor environment, nearly uniform illumination and uniform background). During each shot, the subject utters the digits '0' to '9' in his/her native language (mostly French) and rotates the head by 90 degrees towards the left and the right.

3   **XM2VTS (Extended Multi Modal Verification for Teleservices and Security applications) database**: The XM2VTS database (Messer et al., 1999) is a bimodal biometric database with face and voice modalities. It consists of synchronized video and audio data as well as image sequences corresponding to multiple views of the subject's face. This database has video and speech recordings of 295 subjects collected over a period of four months. The recordings were carried out in four sessions at one month intervals with two recordings of the subject in each session. Uniform illumination and a plain blue background were used during the recording. The subject was asked to read three sentences (two digit sequences along with a phonetically balanced sentence) and a video of the frontal face was recorded as the subject reads the sentences. Subsequently, the subject was asked to rotate his/her head from the center to the left, right, up and down before finally returning to the center. Based

on the XM2VTS database, Poh and Bengio, 2005a have developed a benchmark database of match scores that can be used to compare different score level fusion techniques. Eight baseline biometric matchers (five for face and three for voice) were used to generate the match scores in the benchmark database.

4 **BANCA database**: The BANCA database (Bailly-Bailliere et al., 2003) is a challenging bimodal audio-visual database recorded in three different scenarios, namely, controlled, degraded and adverse. Audio and video data from 208 subjects was obtained over a period of three months. For each of the four different native languages (English, French, Italian and Spanish), video and speech data were collected from 52 subjects over 12 sessions. In the first four sessions, the video was recorded in controlled conditions using a high quality digital camera with uniform illumination and plain background. The next four sessions correspond to the degraded scenario where the video was recorded using an analog web camera. The final four sessions were recorded in adverse conditions using the high quality digital camera with changes in illumination and complex background scenes. In each of the 12 sessions, the subject was prompted to say a random 12 digit number, his/her name, address and date of birth. The audio data was recorded using both a low quality and a high quality microphone.

5 **BIOMET multimodal database**: The BIOMET multimodal database has five biometric modalities, namely, face, voice, fingerprint, hand image and online-signature (Garcia-Salicetti et al., 2003). This database was collected in three different sessions with three and five months spacing between them. The number of subjects in the three sessions was 130, 106 and 91. The face database includes video recordings of the frontal and profile views of the face, the frontal face images of the subject captured using an active differential imaging device (referred to as "Infrared Camera device" in Garcia-Salicetti et al., 2003) and facial surface data captured using a 3D acquisition system. The video recordings also have synchronized audio recordings of the subject pronouncing his/her identification number, digits 0 to 9, "oui", "non", and 12 phonetically balanced sentences in French. Two-dimensional images of the subject's left hand were captured using a scanner. The x and y coordinates (over time) of the subject's signature were recorded at a rate of 200 Hz using a digitizing tablet. Along with the x and y coordinates, the pressure applied on the writing device, the azimuth and the altitude of the pen were also recorded. Optical and capacitive fingerprint sensors were used to capture images of the index and middle fingers of the subject's right hand.

6 **MCYT (Ministerio de Ciencia y Tecnologia, Spanish Ministry of Science and Technology) baseline corpus**: The MCYT bimodal database (Ortega-Garcia et al., 2003) has face and signature biometric modalities collected from 330 subjects. Fingerprint images of all 10 fingers were collected using both optical and capacitive sensors. Twelve impressions were collected for each finger on both the sensors. In the case of signature modality, 25 samples were collected for each subject. Further, for each subject 25 highly-skilled forgeries were obtained. Both online signature information such as the trajectory (x and y coordinates) of the pen, pen pressure and pen azimuth/altitude and offline information (image of the signature) are stored in the database.

7 **UND (University of Notre Dame) biometric database**: The UND biometric database (Flynn et al., 2005) is a collection of several small multimodal databases with face and ear modalities. Since the images in this database were captured using cameras operating in the visible and infra-red spectral regions and a 3D range scanner, this database can also be used for the design and evaluation of multi-sensor biometric systems. The number of subjects in this database varies from 80 to 350. A subset of the UND biometric database has been used in the Face Recognition Grand Challenge (FRGC) experiments (Phillips et al., 2005). The FRGC database includes high resolution 2D still face images obtained in controlled (studio

setting) and uncontrolled (e.g., hallways and outdoors) illumination conditions as well as 3D face images obtained using a range scanner.

8 **NIST BSSR1 (Biometric Scores Set - Release 1)**: The NIST BSSR1 (National Institute of Standards and Technology, 2004) is a multimodal biometric match score database. The NIST BSSR1 consists of fingerprint and face match scores of 517 subjects. Note that face and fingerprint images of the subject are not available. One fingerprint score was obtained by comparing a pair of impressions of the left index finger and another score was obtained by comparing impressions of the right index finger. Two different face matchers (referred to as 'C' and 'G') were applied to compute the similarity between two frontal face images. So, there are four match scores for each subject (one for each modality). Although the number of subjects in the NIST BSSR1 is the largest among all the public-domain true multimodal biometric databases, there are only two samples per subject. Thus, only a single genuine match score is available for a subject in each modality.

Apart from the eight multimodal biometric databases described above, several unimodal biometric databases are also available in the public domain. Some of the commonly used unimodal biometric databases are the Fingerprint Verification Competition (FVC) databases (Maio et al., 2002; Maio et al., 2004), the Carnegie Mellon University Pose, Illumination, and Expression (CMU-PIE) face database (Sim et al., 2003), the FERET face database (Phillips et al., 2000b) and the Chinese Academy of Sciences - Institute of Automation (CASIA) iris image database (Ma et al., 2003). These unimodal biometric databases can be used for evaluating multi-sensor, multi-instance, multi-sample and multi-algorithm biometric systems.

References

Abidi, M. A. and Gonzalez, R. C. (1992). *Data Fusion in Robotics and Machine Intelligence.* Academic Press, New York, USA.

Adler, A. (2003). Can Images be Regenerated from Biometric Templates? In *Special Session on Research at The Biometric Consortium Conference (BC2003)*, Arlington, USA.

Agresti, A. (1996). *An Introduction to Categorical Data Analysis.* Wiley.

Aillisto, H., Lindholm, M., Makela, S. M., and Vildjiounaite, E. (2004). Unobtrusive User Identification with Light Biometrics. In *Proceedings of the Third Nordic Conference on Human-Computer Interaction*, pages 327–330, Tampere, Finland.

Aizerman, M., Braverman, E., and Rozonoer, L. (1964). Theoretical Foundations of the Potential Function Method in Pattern Recognition Learning. *Automation and Remote Control*, 25:821–837.

American National Standards Institute (2003). Biometric Information Management and Security for the Financial Services Industry. Technical Report ANSI X9.84-2003, ANSI.

Arrow, K. J. (1963). *Social Choice and Individual Values.* John Wiley and Sons, Inc., New York, USA, Second edition.

Ashbourn, J. (2003). *Practical Biometrics: From Aspiration to Implementation.* Springer.

Atick, J. (2002). Biometrics in the Age of Heightened Security and Privacy. Available at `http://www.itl.nist.gov/div895/isis/bc/bc2001/EDIT_FINAL_DR.AT%ICK.pdf`.

Bailly-Bailliere, E., Bengio, S., Bimbot, F., Hamouz, M., Kittler, J., Mariethoz, J., Matas, J., Messer, K., Popovici, V., Poree, F., Ruiz, B., and Thiran, J.-P. (2003). The BANCA Database and Evaluation Protocol. In *Fourth International Conference on Audio- and Video-based Biometric Person Authentication (AVBPA)*, pages 625–638, Guildford, UK.

Baker, J. P. and Maurer, D. E. (2005). Fusion of Biometric Data with Quality Estimates via a Bayesian Belief Network. In *Special Session on Research at The Biometric Consortium Conference (BC2005)*, pages 21–22, Arlington, USA.

Balci, K. and Atalay, V. (2002). PCA for Gender Estimation: Which Eigenvectors Contribute? In *Proceedings of Sixteenth International Conference on Pattern Recognition (ICPR)*, volume 3, pages 363–366, Quebec City, Canada.

Beattie, M., Kumar, B. V. K. V., Lucey, S., and Tonguz, O. K. (2005). Combining Verification Decisions in a Multi-vendor Environment. In *Proceedings of Fifth International Conference on Audio- and Video-Based Biometric Person Authentication (AVBPA)*, pages 406–415, Rye Brook, USA.

Ben-Yacoub, S., Abdeljaoued, Y., and Mayoraz, E. (1999). Fusion of Face and Speech data for Person Identity Verification. *IEEE Transactions on Neural Networks*, 10(5):1065–1075.

Bendjebbour, A., Delignon, Y., Fouque, L., Samson, V., and Pieczynski, W. (2001). Multisensor Image Segmentation using Dempster Shafer Fusion in Markov Fields Context. *IEEE Transactions on Geoscience and Remote Sensing*, 39(8):1789–1798.

Benediktsson, J. A. and Swain, P. H. (1992). Consensus Theoretic Classification Methods. *IEEE Transactions on Systems, Man and Cybernetics*, 22(4):688–704.

Bertillon, A. (1896). *Signaletic Instructions including the Theory and Practice of Anthropometrical Identification, R.W. McClaughry Translation*. The Werner Company.

Bigun, E. S., Bigun, J., Duc, B., and Fischer, S. (1997). Expert Conciliation for Multimodal Person Authentication Systems using Bayesian Statistics. In *First International Conference on Audio- and Video-based Biometric Person Authentication (AVBPA)*, pages 291–300, Crans-Montana, Switzerland.

Bimbot, F., Magrin-Chagnolleau, I., and Mathan, L. (1995). Second-order Statistical Measure for Text-Independent Speaker Identification. *Speech Communication*, 17(1/2):177–192.

Blum, R. S. and Liu, Z., editors (2006). *Multi-Sensor Image Fusion and Its Applications*. CRC Press, Taylor and Francis Group, Florida, USA.

Bolle, R., Connell, J., Pankanti, S., Ratha, N., and Senior, A. (2003). *Guide to Biometrics*. Springer.

Bolle, R., Connell, J., Pankanti, S., Ratha, N., and Senior, A. (2005). The Relationship Between the ROC Curve and the CMC. In *Proceedings of Fourth IEEE Workshop on Automatic Identification Advanced Technologies (AutoID)*, pages 15–20, Buffalo, USA.

Bolle, R., Pankanti, S., and Yao, Y.-S. (1999). System and Method for Determining the Quality of Fingerprint Images. United States Patent Number US 5963656.

Brunelli, R. and Falavigna, D. (1995). Person Identification Using Multiple Cues. *IEEE Transactions on Pattern Analysis and Machine Intelligence*, 17(10):955–966.

Bunke, H. and Kandel, A., editors (2002). *Hybrid Methods in Pattern Recognition*, volume 47 of *Machine Perception and Artificial Intelligence*. World Scientific.

Burges, C. J. C. (1998). A Tutorial on Support Vector Machines for Pattern Recognition. *Data Mining and Knowledge Discovery*, 2(2):121–167.

Campbell, J. P. (1997). Speaker Recognition: a Tutorial. *Proceedings of the IEEE*, 85(9):1437–1462.

Campbell, W. M., Reynolds, D. A., and Campbell, J. P. (2004). Fusing Discriminative and Generative Methods for Speaker Recognition: Experiments on Switchboard and NFI/TNO Field Data. In *Odyssey: The Speaker and Language Recognition Workshop*, pages 41–44, Toledo, Spain.

Cappelli, R., Maio, D., and Maltoni, D. (2000). Combining Fingerprint Classifiers. In *Proceedings of First International Workshop on Multiple Classifier Systems*, pages 351–361, Cagliari, Italy.

Chang, K., Bowyer, K. W., Sarkar, S., and Victor, B. (2003). Comparison and Combination of Ear and Face Images in Appearance-based Biometrics. *IEEE Transactions on Pattern Analysis and Machine Intelligence*, 25(9):1160–1165.

Chang, K. I., Bowyer, K. W., and Flynn, P. J. (2005). An Evaluation of Multimodal 2D+3D Face Biometrics. *IEEE Transactions on Pattern Analysis and Machine Intelligence*, 27(4):619–624.

Chang, K. I., Bowyer, K. W., Flynn, P. J., and Chen, X. (2004). Multibiometrics Using Facial Appearance, Shape and Temperature. In *Sixth IEEE International Conference on Automatic Face and Gesture Recognition*, pages 43–48, Seoul, Korea.

Chatzis, V., Bors, A. G., and Pitas, I. (1999). Multimodal Decision-level Fusion for Person Authentication. *IEEE Transactions on Systems, Man, and Cybernetics, Part A: Systems and Humans*, 29(6):674–681.

Chen, K., Wang, L., and Chi, H. (1997). Methods of Combining Multiple Classifiers with Different Features and their Applications to Text-Independent Speaker Identification. *International Journal of Pattern Recognition and Artificial Intelligence*, 11(3):417–445.

Chen, X., Flynn, P. J., and Bowyer, K. W. (2005a). IR and Visible Light Face Recognition. *Computer Vision and Image Understanding*, 99(3):332–358.

Chen, Y., Dass, S. C., and Jain, A. K. (2005b). Fingerprint Quality Indices for Predicting Authentication Performance. In *Proceedings of Fifth International Conference on Audio- and Video-Based Biometric Person Authentication (AVBPA)*, pages 160–170, Rye Brook, USA.

Chen, Y., Dass, S. C., and Jain, A. K. (2006). Localized Iris Image Quality Using 2-D Wavelets. In *IAPR International Conference on Biometrics (ICB)*, pages 373–381, Hong Kong, China.

Cherubini, U., Luciano, E., and Vecchiato, W. (2004). *Copula Methods in Finance*. Wiley.

Cheung, M., Yiu, K., Mak, M., and Kung, S. (2004). Multi-Sample Fusion with Constrained Feature Transformation for Robust Speaker Verification. In *Eighth International Conference on Spoken Language Processing (ICSLP)*, pages 1813–1816, Jeju Island, Korea.

Chiang, C. and Fu, H. (1994). A Divide-and-Conquer Methodology for Modular Supervised Neural Network Design. In *Proceedings of World Congress on Computational Intelligence*, pages 119–124, Orlando, USA.

Chibelushi, C. C., Mason, J. S. D., and Deravi, F. (1997). Feature-level Data Fusion for Bimodal Person Recognition. In *Proceedings of the Sixth International Conference on Image Processing and Its Applications*, volume 1, pages 399–403, Dublin, Ireland.

Choi, K., Choi, H., and Kim, J. (2005). Fingerprint Mosaicking by Rolling and Sliding. In *Proceedings of Fifth International Conference on Audio- and Video-Based Biometric Person Authentication (AVBPA)*, pages 260–269, Rye Brook, USA.

Clemen, R. T. (1989). Combining Forecasts: A Review and Annotated Bibliography. *International Journal of Forecasting*, 5:559–583.

Czyz, J., Kittler, J., and Vandendorpe, L. (2004). Multiple Classifier Combination for Face-based Identity Verification. *Pattern Recognition*, 37(7):1459–1469.

Dasarathy, B. V. and Sheela, B. V. (1979). A Composite Classifier System Design: Concepts and Methodology. *Proceedings of the IEEE*, 67(5):708–713.

Dass, S. C., Nandakumar, K., and Jain, A. K. (2005). A Principled Approach to Score Level Fusion in Multimodal Biometric Systems. In *Proceedings of Fifth International Conference on Audio- and Video-based Biometric Person Authentication (AVBPA)*, pages 1049–1058, Rye Brook, USA.

Daugman, J. (1999). Recognizing Persons by their Iris Patterns. In Jain, A. K., Bolle, R., and Pankanti, S., editors, *Biometrics: Personal Identification in Networked Society*, pages 103–122. Kluwer Academic Publishers, London, UK.

Daugman, J. (2000). Combining Multiple Biometrics. Available at http://www.cl.cam.ac.uk/users/jgd1000/combine/combine.html.

Daugman, J. (2001). Statistical Richness of Visual Phase Information: Update on Recognizing Persons by Iris Patterns. *International Journal on Computer Vision*, 45(1):25–38.

Daugman, J. (2004). How Iris Recognition Works? *IEEE Transactions on Circuits and Systems for Video Technology*, 14(1):21–30.

Davies, S. (1994). Touching Big Brother: How Biometric Technology Will Fuse Flesh and Machine. *Information Technology and People*, 7(4).

Doddington, G., Liggett, W., Martin, A., Przybocki, M., and Reynolds, D. (1998). Sheep, Goats, Lambs and Wolves: A Statistical Analysis of Speaker Performance in the NIST 1998 Speaker Recognition Evaluation. In *CD-ROM Proceedings of the Fifth International Conference on Spoken Language Processing (ICSLP)*, Sydney, Australia.

Domingos, P. and Pazzani, M. (1997). On the Optimality of the Simple Bayesian Classifier under Zero-One Loss. *Machine Learning*, 29(2-3):103–130.

Drucker, H., Cortes, C., Jackel, L. D., LeCun, Y., and Vapnik, V. (1994). Boosting and Other Ensemble Methods. *Neural Computation*, 6(6):1289–1301.

Duda, R. O., Hart, P. E., and Stork, D. G. (2001). *Pattern Classification*. John Wiley & Sons.

Duta, N., Jain, A. K., and Mardia, K. V. (2002). Matching of Palmprints. *Pattern Recognition*, 23(4):477–485.

Egan, J. (1975). *Signal Detection Theory and ROC Analysis*. Academic Press, New York.

Eriksson, A. and Wretling, P. (1997). How Flexible is the Human Voice? A Case Study of Mimicry. In *Proceedings of the European Conference on Speech Technology*, pages 1043–1046, Rhodes.

Ernst, R. H. (1971). Hand ID System. United States patent number US 3576537.

Fancourt, C. L., Bogoni, L., Hanna, K. J., Guo, Y., Wildes, R. P., Takahashi, N., and Jain, U. (2005). Iris Recognition at a Distance. In *Fifth International Conference on Audio- and Video-based Biometric Person Authentication (AVBPA)*, pages 1–13, Rye Brook, USA.

Fang, Y., Tan, T., and Wang, Y. (2002). Fusion of Global and Local Features for Face Verification. In *Sixteenth International Conference on Pattern Recognition (ICPR)*, volume 2, pages 382–385, Quebec City, Canada.

Faulds, H. (1880). On the Skin Furrows of the Hand. *Nature*, 22:605.

Feng, G., Dong, K., Hu, D., and Zhang, D. (2004). When Faces are Combined with Palmprints: A Novel Biometric Fusion Strategy. In *First International Conference on Biometric Authentication (ICBA)*, pages 701–707, Hong Kong, China.

Fierrez-Aguilar, J., Chen, Y., Ortega-Garcia, J., and Jain, A. K. (2006). Incorporating Image Quality in Multi-algorithm Fingerprint Verification. In *IAPR International Conference on Biometrics (ICB)*, pages 213–220, Hong Kong, China.

Fierrez-Aguilar, J., Garcia-Romero, D., Ortega-Garcia, J., and Gonzalez-Rodriguez, J. (2005a). Bayesian Adaptation for User-Dependent Multimodal Biometric Authentication. *Pattern Recognition*, 38(8):1317–1319.

Fierrez-Aguilar, J., Nanni, L., Lopez-Penalba, J., Ortega-Garcia, J., and Maltoni, D. (2005b). An On-line Signature Verification System based on Fusion of Local and Global Information. In *Fifth International Conference on Audio- and Video-based Biometric Person Authentication (AVBPA)*, pages 523–532, Rye Brook, USA.

Fierrez-Aguilar, J., Ortega-Garcia, J., Gonzalez-Rodriguez, J., and Bigun, J. (2005c). Discriminative Multimodal Biometric Authentication based on Quality Measures. *Pattern Recognition*, 38(5):777–779.

Flynn, P. J., Bowyer, K. W., and Chawla, N. (2005). University of Notre Dame Biometrics Database. Available at http://www.nd.edu/~cvrl/UNDBiometricsDatabase.html.

Frischholz, R. and Dieckmann, U. (2000). BioID: A Multimodal Biometric Identification System. *IEEE Computer*, 33(2):64–68.

Fuentes, M., Garcia-Salicetti, S., and Dorizzi, B. (2002). On-line Signature Verification: Fusion of a Hidden Markov Model and a Neural Network via a Support Vector Machine. In *Eighth International Workshop on Frontiers in Handwriting Recognition*, pages 253–258, Ontario, Canada.

Galton, F. (1888). Personal Identification and Description. *Nature*, 38:173–177.

Garcia-Salicetti, S., Beumier, C., Chollet, G., Dorizzi, B., Jardins, J. L. L., Lunter, J., Ni, Y., and Petrovska-Delacretaz, D. (2003). BIOMET: A Multimodal Person Authentication Database Including Face, Voice, Fingerprint, Hand and Signature Modalities. In *Fourth International Conference on Audio- and Video-based Biometric Person Authentication (AVBPA)*, pages 845–853, Guildford, UK.

Garcia-Salicetti, S., Mellakh, M. A., , Allano, L., and Dorizzi, B. (2005). A Generic Protocol for Multibiometric Systems Evaluation on Virtual and Real Subjects. In *Fifth International*

Conference on Audio- and Video-based Biometric Person Authentication (AVBPA), pages 494–502, Rye Brook, USA.

Garris, M. D., Watson, C. I., and Wilson, C. L. (2004). Matching Performance for the US-Visit IDENT System Using Flat Fingerprints. Technical Report 7110, National Institute of Standards and Technology (NIST). NIST Internal Report 7110.

Ghosh, J. (2002). Multiclassifier Systems: Back to the Future. In *Proceedings of Third International Workshop on Multiple Classifier Systems*, pages 1–15, Cagliari, Italy.

Giacinto, G. and Roli, F. (2001). Dynamic Classifier Selection Based on Multiple Classifier Behaviour. *Pattern Recognition*, 34(9):1879–1881.

Givens, G., Beveridge, J. R., Draper, B. A., Grother, P., and Phillips, P. J. (2004). How Features of the Human Face Affect Recognition: a Statistical Comparison of Three Face Recognition Algorithms. In *Proceedings of the IEEE Computer Society Conference on Computer Vision and Pattern Recognition (CVPR)*, volume 2, pages 381–388, Washington D.C., USA.

Golfarelli, M., Maio, D., and Maltoni, D. (1997). On the Error-Reject Tradeoff in Biometric Verification Systems. *IEEE Transactions on Pattern Analysis and Machine Intelligence*, 19(7):786–796.

Grasselli, A. (1969). On the Automatic Classification of Fingerprints - Some Considerations on the Linguistic Interpretation of Pictures. In Watanabe, S., editor, *Methodologies of Pattern Recognition*, pages 253–273. Academic Press.

Grother, P. and Phillips, P. J. (2004). Models of Large Population Recognition Performance. In *Proceedings of the IEEE Computer Society Conference on Computer Vision and Pattern Recognition (CVPR)*, volume 2, pages 68–75, Washington D.C., USA.

Gunatilaka, A. H. and Baertlein, B. A. (2001). Feature-level and Decision-level Fusion of Non-coincidentally Sampled Sensors for Land Mine Detection. *IEEE Transactions on Pattern Analysis and Machine Intelligence*, 23(6):577–589.

Gutta, S., Huang, J. R. J., Phillips, P. J., and Wechsler, H. (2000). Mixture of Experts for Classification of Gender, Ethnic Origin, and Pose of Human Faces. *IEEE Transactions on Neural Networks*, 11(4):948–960.

Hampel, F. R., Rousseeuw, P. J., Ronchetti, E. M., and Stahel, W. A. (1986). *Robust Statistics: The Approach Based on Influence Functions*. John Wiley & Sons.

Han, J. and Bhanu, B. (2005). Gait Recognition by Combining Classifiers Based on Environmental Contexts. In *Proceedings of Fifth International Conference on Audio- and Video-Based Biometric Person Authentication (AVBPA)*, pages 416–425, Rye Brook, USA.

Hansen, J. H. L. and Arslan, L. (1995). Foreign Accent Classification using Source Generator based Prosodic Features. In *Proceedings of IEEE International Conference on Acoustics, Speech, and Signal Processing (ICASSP)*, pages 836–839, Detroit, USA.

Harrison, W. R. (1981). *Suspect Documents, their Scientific Examination*. Nelson-Hall Publishers.

Heckathorn, D. D., Broadhead, R. S., and Sergeyev, B. (2001). A Methodology for Reducing Respondent Duplication and Impersonation in Samples of Hidden Populations. *Journal of Drug Issues*, 31:543–564.

Heo, J., Kong, S., Abidi, B., and Abidi, M. (2004). Fusion of Visual and Thermal Signatures with Eyeglass Removal for Robust Face Recognition. In *IEEE Workshop on Object Tracking and Classification Beyond the Visible Spectrum*, pages 94–99, Washington D.C., USA.

Herschel, W. (1880). Skin Furrows of the Hand. *Nature*, 23:76.

Hill, C. J. (2001). Risk of Masquerade Arising from the Storage of Biometrics. Master's thesis, The Department of Computer Science, Australian National University.

Hill, H., Schyns, P. G., and Akamatsu, S. (1997). Information and Viewpoint Dependence in Face Recognition. *Cognition*, 62(2):201–222.

Ho, T. K. (2002). Multiple Classifier Combination: Lessons and Next Steps. In Bunke, H. and Kandel, A., editors, *Hybrid Methods in Pattern Recognition*, volume 47 of *Machine Perception and Artificial Intelligence*, pages 171–198. World Scientific.

Ho, T. K., Hull, J. J., and Srihari, S. N. (1994). Decision Combination in Multiple Classifier Systems. *IEEE Transactions on Pattern Analysis and Machine Intelligence*, 16(1):66–75.

Hong, L. and Jain, A. K. (1998). Integrating Faces and Fingerprints for Personal Identification. *IEEE Transactions on Pattern Analysis and Machine Intelligence*, 20(12):1295–1307.

Hong, L., Jain, A. K., and Pankanti, S. (1999). Can Multibiometrics Improve Performance? In *Proceedings of IEEE Workshop on Automatic Identification Advanced Technologies (AutoID)*, pages 59–64, New Jersey, USA.

Hong, L., Wan, Y., and Jain, A. K. (1998). Fingerprint Image Enhancement: Algorithms and Performance Evaluation. *IEEE Transactions on Pattern Analysis and Machine Intelligence*, 20(8):777–789.

Hsu, R.-L. (2002). *Face Detection and Modeling for Recognition*. PhD thesis, Department of Computer Science and Engineering, Michigan State University.

Huang, Y. S. and Suen, C. Y. (1995). Method of Combining Multiple Experts for the Recognition of Unconstrained Handwritten Numerals. *IEEE Transactions on Pattern Analysis and Machine Intelligence*, 17(1):90–94.

Huber, P. J. (1981). *Robust Statistics*. John Wiley & Sons.

Indovina, M., Uludag, U., Snelick, R., Mink, A., and Jain, A. K. (2003). Multimodal Biometric Authentication Methods: A COTS Approach. In *Proceedings of Workshop on Multimodal User Authentication (MMUA)*, pages 99–106, Santa Barbara, USA.

International Biometric Group (2005). Independent Testing of Iris Recognition Technology: Final Report. Available at `http://www.biometricgroup.com/reports/public/ITIRT.html`.

Iyengar, S. S., Prasad, L., and Min, H. (1995). *Advances in Distributed Sensor Technology*. Prentice Hall.

Jacobs, R. A., Jordan, M. I., Nowlan, S. J., and Hinton, G. E. (1991). Adaptive Mixtures of Local Experts. *Neural Computation*, 3(1):79–87.

Jacoby, I. H., Giordano, A. J., and Fioretti, W. H. (1972). Personnel Identification Apparatus. United States patent number US 3648240.

Jain, A. K., Bolle, R., and Pankanti, S., editors (1999a). *Biometrics: Personal Identification in Networked Society*. Kluwer Academic Publishers.

Jain, A. K. and Chandrasekaran, B. (1982). Dimensionality and Sample Size Considerations in Pattern Recognition Practice. In Krishnaiah, P.R. and Kanal, L. N., editors, *Handbook of Statistics*, volume 2, pages 835–855. North-Holland, Amsterdam.

Jain, A. K., Duin, R. P. W., and Mao, J. (2000a). Statistical Pattern Recognition: A Review. *IEEE Transactions on Pattern Analysis and Machine Intelligence*, 22(1):4–37.

Jain, A. K., Hong, L., and Bolle, R. (1997a). On-line Fingerprint Verification. *IEEE Transactions on Pattern Analysis and Machine Intelligence*, 19(4):302–314.

Jain, A. K., Hong, L., and Kulkarni, Y. (1999b). A Multimodal Biometric System using Fingerprint, Face and Speech. In *Second International Conference on Audio- and Video-based Biometric Person Authentication (AVBPA)*, pages 182–187, Washington D.C., USA.

Jain, A. K., Hong, L., Pankanti, S., and Bolle, R. (1997b). An Identity Authentication System Using Fingerprints. *Proceedings of the IEEE*, 85(9):1365–1388.

Jain, A. K., Nandakumar, K., Lu, X., and Park, U. (2004a). Integrating Faces, Fingerprints and Soft Biometric Traits for User Recognition. In *Proceedings of ECCV International Workshop on Biometric Authentication (BioAW)*, volume LNCS 3087, pages 259–269, Prague, Czech Republic. Springer.

Jain, A. K., Nandakumar, K., and Ross, A. (2005). Score Normalization in Multimodal Biometric Systems. *Pattern Recognition*, 38(12):2270–2285.

Jain, A. K., Pankanti, S., Prabhakar, S., Hong, L., and Ross, A. (2004b). Biometrics: A Grand Challenge. In *Proceedings of International Conference on Pattern Recognition (ICPR)*, volume 2, pages 935–942, Cambridge, UK.

Jain, A. K., Prabhakar, S., and Chen, S. (1999c). Combining Multiple Matchers for a High Security Fingerprint Verification System. *Pattern Recognition Letters*, 20(11-13):1371–1379.

Jain, A. K., Prabhakar, S., Hong, L., and Pankanti, S. (2000b). Filterbank-based Fingerprint Matching. *IEEE Transactions on Image Processing*, 9(5):846–859.

Jain, A. K. and Ross, A. (2002a). Fingerprint Mosaicking. In *IEEE International Conference on Acoustics, Speech, and Signal Processing (ICASSP)*, volume 4, pages 4064–4067, Orlando, USA.

Jain, A. K. and Ross, A. (2002b). Learning User-specific Parameters in a Multibiometric System. In *Proceedings of International Conference on Image Processing (ICIP)*, pages 57–60, Rochester, USA.

Jain, A. K., Ross, A., and Pankanti, S. (1999d). A Prototype Hand Geometry-based Verification System. In *Proceedings of Second International Conference on Audio- and Video-based Biometric Person Authentication (AVBPA)*, pages 166–171, Washington D.C., USA.

Jain, A. K., Ross, A., and Prabhakar, S. (2004c). An Introduction to Biometric Recognition. *IEEE Transactions on Circuits and Systems for Video Technology, Special Issue on Image- and Video-Based Biometrics*, 14(1):4–20.

Jain, A. K. and Zongker, D. (1997). Feature Selection: Evaluation, Application, and Small Sample Performance. *IEEE Transactions on Pattern Analysis and Machine Intelligence*, 19(2):153–158.

Jiang, X. and Ser, W. (2002). Online Fingerprint Template Improvement. *IEEE Transactions on Pattern Analysis and Machine Intelligence*, 24(8):1121–1126.

Jin, A. T. B., Ling, D. N. C., and Goh, A. (2004). An Integrated Dual Factor Authenticator Based On The Face Data And Tokenised Random Number. In *First International Conference on Biometric Authentication*, pages 117–123, Hong Kong, China.

Kale, A., RoyChowdhury, A. K., and Chellappa, R. (2004). Fusion of Gait and Face for Human Identification. In *IEEE International Conference on Acoustics, Speech, and Signal Processing (ICASSP)*, volume 5, pages 901–904, Montreal, Canada.

Kanade, T. (1973). *Picture Processing System by Computer Complex and Recognition of Human Faces*. PhD thesis, Department of Information Science, Kyoto University.

Kenny, S. and Borking, J. J. (2002). The Value of Privacy Engineering. *The Journal of Information, Law and Technology (JILT)*, 7(1).

Kent, S. and Millett, L. (2003). *Who Goes There? Authentication Technologies through the Lens of Privacy*. National Academy Press.

Kersta, L. G. (1962). Voiceprint Identification. *Nature*, 196:1253–1257.

Kim, J.-S., Hyeon, D.-H., Choi, J.-S., Kim, J.-W., Choi, B.-H., and Jung, H.-K. (2002). Object Extraction for Superimposition and Height Measurement. In *Proceedings of Eighth Korea-Japan Joint Workshop On Frontiers of Computer Vision*, pages 7–12, Sapporo, Japan.

Kinnunen, T., Hautamaki, V., and Franti, P. (2004). Fusion of Spectral Feature Sets for Accurate Speaker Identification. In *Ninth Conference on Speech and Computer*, pages 361–365, Saint-Petersburg, Russia.

Kittler, J., Hatef, M., Duin, R. P., and Matas, J. G. (1998). On Combining Classifiers. *IEEE Transactions on Pattern Analysis and Machine Intelligence*, 20(3):226–239.

Kittler, J. and Sadeghi, M. (2004). Physics-based Decorrelation of Image Data for Decision Level Fusion in Face Verification. In *Fifth International Workshop on Multiple Classifier Systems*, pages 354–363, Cagliari, Italy.

Krawczyk, S. and Jain, A. K. (2005). Securing Electronic Medical Records using Biometric Authentication. In *Proceedings of Fifth International Conference on Audio- and Video-based Biometric Person Authentication (AVBPA)*, pages 1110–1119, Rye Brook, USA.

Kumar, A., Wong, D. C. M., Shen, H. C., and Jain, A. K. (2003). Personal Verification Using Palmprint and Hand Geometry Biometric. In *Fourth International Conference on Audio- and Video-based Biometric Person Authentication (AVBPA)*, pages 668–678, Guildford, UK.

Kumar, A. and Zhang, D. (2005a). Biometric Recognition Using Feature Selection and Combination. In *Proceedings of Fifth International Conference on Audio- and Video-Based Biometric Person Authentication (AVBPA)*, pages 813–822, Rye Brook, USA.

Kumar, A. and Zhang, D. (2005b). Personal Authentication using Multiple Palmprint Representation. *Pattern Recognition*, 38(10):1695–1704.

Kuncheva, L. I. (2003). That Elusive Diversity in Classifier Ensembles. In *Proceedings of the First Iberian Conference on Pattern Recognition and Image Analysis (IbPRIA)*, pages 1126–1138, Mallorca, Spain.

Kuncheva, L. I. (2004). *Combining Pattern Classifiers - Methods and Algorithms*. Wiley.

Kuncheva, L. I., Bezdek, J. C., and Duin, R. P. W. (2001). Decision Templates for Multiple Classifier Fusion: An Experimental Comparison. *Pattern Recognition*, 34(2):299–314.

Kuncheva, L. I. and Whitaker, C. J. (2003). Measures of Diversity in Classifier Ensembles and Their Relationship with the Ensemble Accuracy. *Machine Learning*, 51(2):181–207.

Kuncheva, L. I., Whitaker, C. J., Shipp, C. A., and Duin, R. P. W. (2000). Is Independence Good for Combining Classifiers? In *Proceedings of International Conference on Pattern Recognition (ICPR)*, volume 2, pages 168–171, Barcelona, Spain.

Kuncheva, L. I., Whitaker, C. J., Shipp, C. A., and Duin, R. P. W. (2003). Limits on the Majority Vote Accuracy in Classifier Fusion. *Pattern Analysis and Applications*, 6(1):22–31.

Kwon, Y. H. and Lobo, N. V. (1994). Age Classification from Facial Images. In *Proceedings of IEEE Conference on Computer Vision and Pattern Recognition (CVPR)*, pages 762–767, Seattle, USA.

Lades, M., Vorbruggen, J., Buhmann, J., Lange, J., Malburg, C. V. D., and Wurtz, R. (1993). Distortion Invariant Object Recognition in the Dynamic Link Architecture. *IEEE Transactions on Computers*, 42(3):300–311.

Lam, L. and Suen, C. Y. (1995). Optimal Combination of Pattern Classifiers. *Pattern Recognition Letters*, 16:945–954.

Lam, L. and Suen, C. Y. (1997). Application of Majority Voting to Pattern Recognition: An Analysis of its Behavior and Performance. *IEEE Transactions on Systems, Man, and Cybernetics, Part A: Systems and Humans*, 27(5):553–568.

Lanitis, A., Draganova, C., and Christodoulou, C. (2004). Comparing Different Classifiers for Automatic Age Estimation. *IEEE Transactions on Systems, Man, and Cybernetics, Part B: Cybernetics*, 34(1):621–628.

Lee, L., Berger, T., and Aviczer, E. (1996). Reliable On-Line Human Signature Verification Systems. *IEEE Transactions on Pattern Analysis and Machine Intelligence*, 18(6):643–647.

Lehmann, E. L. and Romano, J. P. (2005). *Testing Statistical Hypotheses*. Springer.

Li, S. Z. and Jain, Anil K., editors (2005). *Handbook of Face Recognition*. Springer-Verlag.

Li, Y., Gong, S., and Liddell, H. (2003). Constructing Facial Identity Surfaces for Recognition. *International Journal of Computer Vision*, 53(1):71–92.

Liu, X. and Chen, T. (2003). Geometry-assisted Statistical Modeling for Face Mosaicing. In *Proceedings of IEEE International Conference on Image Processing (ICIP)*, volume 2, pages 883–886, Barcelona, Spain.

Liu, X. and Chen, T. (2005). Pose-Robust Face Recognition Using Geometry Assisted Probabilistic Modeling. In *Proceedings of IEEE Computer Society Conference on Computer Vision and Pattern Recognition (CVPR)*, volume 1, pages 502–509, San Diego, USA.

Lu, X. and Jain, A. K. (2004). Ethnicity Identification from Face Images. In *Proceedings of SPIE Conference on Biometric Technology for Human Identification*, volume 5404, pages 114–123, Orlando, USA.

Lu, X. and Jain, A. K. (2005). Integrating Range and Texture Information for 3D Face Recognition. In *IEEE Computer Society Workshop on Application of Computer Vision (WACV)*, pages 156–163, Breckenridge, USA.

Lu, X., Wang, Y., and Jain, A. K. (2003). Combining Classifiers for Face Recognition. In *IEEE International Conference on Multimedia and Expo (ICME)*, volume 3, pages 13–16, Baltimore, USA.

Luck, J. (1969). Automatic Speaker Verification Using Cepstral Measurements. *Journal of the Acoustic Society of America*, 46:1026–1031.

Ma, L., Tan, T., Wang, Y., and Zhang, D. (2003). Personal Identification Based on Iris Texture Analysis. *IEEE Transactions on Pattern Analysis and Machine Intelligence*, 25(12):1519–1533.

Ma, Y., Cukic, B., and Singh, H. (2005). A Classification Approach to Multi-biometric Score Fusion. In *Fifth International Conference on Audio- and Video-based Biometric Person Authentication (AVBPA)*, pages 484–493, Rye Brook, USA.

Maio, D., Maltoni, D., Cappelli, R., Wayman, J. L., and Jain, A. K. (2004). FVC2004: Third Fingerprint Verification Competition. In *Proceedings of International Conference on Biometric Authentication (ICBA)*, pages 1–7, Hong Kong, China.

Maio, D., Maltoni, D., Wayman, J. L., and Jain, A. K. (2002). FVC2004: Second Fingerprint Verification Competition. In *Proceedings of International Conference on Pattern Recognition (ICPR)*, pages 811–814, Quebec City, Canada.

Mallet, S. (1998). *A Wavelet Tour of Signal Processing*. Academic Press.

Maltoni, D., Maio, D., Jain, A. K., and Prabhakar, S. (2003). *Handbook of Fingerprint Recognition*. Springer-Verlag.

Mansfield, A. J. and Wayman, J. L. (2002). Best Practices in Testing and Reporting Performance of Biometric Devices, Version 2.01. Technical Report NPL Report CMSC 14/02, National Physical Laboratory.

Marcialis, G. L. and Roli, F. (2004a). Fingerprint Verification by Fusion of Optical and Capacitive Sensors. *Pattern Recognition Letters*, 25(11):1315–1322.

Marcialis, G. L. and Roli, F. (2004b). Fusion of Appearance-based Face Recognition Algorithms. *Pattern Analysis and Applications*, 7(2):151–163.

Marcialis, G. L. and Roli, F. (2005). Fusion of Multiple Fingerprint Matchers by Single-layer Perceptron with Class-separation Loss Function. *Pattern Recognition Letters*, 26(12):1830–1839.

Martin, A., Doddington, G., Kam, T., Ordowski, M., and Przybocki, M. (1997). The DET Curve in Assessment of Detection Task Performance. In *Proceedings of the Fifth European Conference on Speech Communication and Technology*, volume 4, pages 1895–1898, Rhodes, Greece.

Martin, A., Przybocki, M., Doddington, G., and Reynolds, D. (2000). The NIST Speaker Recognition Evaluation - Overview, Methodology, Systems, Results, Perspectives. *Speech Communications*, 31:225–254.

Mason, J. S. D., Deravi, F., Chibelushi, C. C., and Gandon, S. (1996). DAVID (Digital Audio Visual Integrated Database): Final Report. Technical Report, University of Wales Swansea.

Matsumoto, T., Hirabayashi, M., and Sato, K. (2004). A Vulnerability Evaluation of Iris Matching (Part 3). In *Proceedings of the 2004 Symposium on Cryptography and Information Security*, pages 701–706, Iwate, Japan.

Matsumoto, T., Matsumoto, H., Yamada, K., and Hoshino, S. (2002). Impact of Artificial Gummy Fingers on Fingerprint Systems. In *Optical Security and Counterfeit Deterrence Techniques IV, Proceedings of SPIE*, volume 4677, pages 275–289, San Jose, USA.

Messer, K., Matas, J., Kittler, J., Luettin, J., and Maitre, G. (1999). XM2VTSDB: The Extended M2VTS Database. In *Proceedings of Second International Conference on Audio- and Video-Based Biometric Person Authentication (AVBPA)*, pages 72–77, Washington D.C., USA.

Miller, R. P. (1971). Finger Dimension Comparison Identification System. United States patent number US 3576538.

Minematsu, N., Yamauchi, K., and Hirose, K. (2003). Automatic Estimation of Perceptual Age Using Speaker Modeling Techniques. In *Proceedings of the Eighth European Conference on Speech Communication and Technology*, pages 3005–3008, Geneva, Switzerland.

Minsky, M. (1991). Logical Versus Analogical or Symbolic Versus Connectionsit or Neat Versus Scruffy. *AI Magazine*, 12:34–51.

Moenssens, A. A. (1971). *Fingerprint Techniques*. Chilton Book Company.

Moghaddam, B. and Yang, M. H. (2002). Learning Gender with Support Faces. *IEEE Transactions on Pattern Analysis and Machine Intelligence*, 24(5):707–711.

Monrose, F. and Rubin, A. (1997). Authentication Via Keystroke Dynamics. In *Proceedings of Fourth ACM Conference on Computer and Communications Security*, pages 48–56, Zurich, Switzerland.

Moon, H. and Phillips, P. J. (2001). Computational and Performance Aspects of PCA-based Face Recognition Algorithms. *Perception*, 30(5):303–321.

Moon, Y. S., Yeung, H. W., Chan, K. C., and Chan, S. O. (2004). Template Synthesis and Image Mosaicking for Fingerprint Registration: An Experimental Study. In *IEEE International Conference on Acoustics, Speech, and Signal Processing (ICASSP)*, volume 5, pages 409–412, Montreal, Canada.

Most, M. (2003). Battle of the Biometrics. *Digital ID World Magazine*, pages 16–18.

Mosteller, F. and Tukey, J. W. (1977). *Data Analysis and Regression: A Second Course in Statistics*. Addison-Wesley.

Nalwa, V. S. (1997). Automatic On-Line Signature Verification. *Proceedings of the IEEE*, 85(2):215–239.

National Institute of Standards and Technology (2004). NIST Biometric Scores Set. Available at http://http://www.itl.nist.gov/iad/894.03/biometricscores.

Negin, M., Chmielewski, T. A., Salganicoff, M., Camus, T. A., von Seelan, U. M. C., Venetianer, P. L., and Zhang, G. G. (2000). An Iris Biometric System for Public and Personal Use. *IEEE Computer*, 33(2):70–75.

Nelsen, R. B. (1999). *An Introduction to Copulas*. Springer.

Newham, E. (1995). The Biometrics Report. SJB Services.

Nixon, M. S., Carter, J. N., Cunado, D., Huang, P. S., and Stevenage, S. V. (1999). Automatic Gait Recognition. In Jain, A. K., Bolle, R., and Pankanti, S., editors, *Biometrics: Personal Identification in Networked Society*, pages 231–249. Kluwer Academic Publishers, London, UK.

O'Gorman, L. (2002). Seven Issues with Human Authentication Technologies. In *Proc. of Workshop on Automatic Identification Advanced Technologies (AutoID)*, pages 185–186, Tarrytown, USA.

O'Gorman, L. (2003). Comparing Passwords, Tokens, and Biometrics for User Authentication. *Proceedings of the IEEE*, 91(12):2019–2040.

Ortega-Garcia, J., Fierrez-Aguilar, J., Simon, D., Gonzalez-Rodriguez, J., Faundez, M., Espinosa, V., Satue, A., Hernaez, I., Igarza, J.-J., Vivaracho, C., Escudero, D., and Moro, Q.-I. (2003). MCYT Baseline Corpus: A Bimodal Biometric Database. *IEE Proceedings on Vision, Image and Signal Processing, Special Issue on Biometrics on the Internet*, 150(6):395–401.

O'Toole, A., Bulthoff, H., Troje, N., and Vetter, T. (1995). Face Recognition across Large Viewpoint Changes. In *Proceedings of the International Workshop on Automatic Face- and Gesture-Recognition (IWAFGR)*, pages 326–331, Zurich, Switzerland.

Oviatt, S. (2003). Advances in Robust Multimodal Interface Design. *IEEE Computer Graphics and Applications*, 23(5):62–68.

Palmer, T. N. (2000). Predicting Uncertainty in Forecasts of Weather and Climate. *Reports on Progress in Physics*, 63:71–116.

Pankanti, S., Prabhakar, S., and Jain, A. K. (2002). On the Individuality of Fingerprints. *IEEE Transactions on Pattern Analysis and Machine Intelligence*, 24(8):1010–1025.

Parke, F. I. and Waters, K. (1996). *Computer Facial Animation*. A. K. Peters.

Parris, E. S. and Carey, M. J. (1996). Language Independent Gender Identification. In *Proceedings of IEEE International Conference on Acoustics, Speech, and Signal Processing (ICASSP)*, pages 685–688, Atlanta, USA.

Penslar, R. L. (1993). Protecting Human Research Subjects: Institutional Review Board Guidebook. Available at http://www.hhs.gov/ohrp/irb/irb_guidebook.htm.

Phillips, P. J., Flynn, P. J., Scruggs, T., Bowyer, K. W., Chang, J., Hoffman, K., Marques, J., Min, J., and Worek, W. (2005). Overview of the Face Recognition Grand Challenge. In *Proceedings of IEEE Computer Society Conference on Computer Vision and Pattern Recognition (CVPR)*, volume 1, pages 947–954, San Diego, USA.

Phillips, P. J., Grother, P., Micheals, R. J., Blackburn, D. M., Tabassi, E., and Bone, J. M. (2003). FRVT2002: Overview and Summary. Available at http://www.frvt.org/FRVT2002.

Phillips, P. J., Martin, A., Wilson, C. L., and Przybocki, M. (2000a). An Introduction to Evaluating Biometric Systems. *IEEE Computer*, 33(2):56–63.

Phillips, P. J., Moon, H., Rauss, P. J., and Rizvi, S. (2000b). The FERET Evaluation Methodology for Face Recognition Algorithms. *IEEE Transactions on Pattern Analysis and Machine Intelligence*, 22(10):1090–1104.

Pigeon, S. and Vandendrope, L. (1996). M2VTS Multimodal Face Database Release 1.00. Available at http://www.tele.ucl.ac.be/PROJECTS/M2VTS/m2fdb.html.

Podio, F. L., Dunn, J. S., Reinert, L., Tilton, C. J., O'Gorman, L., Collier, P., and Jerde, M.and Wirtz, B. (2001). Common Biometric Exchange File Format (CBEFF). Technical Report NISTIR 6529, NIST.

Poh, N. and Bengio, S. (2005a). A Score-Level Fusion Benchmark Database for Biometric Authentication. In *Fifth International Conference on Audio- and Video-based Biometric Person Authentication (AVBPA)*, pages 1059–1070, Rye Brook, USA.

Poh, N. and Bengio, S. (2005b). An Investigation of F-ratio Client-Dependent Normalisation on Biometric Authentication Tasks. In *Proceedings of IEEE International Conference on Acoustics, Speech, and Signal Processing (ICASSP)*, volume 1, pages 721–724, Philadelphia, USA.

Poh, N. and Bengio, S. (2005c). Can Chimeric Persons Be Used in Multimodal Biometric Authentication Experiments? In *Second International Machine Learning and Multimodal Interaction Workshop (MLMI)*, Edinburgh, UK.

Poh, N. and Bengio, S. (2005d). How Do Correlation and Variance of Base-Experts Affect Fusion in Biometric Authentication Tasks? *IEEE Transactions on Signal Processing*, 53(11):4384–4396.

Poh, N. and Bengio, S. (2005e). Improving Fusion with Margin-Derived Confidence in Biometric Authentication Tasks. In *Fifth International Conference on Audio- and Video-based Biometric Person Authentication (AVBPA)*, pages 474–483, Rye Brook, USA.

Prabhakar, S. and Jain, A. K. (2002). Decision-level Fusion in Fingerprint Verification. *Pattern Recognition*, 35(4):861–874.

Prabhakar, S., Pankanti, S., and Jain, A. K. (2003). Biometric Recognition: Security and Privacy Concerns. *IEEE Security and Privacy Magazine*, 1(2):33–42.

Pruzansky, S. (1963). Pattern-Matching Procedure for Automatic Talker Recognition. *Journal of the Acoustic Society of America*, 35:354–358.

Przybocki, M. and Martin, A. (2004). NIST Speaker Recognition Evaluation Chronicles. In *Odyssey: The Speaker and Language Recognition Workshop*, pages 12–22, Toledo, Spain.

Pudil, P., Novovicova, J., and Kittler, J. (1994). Floating Search Methods in Feature Selection. *Pattern Recognition Letters*, 15(11):1119–1124.

Rao, N., Protopopescu, P., Barhen, J., and Seetharaman, G., editors (1996). *Workshop on Foundations of Information/Decision Fusion With Applications to Engineering Problems*. Washington, D.C., USA.

Ratha, N. K., Connell, J. H., and Bolle, R. M. (1998). Image Mosaicing For Rolled Fingerprint Construction. In *Proceedings of Fourteenth International Conference on Pattern Recognition (ICPR)*, volume 2, pages 1651–1653, Brisbane, Australia.

Ratha, N. K., Connell, J. H., and Bolle, R. M. (2001). An Analysis of Minutiae Matching Strength. In *Proceedings of Third International Conference on Audio- and Video-Based Biometric Person Authentication (AVBPA)*, pages 223–228, Halmstad, Sweden.

Rejman-Greene, M. (2005). Privacy Issues in the Application of Biometrics: A European Perspective. In Wayman, J. L., Jain, A. K., Maltoni, D., and Maio, D., editors, *Biometric Systems: Technology, Design and Performance Evaluation*, pages 335–359. Springer.

Reynolds, D., Andrews, W., Campbell, J., Navratil, J., Peskin, B., Adami, A., Jin, Q., Klusacek, D., Abramson, J., Mihaescu, R., Godfrey, J., Jones, D., and Xiang, B. (2003). The SuperSID Project: Exploiting High-level Information for High-accuracy Speaker Recognition. In *IEEE International Conference on Acoustics, Speech, and Signal Processing (ICASSP)*, pages 784–787, Hong Kong, China.

Rodriguez-Linares, L., Garcia-Mateo, C., and Alba-Castro, J. L. (2003). On Combining Classifiers for Speaker Authentication. *Pattern Recognition*, 36(2):347–359.

Rogova, G. (1994). Combining the Results of Several Neural Network Classifiers. *Neural Networks*, 7(5):777–781.

Roli, F. and Fumera, G. (2002). Analysis of Linear and Order Statistics Combiners for Fusion of Imbalanced Classifiers. In *Third International Workshop on Multiple Classifier Systems (MCS)*, pages 252–261, Cagliari, Italy.

Ross, A. and Govindarajan, R. (2005). Feature Level Fusion Using Hand and Face Biometrics. In *Proceedings of SPIE Conference on Biometric Technology for Human Identification II*, volume 5779, pages 196–204, Orlando, USA.

Ross, A. and Jain, A. K. (2003). Information Fusion in Biometrics. *Pattern Recognition Letters*, 24(13):2115–2125.

Ross, A. and Jain, A. K. (2004). Biometric Sensor Interoperability: A Case Study in Fingerprints. In *Proceedings of ECCV International Workshop on Biometric Authentication (BioAW)*, volume LNCS 3087, pages 134–145, Prague, Czech Republic. Springer.

Ross, A., Jain, A. K., and Reisman, J. (2003). A Hybrid Fingerprint Matcher. *Pattern Recognition*, 36(7):1661–1673.

Ross, A., Shah, J., and Jain, A. K. (2005). Towards Reconstructing Fingerprints from Minutiae Points. In *Proceedings of SPIE Conference on Biometric Technology for Human Identification II*, volume 5779, pages 68–80, Orlando, USA.

Sanderson, C. and Paliwal, K. K. (2001). Information Fusion for Robust Speaker Verification. In *Seventh European Conference on Speech Communication and Technology*, pages 755–758, Aalborg, Denmark.

Sanderson, C. and Paliwal, K. K. (2002). Information Fusion and Person Verification Using Speech and Face Information. Research Paper IDIAP-RR 02-33, IDIAP.

Shakhnarovich, G., Lee, L., and Darrell, T. J. (2001). Integrated Face and Gait Recognition from Multiple Views. In *IEEE Conference on Computer Vision and Pattern Recognition (CVPR)*, pages 439–446, Hawaii, USA.

Shakhnarovich, G., Viola, P., and Moghaddam, B (2002). A Unified Learning Framework for Real Time Face Detection and Classification. In *Proceedings of International Conference on Automatic Face and Gesture Recognition*, pages 16–26, Washington D.C., USA.

Sharma, R., Pavlovic, V. I., and Huang, T. S. (1998). Toward Multimodal Human–Computer Interface. *Proceedings of the IEEE*, 86(5):853–869.

Shelman, C. B. (1967). Machine Classification of Fingerprints. In *Proceedings of the First National Symposium on Law Enforcement Science and Technology*, pages 467–477, Chicago, USA.

Sim, T., Baker, S., and Bsat, M. (2003). The CMU Pose, Illumination, and Expression Database. *IEEE Transactions on Pattern Analysis and Machine Intelligence*, 25(12):1615–1618.

Snelick, R., Indovina, M., Yen, J., and Mink, A. (2003). Multimodal Biometrics: Issues in Design and Testing. In *Proceedings of Fifth International Conference on Multimodal Interfaces (ICMI)*, pages 68–72, Vancouver, Canada.

Snelick, R., Uludag, U., Mink, A., Indovina, M., and Jain, A. K. (2005). Large Scale Evaluation of Multimodal Biometric Authentication Using State-of-the-Art Systems. *IEEE Transactions on Pattern Analysis and Machine Intelligence*, 27(3):450–455.

Socolinsky, D. A. and Selinger, A. (2004). Thermal Face Recognition Over Time. In *Proceedings of the Seventeenth International Conference on Pattern Recognition (ICPR)*, volume 4, pages 187–190.

Socolinsky, D. A., Selinger, A., and Neuheisel, J. D. (2003). Face Recognition with Visible and Thermal Infrared Imagery. *Computer Vision and Image Understanding*, 91(1-2):72–114.

Son, B. and Lee, Y. (2005). Biometric Authentication System Using Reduced Joint Feature Vector of Iris and Face. In *Proceedings of Fifth International Conference on Audio- and Video-Based Biometric Person Authentication (AVBPA)*, pages 513–522, Rye Brook, USA.

Sung, H., Lim, J., Park, J, and Lee, Y. (2004). Iris Recognition Using Collarette Boundary Localization. In *Seventeenth International Conference on Pattern Recognition (ICPR)*, volume 4, pages 857–860, Cambridge, UK.

Swets, J. A., Tanner, W. P., and Birdsall, T. G. (1961). Decision Processes in Perception. *Psychological Review*, 68(5):301–340.

Tabassi, E., Wilson, C., and Watson, C. (2004). Fingerprint Image Quality. Technical Report 7151, National Institute of Standards and Technology (NIST).

Tan, M. (1997). Multi-Agent Reinforcement Learning: Independent vs. Cooperative Learning. In Huhns, M. N. and Singh, M. P., editors, *Readings in Agents*, pages 487–494. Morgan Kaufmann, San Francisco, USA.

Toh, K.-A., Jiang, X., and Yau, W.-Y. (2004). Exploiting Global and Local Decisions for Multimodal Biometrics Verification. *IEEE Transactions on Signal Processing, (Supplement on Secure Media)*, 52(10):3059–3072.

Toh, K.-A., Xiong, W., Yau, W.-Y., and Jiang, X. (2003). Combining Fingerprint and Hand-Geometry Verification Decisions. In *Fourth International Conference on Audio- and Video-based Biometric Person Authentication (AVBPA)*, pages 688–696, Guildford, UK.

Toh, K.-A. and Yau, W.-Y. (2005). Fingerprint and Speaker Verification Decisions Fusion Using a Functional Link Network. *IEEE Transactions on Systems, Man, and Cybernetics, Part A: Applications and Reviews*, 35(3):357–370.

Trauring, M. (1963). Automatic Comparison of Finger-ridge Patterns. *Nature*, 197:938–940.

Tumer, K. and Ghosh, J. (1999). Linear and Order Statistics Combiners for Pattern Classification. In Sharkey, A., editor, *Combining Artificial Neural Nets*, pages 127–161. Springer-Verlag, London, UK.

Turk, M. and Pentland, A. (1991). Eigenfaces for Recognition. *Journal of Cognitive Neuroscience*, 3(1):71–86.

Uludag, U. and Jain, A. K. (2004). Attacks on Biometric Systems: A Case Study in Fingerprints. In *Proc. SPIE-EI 2004, Security, Seganography and Watermarking of Multimedia Contents VI*, pages 622–633, San Jose, USA.

Uludag, U., Ross, A., and Jain, A. K. (2004). Biometric Template Selection and Update: A Case Study in Fingerprints. *Pattern Recognition*, 37(7):1533–1542.

United Kingdom Biometric Working Group (2003). Biometric Security Concerns. Technical Report, Communications-Electronics Security Group (CESG).

Vachtsevanos, G., Tang, L., and Reimann, J. (2004). An Intelligent Approach to Coordinated Control of Multiple Unmanned Aerial Vehicles. In *60th Annual Forum of the American Helicopter Society*, Baltimore, USA.

Varshney, P. K., Oscadciw, L. A., and Veeramachaneni, K. (2002). Improving Personal Identification Accuracy Using Multisensor Fusion for Building Access Control Applications. In *Fifth International Conference on Information Fusion*, volume 2, pages 1176–1183, Annapolis, USA.

Veeramachaneni, K., Oscadciw, L. A., and Varshney, P. K. (2005). An Adaptive Multimodal Biometric Management Algorithm. *IEEE Transactions on Systems, Man, and Cybernetics, Part A: Applications and Reviews*, 35(3):344–356.

Verlinde, P. and Cholet, G. (1999). Comparing Decision Fusion Paradigms using k-NN based Classifiers, Decision Trees and Logistic Regression in a Multi-modal Identity Verification Application. In *Proceedings of Second International Conference on Audio- and Video-Based Biometric Person Authentication (AVBPA)*, pages 188–193, Washington D.C., USA.

Verlinde, P., Druyts, P., Cholet, G., and Acheroy, M. (1999). Applying Bayes based Classifiers for Decision Fusion in a Multi-modal Identity Verification System. In *Proceedings of International Symposium on Pattern Recognition "In Memoriam Pierre Devijver"*, Brussels, Belgium.

Wand, M. P. and Jones, M. C (1995). *Kernel Smoothing*. Chapman & Hall, CRC Press.

Wang, Y., Tan, T., and Jain, A. K. (2003). Combining Face and Iris Biometrics for Identity Verification. In *Fourth International Conference on Audio- and Video-based Biometric Person Authentication (AVBPA)*, pages 805–813, Guildford, UK.

Wasserman, H. P. (1974). *Ethnic Pigmentation*. Elsevier, New York, USA.

Wayman, J. L. (2000). Large-scale Civilian Biometric Systems - Issues and Feasibility. In Wayman, J. L., editor, *National Biometric Test Center Collected Works: 1997-2000*, pages 137–156. Available at http://www.engr.sjsu.edu/biometrics/nbtccw.pdf.

Wayman, J. L., Jain, A. K., Maltoni, D., and Maio, D., editors (2005). *Biometric Systems: Technology, Design and Performance Evaluation*. Springer.

Wessel, F., Schluter, R., Macherey, K., and Ney, H. (2001). Confidence Measures for Large Vocabulary Continuous Speech Recognition. *IEEE Transactions on Speech and Audio Processing*, 9(3):288–298.

Wilson, C., Hicklin, A. R., Bone, M., Korves, H., Grother, P., Ulery, B., Micheals, R., Zoepfl, M., Otto, S., and Watson, C. (2004). Fingerprint Vendor Technology Evaluation 2003: Summary of Results and Analysis Report. NIST Technical Report NISTIR 7123, National Institute of Standards and Technology.

Wolpert, D. H. (1990). Stacked generalization. Technical Report LA-UR-90-3460, Los Alamos National Laboratory.

Woods, K., Bowyer, K., and Kegelmeyer, W. P. (1997). Combination of Multiple Classifiers Using Local Accuracy Estimates. *IEEE Transactions on Pattern Analysis and Machine Intelligence*, 19(4):405–410.

Xia, X. and O'Gorman, L. (2003). Innovations in Fingerprint Capture Devices. *Pattern Recognition*, 36(2):361–369.

Xu, L., Krzyzak, A., and Suen, C. Y. (1992). Methods for Combining Multiple Classifiers and their Applications to Handwriting Recognition. *IEEE Transactions on Systems, Man, and Cybernetics*, 22(3):418–435.

Yang, F., Paindavoine, M., Abdi, H., and Monopoli, A. (2005). Development of a Fast Panoramic Face Mosaicking and Recognition System. *Optical Engineering*, 44(8).

Yang, J., Yang, J.-Y., Zhang, D., and Lu, J.-F. (2003). Feature Fusion: Parallel Strategy vs. Serial Strategy. *Pattern Recognition*, 38(6):1369–1381.

Yau, W.-Y., Toh, K.-A., Jiang, X., Chen, T.-P., and Lu, J. (2000). On Fingerprint Template Synthesis. In *CD-ROM Proceedings of Sixth International Conference on Control, Automation, Robotics and Vision (ICARCV)*, Singapore.

You, J., Kong, W.-K., Zhang, D., and Cheung, K. H. (2004). On Hierarchical Palmprint Coding With Multiple Features for Personal Identification in Large Databases. *IEEE Transactions on Circuits and Systems for Video Technology*, 14(2):234–243.

Zhang, D., Kong, A. W.-K., You, J., and Wong, M. (2003). Online Palmprint Identification. *IEEE Transactions on Pattern Analysis and Machine Intelligence*, 25(9):1041–1050.

Zhang, G. and Salganicoff, M. (1999). Method of Measuring the Focus of Close-Up Image of Eyes. United States patent number US 5953440.

Zhang, Y.-L., Yang, J., and Wu, H. (2005). A Hybrid Swipe Fingerprint Mosaicing Scheme. In *Proceedings of Fifth International Conference on Audio- and Video-Based Biometric Person Authentication (AVBPA)*, pages 131–140, Rye Brook, USA.

Zhou, S., Krueger, V., and Chellappa, R. (2003). Probabilistic Recognition of Human Faces from Video. *Computer Vision and Image Understanding*, 91(1-2):214–245.

Zunkel, R. (1999). Hand Geometry Based Authentication. In Jain, A. K., Bolle, R., and Pankanti, S., editors, *Biometrics: Personal Identification in Networked Society*, pages 87–102. Kluwer Academic Publishers, London, UK.

Index